CW00417465

How she
healed me

OTHER BOOKS BY NAOMI COOK

The Little Bush Nurse Mucky Ucky Teeth

The Little Bush Nurse Lorikeet Won't Sleep
(out December 2017)

How she healed me

A MOTHER'S PROMISE & JOURNEY TO TRANSFORMATION

NAOMI COOK

Foreword by Michael J Tamura

YSH

YSH

First published in Australia in 2017
by Your Soul Health
Copyright text © 2017 Naomi Cook

All rights reserved. No part of this book may be reproduced,
stored in a retrieval system, or transmitted in any form
or by any means, electronic, mechanical, photocopying,
recording or otherwise, without prior permission in writing
from the publisher.

ISBN 978 0 648 1375 0 4 (paperback)
ISBN 978 0 648 1375 0 4 (epub)

Editing: Janet Hutchinson,
Russell Thomson of clearcommunications.net.au
Cover Design: Bespoke Creative
Typesetting: Kirby Jones

In order to fully protect the privacy of the individuals involved in Hana's care and story over the years, names, town and state locations have been changed. Thank you to the individuals who played a role in our story and my healing who have agreed to be named: Dr John Hart, Karen Leadbeater, Dr Fred Kahn, Mark Anthony, Michael Monk.

'If only my love was enough …
a mother's love should be enough.'

Foreword

by Michael J Tamura

Miracles transform our lives. They come not from what we do, but on the wings of validation. Each time life confirms what we hoped was true – but were afraid to believe – a miracle blossoms in our heart. Truth is already within each of us; validation helps us to live it, here on Earth. And the engine that propels us forwards to continue seeking that truth, regardless of the joys or the tragedies that we may face along the way, is none other than love. Love imbues us with the necessary courage and inspiration to go on when all appears lost to us. When we answer love's call, it leads us step by step, even in the darkest of nights, through the most turbulent of seas, to discover for ourselves the miracle waiting to bloom within us. Throughout my life, extraordinary souls have taught me to live that miracle.

Naomi Cook, the author of this remarkable book you now hold in your hands, is an exemplar of such souls who consistently demonstrate the kind of courage required to follow the compass of their own heart, live their own truth and willingly lay down their own life for another. They march forth, where only angels dare to tread. Once you read her story, you will have no doubt about that. I might be tempted to liken Naomi to a female Hercules, completing one seemingly impossible task after another. Although Naomi set out on a perilous journey, desperately in search of *the* miracle that would cure her daughter by answering love's most profound beckoning when all seemed for naught, she discovered an entirely different kind of miracle awaiting her.

Naomi is an exceptional registered nurse, healer, researcher and educator, health activist, published author, wife to a loving husband, and, above all, Mum to two beautiful daughters. Her arduous path began with a devastating tragedy involving her daughter Hana. Hercules, though initially mortal, prevailed through all manner of hardships and trials. Naomi woke herself up each morning from every mother's most dreaded nightmare: witnessing the interminable suffering of her child. Only with the greatest of love could she have undertaken such a Herculean test, much less emerged triumphant. She was willing to offer her own life in exchange for her child's.

Mothers lay down their lives for their children every day, regardless of faith, nationality, race, socio-economic standing or political leanings. There is no greater love than this. The moment a woman discovers she is pregnant, she dies from the person she was, to reincarnate as the mother she will be. Some embrace this dying and rebirth joyously, while others may go kicking and screaming all the way. From the start, some mothers know with absolute certainty, irrespective of what else they may be, do, and have in life, that it is their choice and destiny to be a mother. Other mothers may feel that they had no choice in the matter at all, that motherhood was unfairly thrust upon them. These initial reactions are not all that different than those of soldiers, when they realise that they are dying. Some die knowing that they fulfilled their purpose fighting for their country and defending their loved ones, while others may decide that their lives were short-changed by an unloving god. Our dying takes countless forms, yet despite what our initial reaction may be to making this monumental change in who we think we are and in how we choose to live our lives, every death unfailingly reveals to us what our life is truly about. How long we take to accept it is up to each of us.

All too often, when I ask a mother what she did or what kind of career she had, she would reply, 'Oh, nothing, I'm a stay-at-home mother.' I would laugh, not because I thought being a mother was funny, but because I couldn't fathom having a workload coming close to what an 'average' mother had to do every single day. And that's coming from someone who's worked 80–120 hours a week directing an institute pioneering psychic development that grew from a schoolhouse to a non-profit organisation with a paid staff of 150 and a volunteer staff of 400 during the first 20 years of his career – and who didn't think twice about how challenging that was.

Over my 43 years so far as an adult, I've been known as a spiritual teacher, healer, clairvoyant visionary, author, minister, and pioneer in the fields of healing and psychic development. I've travelled the world over, led groups on pilgrimages, been interviewed or featured on film, TV, radio, and print, and I've helped build communities. I've even died, as in my heart stopped beating and I was not breathing, on five different occasions – and came back each time, conscious of 'where' I'd been. So, I can probably say that I have some experience in dealing with challenges in life. Oh, did I mention that I'm also a dad to two extraordinary sons? Without question, I would easily put being a dad right up there at the top of the scale of difficulty, second only to that of being a mom. Perhaps, that is why I don't recall the high school career counselor ever mentioning being a father or a mother as a career choice. It would be so much easier to opt for becoming a rocket scientist, astronaut, neurosurgeon, or entrepreneur.

Yet, the Oxford English Dictionary defines 'career' as 'an occupation undertaken for a significant period of a person's life and with opportunities for progress'. So, why wouldn't any mother consider motherhood a full career? In fact, it's a career that incorporates the skill-sets, wisdom, and commitment of almost every other conceivable career path: CEO, educator, nurse, physician, counselor, minister, fashion designer, wardrobe coordinator, hygienist, cook, engineer, inventor, artist, therapist, musician, mathematician, business manager, economist, coach, fitness trainer, comedian, laundress, tailor, advocate, and, of course, chief bottle-washer – and healer. It would be safe to say, also, that motherhood is 'undertaken for a significant period of one's life'. But, does it offer 'opportunities for progress'? The world may not yet offer mothers promotions, titles, and pay raises, but in terms of opportunities for spiritual advancement, there are few careers that equal those offered the soul through motherhood.

In this most demanding of life's work, what would be the single most difficult challenge that a mother could possibly face? I think most of us would agree that the death of her child may be a mother's greatest fear. If there is anything that a mother could dread more than the possibility of her child's death, it would be that of helplessly watching her child suffer. In fact, the torture of feeling powerless to mitigate the suffering of others is an experience not only reserved for mothers in relationship to their children, but common to each and every one of us who cares about anyone. The one we love is suffering and we can't seem to do anything to stop it. And, if we feel that we are each a healer in some form, whether a nurse or a minister or a natural healer, that's worse than rubbing salt in our already bleeding wound.

Naomi is a mother, a nurse, a natural healer and a teacher entrusted with the care and healing of the precious lives of two beautiful daughters. One of them, Hana, when she was only five years old, was diagnosed as having a brain tumour requiring surgery to remove it. But it was after the surgery that their real nightmare began. For Hana, the cure may have been worse than the disease. This forced Naomi to undertake the seemingly impossible task – one during which a mere mortal would tear her hair out, gnash her teeth, scream at any god who might listen – the task of piloting a dinghy with her family onboard through a perfect storm of incurable diseases, ignorance, medical bureaucracy, inadequate treatment protocols, scientific competition, desperate measures, and an occasional sliver of hope. Each time she turned into the next onslaught of a monster wave and successfully crested it, wave by wave, she transformed her nightmare into a voyage of discovery.

Once you turn this page, you will open the door to Naomi's heart and, with her, embark upon a profound adventure that will transform the way you see your life. Along the way, you will experience a gut-wrenching medical thriller, a heartbreaking tragedy, a comedy of errors, and perhaps even a touch of the theatre of the absurd. You will certainly shed some tears, smile, laugh, and have your heart warmed, only to have it broken all over again, but, above all else, you will discover a profound and beautiful love story that is Naomi's personal pilgrimage to her innermost shrine.

Each year millions of souls around the world take their spiritual treks, often over great distances and through challenging conditions: El Camino de Santiago de Compostela, the Shikoku O-Hen-Ro, The Hajj Pilgrimage to Mecca, and Pilgrimages to the Holy Land, to name just a few. Eventually, however, each of us must make the ultimate pilgrimage to the inner sanctum of our soul. There is a saying among the Sioux nation, 'The longest journey that you will ever take is the one from your head to your heart.' Naomi has made that trek and here she serves as our guide that we may each find our own way as well.

Michael J Tamura
Spiritual Teacher, Clairvoyant Visionary and
Author of *You Are the Answer.*
www.michaeltamura.com

Chapter One

Just knock her out! End it now!

I wanted to throttle the anaesthetist. Hana, my little girl was fighting with every last inch of her being, screaming as he held the pungent gas over her face. She hated the gas. She'd never liked the gas … she would have had dim memories of going under anaesthesia when she'd severed a lip in two places after falling headfirst into a wooden bed frame in Egypt, aged one. Then for grommets aged two and when, nearly two years ago her ear infections returned, grommets again, aged four. But they were easy-peasy kindergarten surgeries compared to this: this was the real deal.

I should have advocated for her by insisting on an injection – an IV induction – I'd let her down. Now she was writhing in my arms, face red, wild eyed, like a cornered animal as the nurses pinned her down so she'd inhale more of the gas with each scream. But the gas wasn't working and there was nothing I could do.

'Noooooooo!' she screamed, spittle flying out of her mouth, her eyes like slits as she looked sideways at me, but she couldn't see me anymore. Like a punch to my stomach I realised why – she felt betrayed. How could I let this happen to her? She didn't count on me being there anymore because I wasn't ending it for her.

'Darling girl, this has to be done,' I kept singing, calmly, in my low voice as if I couldn't hear her screams. 'Sleepy, sleepy baby.' I kept hoping my words would have a magical effect and soothe her but they didn't.

Hit by another bolt of anger I looked up at the anaesthetist, expecting to see him adjusting his settings to increase the potency of this ridiculous anaesthesia that didn't sedate as much as it stank. But he was just standing there watching, seemingly unfazed by what my daughter was experiencing on that bed. He didn't seem to understand how significant this battle was to me. This was the surgery to remove a life-threatening, tennis-ball-sized tumour that had been discovered only three days earlier. We all knew there was a risk that she may not wake up again … what if these terrible screams were my last memory of my little girl?

'It's OK,' I murmured, stroking her forehead, before quietly singing our song again like a demented broken record. It was the only thing I could do: sing like a demented broken record.

'YUCKY!' she screamed. 'Ssssstop!'

Now the nurses were getting upset too. They were worried I'd lose it – what a test of parental reserve to stay calm while their child screamed for their very lives right before having aggressive neurosurgery.

After what felt like twenty minutes but was more than likely only five, she eventually closed her eyes, her cries turning into watery gurgles in the back of her throat. But first there was the haunting cry she roared heavenwards, the cry that even years later still chills me to my core:

'OH GOD HELP ME!'

It was the last sound she made before the gas knocked her out. A cry to a 'God' that we never discussed or talked about at home. Although Nour, my husband, was a Muslim, I was atheist – completely non-spiritual, and I was very hardcore about that belief. 'God' never came into our conversations, this was simply something Hana wouldn't say.

The room fell to silence. Then, one of the nurses asked sympathetically, 'Are you OK?' before adding, 'Well done.' The unspoken words were: *That was a tough one: you wore it well.*

OH GOD HELP ME.

Her words echoed in my head. Confused, I tried to push them away and 'un-hear' them as I bent down to kiss her cheeks which were wet with tears. The stench of the gas filled my nostrils. As I was a registered nurse I knew she needed to be intubated before her airway closed, so I said my goodbye as quickly as possible.

I got off the bed, dizzy from my brief inhalation of gas and trudged to the door. I was stiff and cold, my arms and legs felt too long on me – awkward, like my body didn't want to work anymore. The world was lopsided by the time I reached the door to the anaesthetic bay, the dizziness increasing as I stumbled down the corridor to find Nour. He was waiting in Recovery for some reason I have never been able to figure out. The nurse waiting with him took one look at my face and grabbed a chair. I slumped into it and fell headfirst – my head onto my knees. Now the world was spinning around me rather blissfully.

'How did it go?' he asked.

There were no words for it. How could I even begin to describe what it had felt like to betray our child while she acted like she was fighting for her life? How the anaesthetist hadn't been moved by her struggle? How she'd looked at me but hadn't 'seen' me? How could I even tell him she had screamed 'GOD HELP ME' when God wasn't part of our daily vocabulary? I didn't think I'd ever be able to put into words how chilling it had sounded and how unsettling it had felt, for as long as I lived.

So I shook my head, no words. I found a flimsy plastic white cup – filled with what I anticipated to be too-sweet lemonade – pushed into my hands.

'Drink,' came the order.

'Don't want to.'

'Drink,' Nour repeated.

'Don't want to be here.'

'Come on, Nounou, drink,' he urged. 'You don't want to faint.'

Oh but I do, husband dear, I thought. *If I could just escape from this body for a few minutes…*

'Drink up,' the nurse repeated.

'Oh, for goodness sake,' I muttered.

I took a sip to appease them. I had been right, it was too-sweet lemonade. Much to my disappointment, the sugar instantly reduced some of the dizziness. I wished everyone would just leave me alone to faint in peace – the last thing I wanted was a crowd around me – the 'weak' mum, collapsing

16

when her daughter goes to surgery. No, that wasn't me. I was the strong one.

However, I still wanted to faint, just with a little privacy if possible.

Clutching the flimsy plastic cup I let the last four days whizz around my head like vultures. It was like watching a movie, none of it seemed real: the kind of movie you watch and afterwards feel so grateful for your lot and hope, desperately, that nothing like that will happen to you.

Only four days ago I'd been sitting in the darkness in our Bondi Junction apartment, curled up by the French windows bawling my eyes out. The following day I would be taking Hana for a CT scan but I already knew what they'd find: I knew she had a brain tumour. What other explanation was there for her symptoms? She was so very unwell and it had happened so quickly over the past three weeks from the moment I'd realised something was wrong – when the quiet nagging in the back of my mind became a loud, audible voice.

'Is she safe to take home?' I'd asked the endocrinologist we'd only managed to sneak in to see at this festive time of year thanks to a friend of a friend.

'She probably has a virus or something, this photophobia – it's usually viral.'

But Hana had just had a random episode of projectile vomiting without nausea as we'd waited for the hand X-ray to check her bone age. I think I'd known even before I'd become a nurse that this was a sign of raised intracranial pressure. Doubting him, I flicked a look at Hana curled up asleep in Maryam's stroller, she only just fitted in. No … there was something wrong and it wasn't a virus. Confident it was autoimmune thyroiditis causing a low thyroid output and her symptoms of thirst, headache and fatigue, he'd written up a script for thyroid medication and said to start taking it once he'd confirmed his diagnosis from the blood tests later that afternoon.

But then, on the way home, he rang me. 'Hold off the thyroid meds,' he said. 'Her levels are normal … low normal, but normal.'

'What do you—' I started to say before he cut me off.

'Er, I also have the bone age back.' There was a short silence. Instinctively I knew he was about to break some bad news. 'Her bone age is 3.5 years.' Hana was five, about to turn six. The world suddenly got so much darker.

'Well, what is wrong with her then?' I asked, my throat tight. I looked at Nour who was driving but listening to everything I was saying.

'I don't know …' he replied. 'We might need to start considering a rarer genetic condition.'

We got home and mechanically put the girls in the bath, the evening routine unfolding. Nour stayed with them while I slipped out to FaceTime my mum who'd just woken up, it was morning in the UK. I told her about Hana's bone age.

'What does that mean, Naomi?' she asked, emphasising every word, as if to say, *Don't you lie to me now. Don't fob me off with an 'everything will be OK'.*

'What does that mean?' she repeated.

My face crumpled and I sank onto the kitchen floor, gritty with toast crumbs I hadn't had the energy to clean up in the stress of Hana's emerging illness. Tears streamed down my face.

'It means there is something very wrong with her, Mum.'

Hana's headache was so severe I wouldn't rest until she'd had a CT scan. Grateful I had a paediatrician who I was able to contact at any time, I emailed her that night. She instantly replied saying she'd put forward an urgent request for a CT at the children's hospital for the next day.

That night before that CT scan, after watching my little girl fall asleep, I went and sat out in the darkness, sobbing my heart out as I let myself imagine what might be about to happen. If I was going to lose her, how could I possibly bear a day in this world without her in it?

Nour had been at the cinema with his parents who were visiting us in Sydney for Christmas. When he came home, shocked to find me in such an uncharacteristic mess, he asked, 'Why are you crying? Tomorrow we will be ruling out a brain tumour—'

'No. Tomorrow isn't to rule out a brain tumour, it is to find if she has one.'

Silence.

'If she has one, if it's a craniopharyngioma, then we can work with that we can—'

'That would be AWFUL!'

He was a little disgusted – he couldn't imagine how I'd been sitting here thinking about the fine details like that.

My research had informed me that craniopharyngiomas originate from embryonic structures usually growing out of the hormone production centre – the pituitary area – deep in the brain. It was a locally invasive tumour, invading and damaging a multitude of brain structures from the optic chiasm, which affects sight, the hypothalamus, which affects an enormous range of bodily functions – weight, appetite, sleep and hormone messaging – as well as the pituitary area itself. But it wasn't a malignant tumour and so didn't spread systemically.

Tutting to himself, Nour went to get a drink in the kitchen.

'She would need hormone replacement for life,' I continued.

'That would be *terrible* – to be on hormone replacement for life,' he protested.

'But she would most likely survive …'

We were speaking over each other but I won and rendered him speechless as he held the glass of water halfway to his open mouth, finally taking on board the fear I had let run through me all evening. I went to bed with rocks in my stomach, but not without kissing Hana again.

The next day I packed her up into the car and headed off to the hospital. After the CT scan, we had to wait in the side room where people are only ever told bad news. I was shaky, even my neck felt shaky, as if I had Parkinson's or some other neurological disorder. There was a toy MRI machine on the floor and Hana put her toy penguin on it, scanned it, followed by her scarf – my old scarf, 'Mummy's Scarf'. I took pictures with my iPhone – memories of the moment *before*.

Then I texted my mum who was staying up late in the UK waiting for news.

Told to wait in side room. Not looking good.

'Hello,' the radiologist said as he came in and delicately sat down on the chair right next to the door as if he wanted to be sure he could make a quick escape if needed. He looked awkward, although he was smiling a little.

'So,' I said brightly, as if I was talking about the weather. I was a nurse, a professional after all. I was not going to show him I was afraid of what he was about to tell me. 'Did you find anything?'

A moment's pause, a moment's hesitation, an infinitesimal blip in time but long enough for me to register it.

'We found a mass.'

Fireworks exploded in my head.

'Where?'

'Just above the pituitary.'

I nodded, and I felt something along the lines of relief.

'It is most likely a cranio—'

'—pharyngioma,' I finished with him.

He nodded, impressed and relieved because I'd made his job so much easier. My relief was short lived as I suddenly found myself rushing to ED – the Emergency Department – in a daze. The tumour was extensive and blocking a ventricle, she had severe 'water on the brain' – 'hydrocephalous', which meant it was imminently life threatening.

ED was dead, apart from one mother sitting with her little girl who most likely did not have a brain tumour. Stumbling over my words and unable to focus on the nursing staff, I got the admission process started when I saw two messages from my mum on my phone.

Am frantic with worry. Have you heard yet?

Then, as if I was in a trance, my fingers found the letters that made the words and I typed it for the first time.

She has a tumour

Nour! I was in such a state of shock, I couldn't believe I hadn't told him. He picked up his phone right away He was at the playground with Maryam, his parents, my brother and my nephew.

'Hello?' he answered, brusquely – it was an *'And?'* more than a hello – he expected the CT results to follow in my reply instantly.

My voice was small, the tone of someone who'd known all along.

'She has a tumour.'

I tasted it on my tongue for the first time, it felt alien. This was my voice saying those words about our beautiful little girl.

They were all looking at him I knew it. I could *hear* their expectant faces as he was hit by my words.

'Tumour,' he relayed flatly, a slight Egyptian accent on the 'r'.

I could see him turn around to face them, resigned somehow as the word came out of his mouth. And I could feel the heavy blackness descending on them in that patch of sun in the playground that had witnessed our hours of fun and games. There was a stricken silence interrupted only by the empty sound of wind blowing into the mic of Nour's phone.

This was the worst movie scene of my life so far. I'd tortured myself, playing out various terrifying scenes in my head before. Scenes where my children are being defibrillated on the resus table, and I'm screaming like a mad woman, pulling at my hair and clothes as my children flatline and go into asystole. Scenes where my children are bald and skinny in the Cancer Ward, isolated with huge, haunted eyes peering out from behind the glass panes.

The fears that haunted me on random sleepless nights, taunting me with the unknown. And here I was living one I'd never seen coming.

GOD HELP ME.

There in Recovery, my head in my lap, still clutching the flimsy white plastic cup — Hana's head was now being drilled opened in theatre. I took another dutiful sip of the too-sweet lemonade that made me want to vomit as much as the circling memories of the last few days.

If only I could kiss the tumour out of her head! It felt instinctual, that my love should be enough to do that. A mother's love should surely be omnipotent? How surprising that it wasn't …

Her scarlet, tear-streaked face, spittle flying out of her mouth, roaring like an animal pushed into the slaughterhouse. The way she'd looked but not seen me — of course, she'd known what was coming …

Deep down inside she'd known, or remembered perhaps, that this was the end of things: *this was where we died.*

23

Chapter Two

There was definitely something metallic about it, the smell or a taste maybe. I had an urge to shift and move about to get away from it, shake it off, but because I was driving I couldn't. There was no way to escape it. It came right out of the blue; out of the impossibly blue and high Australian sky one random day: The warning of what was to come.

I didn't believe in psychic stuff. Besides, my life was perfect. Surely this feeling was just my subconscious being paranoid about just how perfect it was? Yes, that must be it. My life had always been perfect. Perfect, but different.

Of course, I'd felt a little different to my peers, being born into an evangelical Christian family. We were non-affectionately nicknamed 'Bible Bashers' by the local bullies, a bike-riding boy band that sometimes cruised our road. I was certainly guilty of trying to convert my playmates to Christianity while playing on the front lawn: 'Let Jesus into your heart or else you will go to hell!' I warned my five-year-old next door neighbour. When she disappeared inside to tell her mum that 'Jesus was now in her heart' she had to have an early dinner and, funnily enough, I don't think she came out to play much after that.

When I got bored of converting friends to Jesus, I tried to convert them to Vegetarianism and Animal Rights – all of this was before I knew all my times tables. I'm pretty sure I was the youngest to stand at the animal rights – chest high to me – market stall, eagerly asking for papers on animal cruelty and animal rights to add to my growing stash of photocopied leaflets. I know my auntie loved me, but I definitely picked up on some nervousness, as aged nine, I procured some of these anti-factory farming leaflets, with graphic photos of animals being tortured, at a sleepover with my cousin. 'Mum,' my cousin declared after ten minutes with me, 'I'm going vegetarian.' I nodded in fervent agreement. I was born with an inherent aversion to the presence of meat – near me or 'in' me, when aged three I'd pointed to the suspicious brown slab of glistening beef and asked my dad what it was. On hearing is was a 'dead cow' I didn't feel disgusted – just perplexed, how, *how* could it be possible for the flesh of another living being to enter within our own?

Feeling 'different' continued into my teens when I left my closeted private religious school for a local state comprehensive. White, knee-high socks were not considered normal there. It was at this point that I started mentally constructing a list of *Things to Do Before I Die* – after all, the world was my oyster and my future there for the taking.

So, number one:

1. *Study something mind-opening:* A dark period of anorexia nervosa when I was fifteen shook up my so-far-pretty-perfect world a little and I emerged a new person. The new me was passionate about astronomy – I yearned for space and the stars. I'd stand on the front porch of my Oxford home, every inch of me freezing cold, breathless with awe staring up at Betelgeuse, the red giant star in its dying days in the Orion Nebula. Now that I was beginning to get a clearer idea of the enormity of the universe, it simply seemed too vast for the boxed-in Christian idea of God I'd been spoonfed. The Sunday evening church I experienced seemed smug and hypocritical – individuals bent on satisfying themselves rather than changing the world. I left the church and stopped believing in God, just like that. Suddenly my life was mine and mine alone. I choose to be moral because I believed in being good, rather than because I feared the wrath of an almighty being who threatened hell. And this way, I didn't have to repeatedly ask the question: *Why would a God of love, power and knowledge allow so much suffering?* I was free to believe there was no reason for suffering – and this made so much more sense!

You'd have thought that freedom from religion would make me feel more 'normal' – it didn't. My mind, now free, wanted to go places no one else's seemed to want to go. I wanted to know … *everything!* I wanted to travel the universe and see it all, feel it all, know it all – every single little secret hidden in those far-flung galaxies I could see from my freezing porch. The answers to everything were out there, how I wished I could fly through those starry clusters, dipping in my fingers to know their stories. Knowing I would never 'know' everything moved me to tears of frustration sometimes: Yes, I have been known to cry while looking at photos from the Hubble Telescope.

In a desperate, unsuccessful attempt to open my mind and 'know it all', I chose to study Philosophy at the University of Durham as an undergraduate – a degree that raised more questions than the answers I craved. But I relished burying myself in my room with piles of books and ancient texts from the library that analysed meaning, words, and what it meant to be 'good' and 'to be'.

I wasn't really weird, I had a good circle of friends. But I was still different – I thought it better to party without alcohol, which really kind of does make you a teensy bit weird in the booze-drinking scene at uni. I preferred an early night so that I could get up to have a run before a day of study. So, when graduation came and everyone flocked to get their gowns and hats, ready to party, I had no inclination to join them. I simply didn't need the showdown. For me the joy had been in each page read and each thing learnt, the thought of celebrating bored me – I'd celebrated each day for three years! Without a hint of indecision I packed up and went home while my friends graduated.

Now my childhood was well and truly over and I still didn't feel that I fitted in. Maybe I should try living in another country to see if I could fit in there …

2: *Live in an exotic, exciting and mysterious country:* I envisaged myself navigating through smoky souqs with a backdrop of eerie-sounding foreign music, writing incredible stories on the rag-rugged floor of my equally exotic apartment. My love of writing had begun in early childhood when I started journaling at ten and I couldn't wait to indulge my hobby with some Ancient Egyptian inspiration and Middle Eastern flavours! I thought I'd find my pot of gold in Egypt and discover what I was supposed to 'do' with my life and maybe, just maybe, I'd 'fit in' finally.

Five months after graduating I'd saved up enough for my plane ticket to Egypt and first few weeks rent by working gruelling fourteen-hour shifts as an assistant nurse by day and belly dancer in my local Lebanese restaurant by night (and sometimes combining the two – the little old ladies on Bedford Ward loved watching my morning shimmies and hip drops as I drew open their curtains to say good morning). I boarded a British Airways flight ready to take the next step to my destiny …

The wintery arrival to a severely cockroach-infested apartment that didn't even have glass windows fitted over the wooden shutters wasn't the glamorous start I'd imagined. But within a year, I qualified as an English Language Teacher, working at the prestigious British Council in Agouza, along the Nile.

Cairo life was glamorous and quite perfect! I spent my days teaching and at night I hung out with trendy, upper-class Cairenes who spoke a funky mix of American English dotted with Arabic words. We dined at an endless choice of cafés and partied at fairytale weddings for millionaires – the women decked in layers of enormous sparkling diamonds, perfectly manicured nails and hair coiffured to utter perfection. Adventurous weekends were spent travelling to the desert, the mountains of Sinai, the Red Sea and ancient temples with a man I'd found a soulmate in.

3: *Marry a prince:* Ticking off this on the list had looked potentially tricky as I'd never had a chance to meet Prince William who was now officially taken and I didn't know of any other princes. So Nour, a descendent (maybe) of the Pharaohs was a perfect fit. He even looked like Tutankhamen – if you went by the Boy King's death mask. We got engaged and similarly indulged in one of the enormous fairytale weddings we'd been going to for four years together.

But then what next? My mind began to niggle at me again. What are you here for? What do you want to do with your life? It better be something good.

I had continued to work off and on as an assistant nurse in the UK to save sterling from time to time during my years in Egypt. I liked how it felt to help people – this was my next step! But should I choose medicine or nursing? I felt the tempting intellectual pull of medicine and my ego was certainly keen on 'Dr Cook', but I knew, deep in my heart that if I became a nurse I'd find it easier to fulfil two other life dreams: to write and be a fully dedicated stay-at-home mum while still in my twenties.

Nour and I planned an adventure across the world: we applied for Master Degrees at the University of Sydney in Australia – he would study Orthodontics, and I would undertake a two-year Masters of Nursing before, we thought, we'd return to Egypt and put our new education and skills into practice. I had dreams of developing the non-existent primary healthcare sector as a proud Australian-trained nurse, and he dreamed of teaching at Cairo University. And so this led me to the ticking off of a number four:

4. Live by a large expanse of water like the ocean or a big lake: I could see myself going for long thoughtful walks and having deep and meaningful conversations by this large expanse of water. This was inspired, I think, by watching *Dawson's Creek* and perhaps a bit of *Home and Away* as a teenager. Sydney, Australia fitted this bill, perfectly, in my mind.

Soon after we graduated from our Master's Degrees, with hopeful anticipation (in our pyjamas) we watched the Egyptian Revolution unfold on the internet from our airless and overheated Rose Bay apartment. But then the whole of the Middle East fell into tragic upheaval and we changed our immediate plans, becoming triathlon-loving, Bondi Locals – proper Aussies with passports and everything! Meanwhile, I'd ticked off another thing on my list:

5: *Have kids while still young:* This had been a dream since my childhood, inspired by my mum's dedication to me and my brothers. As planned, I had two, two-and-a-half years apart – Hana and Maryam – the girls I'd hoped for. And as I'd always planned, I put my own career aspirations on hold for them so I could be the perfect mum I'd always wanted to be. I set up a blog called 'Nurse Naomi' which gave me a platform to keep writing and put forward my emerging perspectives on health and wellness.

But there were two things left on my list that were yet to be ticked:

6: *Make a difference to the world in some way:* I wasn't sure how, but I desperately wanted to leave my mark so that when I was dead, part of me could live on. I thought that perhaps I could live on by being a writer of great and meaningful things.

Therefore:

7: *Write awesome books* was an essential part of my list of *Things to do Before I Die.* I had grand ideas of cleverly interweaving mind-opening philosophical themes into wow-some page-turning children's books.

So, five years after moving to Australia, in my mid thirties I deduced that four out of six things were perfect start – I felt I could comfortably claim that I was satisfied with my life so far. I could hesitantly say that maybe, just maybe, I finally felt like I was 'fitting in', not so different anymore. I was in full control of my own destiny: Things were good. Perfect even.

But then that dark feeling washed over me at the end of 2013. I was driving into the preschool's driveway, Hana in the back, flushed and happy after a day at school, she was loving her Kindergarten year – I couldn't see darkness on that gloriously sunny day, but I could feel it, hovering a few metres away from me.

Something bad is going to happen.

Immediately I tried to shrug it off. How silly of me! The moment things were coming together, the moment I had an inkling that my life was going pretty much how I'd always wanted it to! I was just being melodramatic; this sense of foreboding couldn't be real.

But it is real, something deep inside told me. *You've been right before.*

Because I didn't believe in a spiritual dimension, I hadn't bothered giving much thought to how psychic stuff could 'work'. Because it didn't make immediate sense to me, I found it much easier to ignore it and disbelieve. But at the same time I couldn't explain two premonitions I'd had before:

Once, in Cairo, on a stinking hot afternoon, waking abruptly from a nap in the filthy, ramshackle apartment I was practically squatting in, simply 'knowing', out of the blue, that something was up with my parents. I immediately called them.

'Is everything alright between you and Dad?'

Silence.

'Errmm.' Her voice was a little shaky, sending off instant alarm bells in my head. 'Actually we've decided to separate.' And then my picture-perfect family began to disintegrate and things at home were never the same again.

The other time had been here in Sydney. In a dream, a close friend told me her dad had died. I hadn't had contact with her for months; I'd had no idea that he was even sick. Eyes still sticky from sleep I'd woken to find an unopened text message on my old Nokia phone. Still in bed I'd opened the message – it was from my friend. But I already knew what the words would tell me as my eyes skimmed over them: she wanted to let me know that her dad had died. The adrenalin surge and rush of confusion was initially stronger than my sadness for her as I stumbled out of the bedroom like a drunkard looking for Nour so I could share my disbelief.

Darkness fell over the car as I drove into the underground car park. Uneasy, I pulled up to my favourite parking spot willing the feeling to go away. But it lingered there. I could feel it curling in my belly and my skin was silently buzzing as if it was covered in static electricity. I had an urge to ring Nour and tell him, but how silly would I sound saying it?

'Hi, habiby. I've got this dodgy feeling that something bad is going to happen. I have no idea what it could be though … do you?'

Somehow I knew the feeling would dissipate. I knew that I'd forget about it and, if the bad thing did happen, I probably wouldn't even remember this moment. Or at least I hoped that I wouldn't and that made me feel a little better. So I got out of the car and let Hana out. She jumped down, excited about going to get Maryam; she loved her little sister.

'Lift or stairs?' she asked; she always asked even though she knew the answer, it was the same every time.

'Stairs, of course! We've got good legs, let's use them!' I said, grateful for the distraction. And, as usual, I mentally congratulated myself for that interchange – I believed I was further ingraining a lust for activity, for movement, for a healthy, strong body! I thought it was so important, especially these days when so many kids had far too much screen time and not enough active play. Not my kids! I'd chosen to invest in them in these early years for a good reason. In the corner of my eye I saw some other parents choosing the lift.

'Yes, good strong legs!' I affirmed smugly as Hana watched the lift door close on them and we embarked on the steep concrete steps, steps that in only a few months from then on would become impossible for my little girl to climb and I would become one of those parents that chose the lift.

The higher we climbed the more the bad feeling began to ebb away. We scooped up a hot, sweaty, suncream-scented Maryam and jumped back in the car planning our swim; we'd bring down the hoops and noodles today! Once the music was back on I felt calmness seep through me.

The sun felt good on my arms, the sky higher than ever, open with endless possibilities in a way the sky back in England never seemed to feel. I glanced in the mirror and saw Hana and Maryam holding hands over the middle seat, they were both grinning like Cheshire Cats, they knew I found this ridiculously cute.

Yes. Things are really good right now. And I couldn't wait to get stuck into tomorrow – into the future. I just knew that was going to be awesome too.

Chapter Three

'Hello, baby.' I leaned over Hana and kissed her cool, pale cheek. The stench of anaesthetic gas leaked out of her mouth and nose. Her eyes were open but she didn't say anything. She darted her eyes left, then right, seeing but not seeing.

Where is she?

I looked deeper into her eyes, hit by a bolt of panic – her eyes were empty of … Hana!

Then I admonished myself for expecting too much. The kid had just come out of massive brain surgery, of course I couldn't expect her to smile and say, 'Hi, Mummy!' All the same, I ached to whisper to her, 'Don't be gone …'

The next few hours were a series of gut-wrenching screams and tubes as Hana was taken to Intensive Care (ICU) and stabbed unsuccessfully multiple times in her ankle for a peripheral line – a tube that must be pushed deep into a leg vein as an access point for medications. They had forgotten to place it in theatre, when she had been unconscious. Then to top it all off, her catheter fell out and she needed a new one to monitor her urine output as we waited for the onset of complete pituitary failure. The first symptom would be diabetes insipidus, a lifelong condition where the body stops producing antidiuretic hormones, meaning it can no longer hold onto any fluids without a medicine called DDAVP, or Minirin. Untreated diabetes insipidus can lead to rapid death through excessive water loss in urine. So, after the repeated sharp needle sticks and tubes being pushed into her leg veins for the peripheral line she now had the medical team crowding over her genitals, holding back and pulling open her little legs wide in order insert the tube into her urethra. Her cries were high pitched, shaky and continuous.

'Nononononono.'

Eventually Nour and I were asked to leave so the doctors could continue without us looking on – the pressure of us being there was simply too much, after shaky, repeated failed attempts. I could hear her screams echoing down the corridor. I raised my hands to my ears and clenched my fists, close to punching the resus trolley I was standing next to.

'SSSSSTOP!' I hissed, seething that my baby was being subjected to this so soon after having her head opened in theatre.

Earlier that day the surgeon had walked out of Recovery, bearing the good news that the tumour had been fully removed or 'resected', his chest was puffed out, literally beaming with pride. There'd been very little blood lost, he said, and he was adamant the tumour would not grow back – he was sure he'd picked up all of it. Tears of joy rained down my face, it was over! The hell was over. How *lucky* we had been, I thought.

How very, very stupid of me.

The hell was only just beginning.

Hana was delirious and had no working memory.

'Hana has to go to hospital tomorrow because she has a brain tumour and the doctors and nurses need to take it out …' Her words tumbled out rapidly, her pupils pinpricks from the morphine and she stared out at nothingness.

'Do you know where you are, Hana?' I asked.

'On a boat. It's cold. Can you close the balcony door?'

She couldn't sleep, for nearly two weeks she had micronaps, for only minutes at a time, never getting into deep nourishing sleep and her sleep-deprived world became even more colourful as she saw orange worms in her bed and spoke gently to a 'prince' in a wound on her arm.

Then the rage started. Out of the blue she began shouting and started to hit me. Her monitors began beeping, flashing the ominous *Extreme Tachycardia* warning as her heart rate skyrocketed. She'd lost too much urine, late for a dose of Minirin that she now needed to retain fluid after the damage to her pituitary gland. Now after peeing too much, she was dangerously dehydrated, her blood sodium seizure level high and rage was the first symptom.

It took days to rehydrate her safely and get her sodium down – her heart rate too high for her little body. Rehydration had to be done slowly to avoid fluid overload – another life-threatening condition that could lead to death from swelling in the brain. As the hospital was a couple of hours drive from our home, we were staying in local serviced apartments. Nour still had to work, he was booked back to back with patients – holidays were his busiest time of year. So once he'd arrive at the hospital around 7pm to take care of Hana at night, I'd take Maryam back to the apartments to sleep fitfully with her curled next to me. When my alarm went off only a few hours later, I'd wake up heavy with nausea, head spinning with dizziness and sleep deprivation. I'd jump into the shower, stomach churning as the warm water streamed over me, then I'd head into the kitchen and prepare meals for the girls for the day. Due to our food sensitivities, I couldn't rely on the hospital canteen and so every meal and snack was pre-planned and prepared by 5.30 in the morning. Then, I'd wake up a warm and slightly vinegar-scented Maryam and hail a taxi back to the hospital.

I'd start increasing the pace of my walk to a trot once inside the building, pushing Maryam in the stroller that was laden with bags of food – the panic of getting back to Hana in ICU as soon as possible increasing like steam in a pressure cooker. I'd arrive breathless, greet a dark-eyed Nour who would already be showered and suited up, ready to leave for work. I'd rush to look at her monitor, my morning nausea increasing as the frequent, thin fluoro spikes that revealed how fast her heart was beating glowed in the darkness.

But even with cautious rehydration, the hell continued – no one could figure out why her dehydration would lead to over-hydration. Her body held onto too much water and her sodium swung too low – seizure level low. Getting the balance of medication to control her diabetes insipidus seemed an impossible feat – we felt it was due to the sheer number of medical personnel involved in managing her care. There were simply too many opinions, too many changes to her regime and too many barriers to accessing medications when they were needed.

I vigilantly stood by her catheter bag, watching for the urine to go pale, the sign of a 'breakthrough', the word we would use for when the antidiuretic medication wore off, meaning she needed another dose to stop dehydration. One afternoon it suddenly went pale and began to pour down the thick plastic tubing.

'Is this a breakthrough?' I pointed it out to one of the doctors as they popped in.

'We need more than 200ml in an hour for breakthrough,' he said.

I began to get anxious. I knew the routine now – if we waited for the full 200ml before taking action, another 200ml would be lost before the nurse would be able to call the doctor to write up the next dose, prepare it, administer it and wait for it to kick in. Then I'd have another feral, dehydrated or 'hypernatremic' child close to seizure on my hands again.

Another doctor popped in. 'I think this is the breakthrough,' I said, my worry growing as I showed him the pale urine.

'Umm, yes but we still need another 100ml,' he said.

Two hours later, as I'd predicted, Hana's heart rate skyrocketed again and the battle to lower her sodium was back on.

'With hindsight, we could have ...' began one registrar, explaining to the consultant the events of the day.

'Not at all,' he began, immediately shrugging off the incident – there was no blame to be placed. I sat in my chair in the dark corner of the room and flinched. Hospital suddenly didn't feel like the home it was to me as 'Nurse Naomi'. As my trust was diminishing, my feeling of imminent danger was growing. It made me feel itchy in my skin.

'You need to sit back and be a consumer,' one of our medical friends poignantly advised me by Hana's bedside one evening. 'I know you and Nour are both medical, but you can't have a clear head when it's your own children, this is when you take the back seat and let the experts run the show.'

And the hunger – the all-consuming hunger – began its torment while she lay tangled in those white sheets, tubes and wires.

'I'm hungry. When can I eat?'

'You just had dinner, lovely.' *Oh no, not again …*

'EAAAAAAAAT!' she'd scream, turning to hit me, or scratch me. A monster had stolen my child. 'FOOOOOOD!'

I utilised her micro-naps for reading time, pouring over medical journals and articles on craniopharyngioma. It was there that I quietly discovered the fallout frequently encountered by those who undergo radical resections of this tumour: *hypothalamic obesity*. A hellish condition characterised by hunger that is never satiated and, to pack even more hellish punch, destroyed the patient's ability to metabolise food for energy. The bodies of these poor individuals would go into storage mode, putting on every calorie consumed as fat in rapid, unrelenting weight gain. There was a case report of one teenage boy who'd been practically starved on a diet in hospital in order to combat his obesity but even with severe caloric restriction and an enforced exercise regime he still gained weight. Within six months, Hana could go from being the tiny little five-year-old with 3.5-year-old skeletal age to a morbidly obese child – regardless of how restricted her diet was or how much exercise she did.

'It could just be the high-dose steroids she needs for the brain inflammation,' one registrar informed me after I questioned her about the hunger. But the high-dose steroids were being lowered now, rapidly, and, instead of diminishing, the hunger was increasing.

It had been ten days since the surgery and Hana was still

wired up to multiple monitors, cannulated in multiple veins and catheterised.

'I want the catheter out,' I told the registrar.

'But you'd have to measure each urine output,' he said. 'It's a heavy workload.'

'That's fine,' I said. 'It'll be worth it.'

Next I insisted she have her cannulas removed and I forced Hana to drink the litres of fluid a day she needed to stay hydrated with diabetes insipidus – even with Minirin to reduce the urine output, it seemed she'd still always pee more than someone with a functioning pituitary gland. I trawled over her medications sheet and learnt the dosages of the other hormones she now needed to stay alive. She needed Thyroxin, a thyroid replacement therapy to compensate for the hormones she lacked that would prompt her thyroid to work and steroid replacement therapy. Steroids were needed to replace her cortisol, a natural stress hormone that is needed for life sustenance – even without 'stressors' the human body still needs small amounts of cortisol to get through each day. Her daily steroids would replace that missing cortisol. Yet, if her body was suddenly exposed to a huge stress like an injury or severe illness, she could go into a life-threatening adrenal crisis, her body suddenly going into fatal collapse if her steroid coverage became inadequate. I needed to carry an emergency injection in my handbag, a high dose of steroid to be given into a muscle in her leg that could keep her alive if this ever happened.

After nearly two weeks we were allowed to leave ICU for a neurosurgical ward without the intensive nursing care. But even two weeks later, Hana was still *gone*. There was nothing about this little girl that resembled the child I had taken into hospital two weeks before, except in how she looked — although even that had changed. She was pale and anaemic now from the all the blood taken for testing, her little legs wobbled like jelly when she put weight on them and giddy. She would need someone to escort her if she wanted to move around. But I thought that *If I could just get her home,* I'd be able to get her back. Maybe I'd see her once again, in her eyes, instead of that hazy distant, coldness that I encountered when we made eye contact now.

'I want to take her home.' It came out a little more assertively that I'd intended but I wasn't the type of person to beat about the bush. My statement shocked the registrar so much he actually took a step back, recoiling a little. 'I can do it, I can take care of her.'

'Oh, um,' he fumbled for an answer. 'We'll have to ask Dr Maxwell about that,' and he made a quick exit.

Soon afterwards, the surgeon, Dr Maxwell walked in with the same registrar. They'd been talking, I could tell. There was a funny look in his eye — curiosity, definitely, but also something else. I wasn't sure I liked it.

'I want to take her home,' I repeated. 'I can look after her.'

'Well, do you have a machine to measure her sodiums?' he half-laughed, half-scoffed.

Now it was my turn to step back — I hadn't been expecting him to laugh at me. I'd thought he'd understand and I'd thought he'd see the truth, that I was more than capable of looking after her. I glanced at Nour but he kept his face carefully passive.

'N-no,' I stuttered, suddenly fishing for my shattered self-confidence. 'But I can measure her urine output, fluids and get regular blood tests. We have a pathology lab on our street.' I added, 'The team here can't control her hydration because there are simply too many people involved from the decision to medicate through to the actual administering of her medication!' I was, of course, referring to the constant changing circuit of doctors and opinions that differed as often as the tides, the result had manifested in a wild, dangerous two weeks in ICU – and he was more than aware of it.

'We need to move on from that,' he ordered brusquely, literally bulldozing down the circus of the past two weeks and the life-threatening implications there had been for Hana.

'Look,' he said, puffing up his chest, 'let's have a trial to see if you can manage her – if you can control her sodiums over the next twenty-four hours we can talk about discharge.'

I furrowed my brow and tried very hard not to pout even as my heart sank. It was upsetting, and not only to my pride. I had studied her health conditions like a medical student cramming for final exams next to her bed for a solid two weeks! But it hurt me more as 'Mum'. If I didn't truly believe I could keep my own daughter safe, I would never had suggested taking her away. Now, like a schoolgirl, I had to prove to the grown-ups, the medical team, that I could do this. One final exam in order to get out of school and out into the big wide world.

Nour nodded politely, much more anxious than I was to not seem overbearing. 'And the fits of rage,' he said, 'these are very uncharacteristic. Will they go over time?'

The surgeon chuckled, 'I think these are more of an alpha-personality thing. She certainly doesn't get them from you!' he said, gesturing to Nour.

I was jolted out of my self-pity for a moment. Was that supposed to be a joke? Confused, my mind began to whirl, was he truly relating my daughter's frightening and aggressive brain injury to my assertive push to get her home? I felt myself shrinking and Dr Maxwell grow taller and wider with every remaining minute he spent on the ward.

'Why didn't you also tell him that we were ready to take her home?' I whispered to Nour once Dr Maxwell had left. 'I thought you agreed she'd be safer at home with us!'

'We couldn't both be pushy about it,' he said. 'Good cop, bad cop kinda thing, you know?'

What?

'Why do I have to be the bad cop?' I said tears welling in my eyes. 'They screwed up here big time, he knows that too! We shouldn't have to prove anything to them!'

'We'll just do the trial,' he sighed. 'I'll go and buy some weighing scales and a jug, then in two days we're outta here. OK? Let's just play their games.'

I stuck out my bottom lip like a petulant child. Now I was acting like a schoolgirl as well as being treated like one. I didn't want to play their stupid games, I just wanted my baby home. I was her mum. I knew her best.

So it was later that night, at midnight, that I found myself ringing the hospital number over and over again to get put through to the ward where Nour was sleeping with Hana. He was supposed to be keeping me updated with her medication and, most crucially, her urine output. If by any chance there'd been a slip-up and she was now peeing out into her bed (which had happened the night before), we'd lose our 'trial' and be stuck in that shithole for another week. I was fuming to find that he hadn't been answering his phone so, visions of Hana's bed becoming flooded with urine again were freaking me out and eventually I dragged my heavy body out of bed and rang the ward directly to check.

'Yes, of course she had her evening dose but now your husband is tucked up in bed and fast asleep,' the night nurse said, and then with an edge to her voice, she said, 'Just like you should be. Stop doctoring and leave it up to us!'

Stop doctoring?

The words rang out into the darkness of our rental apartment as vivid as the red glowing numbers glaring into my tired eyes from the microwave and oven clocks.

'We are supposed to be doing a trial – a test.' My voice cracked with fatigue and I was close to shedding frustrated tears. After the sodium swings over the past two weeks, how I could ever leave anything up to them again?

The next morning it was declared that we'd 'passed our test' and we could take her home the next day. The bags were packed and I couldn't believe we'd finally be out of there. Later that evening, before I left for the serviced apartments with an overtired Maryam, I received the evening blood results. Hana's sodium level was a little lower than the normal range, which meant that she was holding onto more fluid than she should be – yet her care plan had been altered and it was written that she should receive her next dose without waiting for the previous dose to wear off. This meant she wouldn't start peeing before her dose was administered. It was clear to me that she should be allowed to have a small breakthrough, or a big pee, before being given the next dose, otherwise she'd most likely end up overly hydrated – meaning a 'low sodium' blood test result – again in the morning. I went to the nursing station. Not a doctor was in sight so a nurse jotted down my concerns, stating that I thought Hana should have a big pee before her evening dose.

'I will be managing her fluids and sodiums at home,' I emphasised. 'I want it to be made clear that if this was up to me, I'd let her pee a bit before giving the next dose.'

'Well, her care plan says to give it anyway without breakthrough, but I do hear your point. I'll pass on your concerns to the evening doctor,' the nurse said.

Happy that it was documented, I scooped up Maryam and went back for our final night in the hotel. The bags were packed and stacked in the apartment lobby early the next morning, and I arrived at Hana's ward early so we could get going home as soon as possible. Nour had taken the day off work and had gone to pick up my mother-in-law and to load up the car with our bags. Just as we were waiting for the discharge papers, the registrar walked in, looking solemn and gloomy.

'She's not able to go home,' he said. 'Her sodium is 121, this is seizure level low. It's simply too dangerous.'

Hana was over-hydrated. I saw red.

'I TOLD them her medication should have been suspended until she broke through last night!' My whole body began to tremble as if I was freezing cold, my neck shaking so much I had to put my hands there to hide it. This may have been the first time I had experienced rage. 'This is completely incompetent! Are they trying to kill her? No way am I leaving her here. They can't look after her!'

And so I began to taste what it felt like to be at odds with the patriarchal healthcare system for the first time. Was I now 'one of those parents'? The ones that get the 'eye rolls' in handover, the ones that were whispered about at the nursing station. It wasn't a nice feeling.

46

'We are going to have to discharge her against medical advice,' I spat down the phone to Nour who was driving back with all our bags. 'This is completely unbelievable, they should have listened to me!'

Hana was dopey and pale, low sodium made her very sleepy and woozy. We loaded her into a wheelchair, signed the 'against medical advice' discharge forms and practically ran out to the car before anyone could stop us. As we were loading her in, another registrar rang me. I let my frustration rip into the mouthpiece:

'She is in danger under the care of this hospital. Two weeks of screwing up her sodiums and now this? I SAID her evening dose should wait yet it was administered anyway!'

'She ... she needs to be in hospital. Can you just confirm that you will be going to another one to get her checked?' The registrar faltered a little as she received the brunt of my wrath. I felt a twinge of guilt – in a way she was a colleague, but I had been through too much to be polite anymore. I would have to be 'one of those parents'.

None of your business, I wanted to snap at her, but of course we were on our way and the '*breakdown in communication between the parents and medical team*' was already being exchanged between hospitals. Our reputation – now officially documented and which would precede us whereever we went – had been declared as we made the mad dash from one medical prison to another.

That night, once the local hospital had agreed she could go home and come back for another test in the morning, with cannula still in situ, we all got ready for bed – back in our own home. Only it was a home that didn't feel as safe and homely as it had just weeks before.

I was brushing Maryam's teeth in the bathroom when I heard a terrible crack, like a coconut dropping on a tiled floor. My heart sank as screams followed.

'Oh God, oh God,' Nour buried his face in his hands before putting his hands on the sobbing Hana.

'What did you DO?' I rushed over to her.

'She fell back, I thought she'd just get into bed, but she whacked her head against the wall … Oh God, oh God.'

In my mind I saw a giant pool of blood form, as the fresh wound from the surgery burst open and leaked into her brain. She could die from a brain haemorrhage tonight and it would be our fault. I sat next to her, the room filled with a horrific, tangible energy – terror. Maryam was now screaming with Hana, her face all eyes and mouth – she *knew*.

Oh, make this disappear, make this go away. I can't bear it.

'What do we do?' I managed to ask Nour eventually. He was sitting on the bed, his head in his hands, unable to fully connect with the moment. 'Do we go back to the local hospital or what? We can't phone the other one! Not after we did a runner like that! We've got no one to ask for help!'

He began to calm down, and looked objectively at Hana – her sobs were settling and we took a deep breath. We'd have to take the risk. She seemed OK, no head pain, no strange new neurological symptoms. Calmed by his sensible observations, I agreed.

'Let's tuck you up,' I said, leaning over her and placing my weight on my right arm to give her a big hug.

'OWWWWWW!'

Fresh tears began spilling again, 'My cannula! You leaned on my cannula!' She was crying, again.

'Oh gosh, I'm so sorry baby!' I whipped my hand off her duvet.

This was like a bad sitcom, a comedy of slapstick errors.

'What sort of parents are we?' Nour moaned, as I tried to soothe her. Now I was the guilty cause of her suffering. I got a picture then, of who we had been and who we were now becoming. The two of us, indestructible in Egypt – climbing giant sand dunes in the desert at sunrise, driving for endless miles in the mountains of Sinai, singing along to Avril Lavigne, dressed up to the nines and dancing till the early hours of the morning at wedding parties – to this pathetic scene, crippled with terror and flooded with self-doubt that we'd ever be able to look after our daughter properly again. Perhaps we had been stupid to discharge her? Maybe she did need hospital care more than ours?

I kept Maryam safely next to me in bed, where she would stay at night for the next two years, safely snug between Nour and I, but always curling up next to me like a little magnetised worm. The nights were too dark, holding unspoken whispered fears for her to sleep alone. If we couldn't comfort her enough by day, maybe my continual presence at night would help to erase her darkest thoughts that she was too young to understand, let alone articulate.

The questions began rolling around my head, the darkness magnifying them: Would Hana pee out overnight and wake up seriously dehydrated? Would she go into adrenal crisis and die in her sleep? Perhaps she had a brain bleed growing right now after the bang against the wall? I heard it again, the sound like a coconut dropping onto a tiled floor …

This is what fear looks like – dark nights with whispering, creeping shadows. You swallow it, like black coffee burning your throat and stomach before it sets your heart racing.

And this suffocating sensation, fear, had walked through the front door with us, it was sitting itself down at the dining-room table, it was loitering in the bathrooms and watching from the corners of the bedrooms as we slept.

The fear wasn't going anywhere soon. It was here to stay.

Chapter Four

'The metastases have already gone to her liver.'

'Does she know?'

'Not yet. He's going to tell her later. I think he chickened out this morning. Can't blame him really.'

'The poor thing. What she'll be leaving behind—'

About six years earlier, the nurse I was shadowing as a student on clinical placements cut off as the phone rang. Horrified at this young mum's prospects, I snuck down the ward to peek into her room, guilty that I knew before she did that her life would soon be ending. She was asleep, her little five-year-old girl, still in school uniform, was in her arms asleep next to her. Meanwhile her premature baby, removed by caesarean section only a few days before was buildings away, lying in an incubator. This tiny baby who grew cozily alongside a deadly bowel cancer would never get to know her mother.

That night I went home to our Rose Bay apartment to make a baby.

I would affirm life while this life was ebbing away, leaving behind two beautiful little girls and a desperate husband. My bringing about a new life would relieve the pain of witnessing this mother slip away from her dear children. Life, not death.

During my two weeks student placement at our local hospital, I fetched this dying mother cabbage leaves to relieve her engorged breasts and I cleared up her chemotherapy-induced vomit, all the while a bundle of cells inside my belly spun and wove themselves into Hana. My baby, life growing inside me, while life was ebbing away around me.

Six weeks later a rice-grain Hana had already made my pancake-flat stomach swell and bulge and it was my turn to vomit. On the bus to my palliative care placement at another local hospital, I'd hold my handbag at the ready to catch a puke if needed before disembarking and pausing to retch on every street corner in Kings Cross as I made my way to the hospice. Then, while caring for the dying, dashing off to the bathroom to spew my guts up every half an hour. My patients were dying, but Hana was growing inside me so ferociously affirming her fragile life that it was making me sick.

I got fat, very fat over nine months – who ever would have thought? I was naturally slender and stayed stick thin through exercise and a strict, healthy diet. But pregnant me was famished, and kept crackers next to her bed for midnight snacks; pregnant me would eat like a horse (and still be hungry). I *felt* like an enormous pregnant horse by the time I went into labour, after a hike to Bondi Beach and back and a 2 km swim at the Icebergs Swimming Pool thrown in for good measure. Three days of wrestling with intermittent painful contractions that felt like they would crack my sacrum, exhausted, I went in for an induction, disappointed as my dreams for an intervention-free, natural labour went out of the window.

A few floors up from the Oncology ward where I'd witnessed one life taken by cancer, after pushing for over an hour and a half, *my* new life emerged – Hana – with a 1.5 litre gush of blood that splattered over the floor. My uterus was too exhausted to contract anymore, the haemorrhage barely registered with me as my blood pressure dropped. Warm and slippery, she let out a small cry as she was passed straight up into my arms. As I pulled her to my breast I felt a jolt of surprise – this was my baby? This was Hana? Out of the corner of my eyes I saw Nour gasp and clap his hands to his mouth, his eyes radiant with joy.

But I'd thought … I didn't know what I'd thought.

I pushed whatever I'd *thought* I'd thought away and murmured my first-ever words of comfort to my baby:

'I know, I know … *It's hard being born.*'

'You'll regret saying that if you find out she has a brain tumour,' I hissed viciously at Nour, days before Hana's CT scan and diagnosis. We were going on a family walk along with cliffs in Maroubra with my in-laws and Nour had declared that we would all enjoy it: so there! Hana was crying softly as she got out of the car.

'Stop being silly!' Nour had warned her, before shooting me a warning look that said *and don't you indulge any of this!*

We had clicked only two weeks ago that something was wrong with Hana. At a GP appointment to check her ears, I'd thrown in my observation that Hana seemed shorter and ever so slightly chubbier than her peers. Even at the end of her first year at school she still had that 'babyish' look of a toddler, yet she was five, nearly six. A height and weight measurement had put her in the 13th percentile for height and 75th for weight.

'She's always looked like this,' the GP had said, unperturbed, as I checked with him before he left for his Christmas holidays.

But back home, sitting in the jacuzzi, the first year of school over and Christmas holidays now in full swing, Nour and I tried to piece the puzzle together. Maryam swam like a fish around Hana who was playing from the swimming pool steps, too tired to swim laps.

'But she's still in the normal ranges,' I protested, weakly.

'You don't just drop off the 50th percentile,' he said. I nodded, grateful for his insight. It was so useful for us both having medical backgrounds – we could easily bounce ideas off each other using jargon, terminology and concepts that someone with a different education would struggle with. In fact, we often used to laugh at how nonsensical medical and biological language sounded to nonmedics by speaking complete and utter nonsense together for fun like, 'The phospholipid bi-layer of your cellular membrane has experienced degranulation in the inflammatory oesophageal region. If we don't treat your cilia, your rods and cones will evaporate.' And, when we were madly in love in Egypt and I had begun studying human biology as a prerequisite for my up-and-coming Masters of Nursing, we'd declare with wild abandonment crazy things like, 'I love you so much I want to phagocytose you.' Or , more lovingly, 'You make me want to degranulate.'

'Hana was a never small as a baby – at some point she's dropped off! And it's the "dropping off" that is the most sinister symptom,' Nour continued. Assessing Growth and Development were crucial aspects of his work as an orthodontist so I trusted his perspective.

I looked over at Hana – she was giggling as Maryam tickled her toes under the water. Pretending her sister was a dog, she threw out a hoop for her to catch.

'Thirst, fatigue, the occasional headache and growth delay …' I mused out loud. 'Thyroid! Maybe she has an underactive thyroid!'

For a few weeks now Hana's thirst had been perplexing me, the increase in thirst had been gradual but now I'd mentioned it, her thirst was totally unnatural; she was always gasping for water on the way home from school and first thing in the morning she'd be literally parched. She was peeing around the clock too, huge dilute wees that would fill the potty to the brim overnight. At first I'd been bemused by these excessive wees, then confused but now …

'You don't get growth delay from an underactive thyroid, do you?' asked Nour, reluctantly pulling himself out of the hot pool to go and punch on the jacuzzi bubbles again.

'Yes, I think you do – let's google it.' I grabbed my phone, and holding it high to avoid the bubbles that were now beginning to spit up around us, I read out the list of symptoms that perfectly fitted our little girl.

'What about the cause?' Nour asked.

I already knew this. Furrowing my brows and looking back at Hana who was now heading our way, I whispered, 'God, autoimmune thyroiditis? Pituitary tumour?' Then I laughed, nervously.

'We need to see an endocrinologist, but no one will be open now it's almost Christmas,' Nour said, picking up his phone and letting out a sigh.

'We can ask Tasha to pull some strings, she's well connected.' I began constructing a text to one of our medical friends. 'At least so we can see someone early in the new year rather than wait for everyone to come back after Australia Day.' Eight years of living in Australia and we were all too familiar with how the country basically shut down from the end of December until after 26 January. Now we'd figured out that something was definitely up with Hana, we couldn't wait that long!

As if we were watching a movie where the heroine fades unrealistically quickly, Hana deteriorated faster than we would have ever imagined. Only a week after that GP appointment for a general check-up, we'd flown to New Zealand for a week's break over the New Year period with my in-laws. Hana was too tired to play in the playground and struggled to keep up with moderate walks. She preferred to sit quietly and colour in, her head aching a little more each day – nothing severe, just a constant, low-grade ache.

There was another moment that I'll never forget. Hana had just eaten a big lunch of soup and pasta and settled down to do some colouring-in at the table. Shortly afterwards, she simply said, 'I'm hungry.' There is no reason on Earth why that should have bothered me – kids get hungry sometimes, unpredictably, right? But for some reason, this 'I'm hungry' hit me like a sledgehammer.

'Hungry? Why?' I snapped my head round to face her. She looked guilty.

Why was she guilty at being hungry? Why would her being hungry bother me? Then it was gone. The fleeting feeling of … what? fear? anticipation? … disappeared as quickly as it came.

Then we passed the point of no return. The week we flew back from New Zealand she was hit with a sudden headache that so severe I was on the brink of taking her to ED.

'The appointment with the endo is in two days,' Nour said, reluctant to overdramatise things. Hana had recently started crying out in pain and was lying in bed as I stroked her forehead.

'My eyes! My *eyes!*' she said. Unable to do anything for her, I got an icepack to hold over her forehead. She lay next to me in my bed, quiet but in pain.

In the two-week wait to see the endocrinologist I'd become well versed in autoimmune thyroiditis and paediatric brain cancers. For fourteen long dark nights I'd trawl though medical sites, absorbing information like a sponge. I'd planned my strategy if it was autoimmune thyroiditis – I'd insist on seeing her levels to make sure she wasn't misdiagnosed as 'normal' when she might be 'subclinically' hypothyroid. I researched the natural desiccated thyroid – porcine or bovine thyroid – over the synthetically produced 'thyroxin' and familiarised myself with the adrenal insufficiency that often accompanied autoimmune thyroiditis. I also researched the array of brain tumours that affect children … especially those that caused pituitary dysfunction, and it was there I met *craniopharyngioma.*

In my initial research there wasn't much that I encountered about the fallout of this locally invasive, non-malignant tumour; only the symptoms of hormone dysregulation. Because it was one of the few paediatric tumours that was benign or didn't metastasise, that is spread to other body parts, it seemed less frightening.

An oppressive heaviness filled those evenings. The girls would fall asleep and I'd immediately open my iPad and get back to my research. It was hot and the air conditioning didn't cool as much as it blew warm dusty air around the apartment. I pushed my duvet to the bottom of my bed, away from my feet that were sweating more with anticipation than heat. The quietness emphasised my heart rate, accelerated my fear as my mind wove itself around the rare conditions that could cause Hana's symptoms – particularly the brain tumours.

The night before Hana's surgery was the darkest, longest night of my life. But if I were to remember it in colour it wouldn't be dark or black but sheer white, like the bathroom wall where my thoughts bounced off the tiles as I showered. White, like the pain of childbirth when the room around you 'fuzzys' then disappears into white noise, your noise as you scream and groan your baby out. Clinical, starched white like the hospital bed my daughter was now sleeping in. I remembered studying Shakespeare's *Henry V* in school and reading about his agonised 'dark night of the soul' before the big battle. My teacher compared it to Jesus in the Garden of Gethsemane, the night before his crucifixion. This was my 'dark night of the soul', my Gethsemane, my darkest, whitest night.

I spent the hours pacing up and down the small living room of the serviced apartments we'd chosen near to the hospital. Then I'd sit on the hard, comfortless couch and cradle my head in my hands, pull tightly on the hair hanging over my ears, my heart racing and stomach knotted like I'd drunk five coffees in a row. Sod's law – that night there were roadworks right outside the bedroom window. Drills cutting deep into the tarmac.

Tack – Tack – Tack

The sound of cracking concrete wracked the stillness, echoing up and down the street at a billion decibels, mocking any suggestion of sleep. But sleep wasn't an option for me anyway – there was no sleep when, in only hours, Hana's skull would be opened in theatre by a drill of a different kind. I imagined what that would sound like. The sound, to the neurosurgeon and the anaesthetist will be a familiar sound, the sound of a drill cutting into bone. A skull. Just another day's work, just another patient, just another skull. Perhaps they would chat about what they watched on TV the night before, or what they had for dinner while they do it. Make small talk to the sound of their drill cutting into my daughter's skull. Her head, her brain, her life in their hands. My head swirled. I imagined myself fainting.

Tack – Tack – Tack

I went back to the bedroom and, eyes impossibly wide with the most powerful adrenalin my body had ever produced, I cradled Maryam in my arms. Her tears were barely dry on her cheeks after she'd cried herself to sleep asking for her sister, Hana. 'I don't understand, Mama,' she'd sobbed as I tried to explain why she'd had her bath alone, that Hana was in hospital with Daddy. Her eyes wide with the 'knowing' that she didn't 'know' what was happening.

The bedroom door was wide open, orange light creeping in from the lounge lamp I'd left on. Like a child scared of bad dreams, I was afraid of the dark that night. I thought the light might quell the rushes and clusters of thoughts rising and then crashing down on me like waves in the ocean. I thought that the darkness alone would bring with it things I didn't want to think. But I was wrong, the light was useless and the thoughts exploded brightly behind my open eyes, like fireworks.

Is the surgeon sleeping well?

Is he at a social function now or in bed? He should *be in bed…*

What if he isn't feeling well tomorrow and has a bad day?

What if it's not a craniopharyngioma? What if it's malignant? What would her life expectancy be if so? How would we spend her last months? What if she wakes up brain damaged? What if she …?

Dark possible worlds wove their way into my exhausted mind like a cancer themselves. Life without Hana? How could I move without her? How could I ever willingly take another breath without her? I imagined a complete world without colour and I saw myself, broken within it.

Chapter Five

'How long now?'

I sigh, again. This was the third time she has asked me in the last five minutes. I couldn't keep the irritation out of my voice. I was putting on my make-up as meticulously as ever – I would never begin a day without a full face on. 'Still ten minutes, Hana.'

'Oh.' She flushes and tears filled her eyes as I let out yet another sigh;

'Come on, let's do something together to distract you.' I finished my last stroke of mascara.

'But I don't like to do anything when I'm hungry.' She stuck out her bottom lip, frowned and crossed her arms. I can feel the mood swing – right around and upside down. It will hang over her now like a rain cloud, nothing I do or say will take it away. I've lost her again.

'You have to try and distract yourself. You can't eat all day every day – we need to space your food. Right?' My stomach clenches, I'm angry that my daughter must live like this. I'm angry that *I* must live like this. And I'm angry that I'm angry.

Even as I say the words I know how stupid they are. The child is brain damaged! Nothing she does to distract herself will change that. *'You try being starving all the time!'* a voice screams at me from inside. *'I KNOW what it's like being starving all the time …'* A sad voice whispers back.

'Oh, Hana…'

This is no life! This had been my recurring motif over the last few weeks since getting Hana home, I can't stop thinking it. *This is no life, this is no life …*

Hana's face crumpled and the tears started pouring down. Then she sobbed. Deep, gut-wrenching sobs coming from a dark place I didn't know could exist in my child. The apartment rocked with her sobs, echoes of a damaged and terrified little girl who is lost somewhere in this unfamiliar body and can't find her way out.

Maryam looked up, worried, put on her well-worn nervous smile and edged towards me. I knew she was wondering whether Hana might hit me or start shouting again. Maryam placed her hands over her ears, her face pale. I wanted to copy her and place my hands over my ears too, hide behind her blanky with her to block it out. I indulged in my new fantasy – I saw myself get up and walk out the front door and slam it shut. I leave this all behind. *This isn't my life.* I saw myself punch the lift buttons defiantly and run out into Bondi – a sun-kissed world that smells of suncream and doesn't hurt so much.

Memories of life before float through my head – bundling the girls into the car for a windy walk on Bondi Beach, watching them both run up to the line where the waves break on the shore then running away screaming with glee as they were chased by the water. Even when we got home we could still taste the salt spray on our lips or strands of hair that made their way into our mouths. Or, perhaps as a change to our daily afternoon swims, I would load them both into the double stroller – the year before Hana started school – walking all the way down to Centennial Park together for a wintery afternoon stroll. Then, pink nosed, we wade back through the bustling Junction to our apartment block, towering over the shops and rush hour hustle ready for a warming dinner of thick lentil and vegetable soup, brussels sprouts and cabbage on the side with homemade buckwheat cookies for dessert. The sun would set over the harbour, turning the neighbouring apartment blocks and trees pink and orange. Bit by bit lights would go on in the matchbox-sized apartments we could see from our bird's-eye view, illuminating those tiny people getting in from work, going about their evening. Floor upon floor: in one home someone would be cooking dinner, in the floor above someone would be brushing their teeth in front of their bathroom mirror, in another, someone lying stretched out on the sofa, remote in hand, TV already on.

Being surrounded by people in their little homes glowing in the darkness felt safe and cosy. Even in the middle of the night, popping into the kitchen for a drink, I would catch a glimpse of these homes, many apartments would still be lit up and moving with people who hadn't yet gone to bed. It was company, in a way. After dinner, I'd clean up, bath the girls, put on classical music and we'd play before the bedtime story. Then, worn out after a day of mothering, I'd tuck them up, grateful to be off duty, and curl up in my own bed to read, exhausted but relaxed, ready for my sacred time of the day.

The only tears I had to deal with then were if one of them tumbled over and grazed their knee, or maybe the frustrated tears of a silly squabble. How simple and easy life seemed to have been back then. The only food I had to think about was how low my lentil-soup stock was getting and whether I needed to make more cookies or homemade bread.

Back to the present – guilt replaced the anger and I hated myself for fantasising about running away from this new life. I took Hana in my arms and soaked up her heaving sobs as if I were a sponge. This was up to me – I needed to be the one to take this away – so I wrapped my body around hers. If I could just absorb enough of her pain, take it away from her, it would hurt me less.

Sometimes the pressure of keeping a cheerful face for Hana and Maryam would just get too much – something small would tip me over the edge and, like an exploding pressure cooker, I would flee into my walk-in wardrobe and scream – over and over again. A hollow, empty sounding repetitive scream that has probably scarred Maryam for life. Once I raked the carpeted floors with my fingers while screaming. My roars distracted me from the fact I'd ripped part of my fingernail off – I didn't notice until fifteen minutes after when I was confused to find blood pouring over my fingers.

You don't how powerful you are, until you lose it. I didn't know how important power over my children's health and wellbeing was to me, until it was gone. When it lay in the hands of doctors, care teams and pharmaceutical companies who had no emotional attachment to her, no fiery passion or love for her, did I truly begin to see what power I had held, *wielded*, before the tumour was diagnosed.

When your power is gone you are hopeless, helpless and you know that all has been lost.

When we walked back through the front door from the hospital, we brought a new child into the home. Easing our new post-brain-tumour Hana through the hallway, I remembered the wobbly feeling I'd had carrying newborn Hana home six years before, my blood loss sending my head spinning as I hiked up the three flights of stairs to the sun-baked top floor of our Rose Bay apartment with my child and my sense of responsibility increasing with each step. Clutching my swaddled baby to my chest, I crossed the threshold, merging my old life with my new, knowing nothing would ever be the same again. I had felt guilty for feeling this sense of anxiety that there was no going back now, not ever.

The last meal I'd cooked Hana at home before her surgery had been baked potatoes and green beans. I'd watched her enjoy her meal, pale faced due to her headache, pleading with the universe that this was not a Last Supper. But it was, in a way. The Hana who walked through the front door now wasn't the Hana we'd taken out three weeks before. Just as I had been weak and giddy when I brought her home swaddled in muslin, this new Hana was wobbly on *her* feet. And like the newborn she'd been, post-brain-tumour Hana didn't know if it was night or day. Nour came home from work one evening, kissed us hello, then went into the bedroom to get changed. He came out a few minutes later to have dinner.

'You had a long lie in today, Daddy,' Hana chuckled, her pen still swishing to and fro, not missing a beat as she intently coloured in a sea turtle with rainbow, fruit-scented Smiggle pens. Nour and I shared a glance – it could be funny, except it was frightening. Would she always be like this? How could she *live* if this was to be the case?

Three weeks after her surgery she spent her sixth birthday only remembering it was her birthday whenever we reminded her it was. People kept asking me – will you give her a party? The word 'party' sounded so ludicrous to me right then. A party with balloons, streamers, cake and celebration when our world had come undone at the seams?

In the first few days and weeks back home after her surgery, she had become obsessed with pens and colouring-in. She spent her days colour grouping her pens and completing one picture after another. No one was allowed to touch her pens or encroach on her area of the table – a form of obsessive compulsive disorder (OCD) that hadn't been there before her surgery. I could understand it – it was if she knew she had lost control over the processes unfolding in her body and by strictly controlling her environment by colour coding and laying her pens with obsessive precision, she could regain some sense of control over things. She wouldn't play with Maryam, or Nour and me – the only thing she wanted to do was colour in. Her eyes were cold and distant and her mind only held one thing – food. I had begun to dread it when she would lay her empty hollow eyes on me, meeting mine – there was no recognition there, no spark of love or connection – I was just the bringer of food, the maker of meals.

Her hunger tormented her from the moment she woke until the moment she fell asleep. She planned one snack or meal – going over it again and again.

'I'm hungry.'

'What's for dinner, Mummy?'

'When's morning tea?'

'When is it lunch? What am I having for lunch?'

'How many minutes now?'

'I'm hungry.'

'I'm really hungry now.'

'When is it morning tea?'

'When is dinner?'

'I'm thinking of food. When can I eat?'

'I can't stop thinking of food.'

'My tummy is saying it's hungry already.'

And my response?

'I know you're hungry. It's one hour and ten minutes now.'

'At ten o'clock.'

'Lunch is at twelve-thirty. You're having soup and salad.'

'Forty-five minutes now.'

'I know, not long now.'

'I know, love, not long now.'

'Morning tea is at ten, that's thirty-five minutes now.'

'Dinner is at five, that's two hours from now. You've just had your afternoon tea.'

'Not long now.' 'Not long now.' I might as well have recorded my voice and put it on replay, this is all I said.

Every other minute, throughout the day, day after day, there was a question about food. Her life, and our lives, revolved around meals, the timing of meals and of what those meals would consist. Then there were times when she'd cut herself off at having to wait. She'd just stare blankly into space.

If I can't eat then I'm not here – 'Mish Mawgood' as we'd say in Arabic: *Not at home.*

And then there were the unpredictable fits of rage.

'FOOOOOOOD!' she'd scream, reaching out to hit me, or scratch me. 'I'M HUNGRY!'

'EAT! I want to EAAAAT!'

One evening, after dinner, when she was angry and thinking of food, I'd encouraged her to grab a large piece of paper and scribble how she felt.

The result was a messy tangle of lines, but the whole while she scribbled she whispered: *'I hate being hungry all the time, I hate having a brain tumour'* over and over again. But she went to bed that night talking of what she'd eat for breakfast the next morning. Sometimes when sleeping, she'd suddenly shoot up in bed, eyes wide and staring into space – still asleep – she'd holler in a panic, *'I want food!'*

In the early days, we had to hide from Hana if we needed to eat and it wasn't time for her scheduled snack or meal. There was something grotesque about little Maryam learning, from very early on to hide, wide eyed on the kitchen floor, guilty for being hungry. Cramming some toast in her mouth before her unpredictable sister spotted her and started shouting about it. Food was the forbidden topic, eating had to be hidden or 'conducted' at the same time as Hana. I had a dreadful sense of foreboding that I was paving the way for Maryam's development of an eating disorder – how could anyone develop normal healthy, eating habits in a house where the day revolved around food and even the word 'food' was practically illicit?

One afternoon, exhausted, I collapsed crying on the floor next to a screaming Hana. Maryam was sobbing in my arms as Hana hit me again and again. I held out my arm for her to hit so she could vent her anger on me rather than punching her own thighs and stomach as she had the night before. I have never, *ever*, felt so alone as I did at the moment – the extreme depth of loneliness while being surrounded by two tiny, frail human beings who needed *me* to be their pillar of strength and inspiring role model was utterly gruelling. While I temporarily collapsed into my grief, unravelled for those few minutes, I wondered how I would pull myself up off that floor and continue on with the day.

But dinner had to be made, the afternoon swim had to be swum and so up I got; the smile etched back on my face – my voice still thick with the despair of the previous minutes, yet now controlled – comforting and reassuring as I got them into their swimming cossies. We laughed about the water woggles and debated what colour goggles they wanted to bring down that day. We had hours of fun memories in that pool, a place we'd religiously spent every afternoon for nearly three years, rain, wind or shine. Just a sniff of the warm, humid, chlorine-scented air as we walked through the door was enough to bring back some of these memories: Hana and Maryam darting along the poolside and jumping in, playing happily for hours together. It wasn't the same sanctuary it used to be now things had changed, once happy-go-lucky Hana now emotionally cold, refusing to play with Maryam, but I still felt so much gratitude to have it as a place to go every day – to get out of our apartment, down through the sunny courtyard to be alongside the dancing blue water. And underwater it was quiet. I would swim under for as long as I could hold my breath, savouring every second that I couldn't hear Hana ask how long we had to go until dinner.

The living agony of watching my daughter's tormented starvation was just the tip of the iceberg. The dark fear that had threaded throughout the house was related to the weighing scales and the unnatural rate that her tiny body was exploding with size. Her weight was shooting up at a rate Nour and I simply could not fathom. How could her heart keep beating in this tremendous physical assault? How *would* her heart keep beating if this continued?

I weighed Hana twice a day, once in the morning to assess for fluid loss overnight while we were still getting used to her dosages of DDAVP or Minirin to control her urine output, and again last thing at night. The numbers went up, never down; my five-year-old little girl who had a skeletal age of a three-year-old was gaining an intractable kilo a week.

24kg, 24.5kg, 25kg, 25.8kg, 26kg, 26.7kg, 28kg, 28.4kg, 29kg – within weeks we hit the 30s. None of her clothes fitted and her belly was ballooning out in front of her. She didn't look like Hana anymore, not only had we 'lost' our daughter during surgery, but we were tortured with the ongoing loss of her every day. Sometimes Nour and I would rub salt into our wounds, trying to 'see' Hana in the rapidly changing face and body in front of us but it was futile – Hana wasn't there, she was gone and going even further away each day.

The cruelty of Hana's relentless weight gain was magnified by the fact she had no issues controlling how much she ate in that she would eat a small meal slowly, delicately and be satisfied with it, and she wouldn't dream of taking any extra food unless I said she could. Some survivors of her type of tumour were unable to control themselves around food – fishing it out of bins, sneaking into the pantry at night but she was so disciplined, we never needed to lock the kitchen cupboards and fridge. She lived on organic buckwheat, cashew nuts, salads, broccoli, lentil soups, peas – she loved her vegetables, and her favourite food was still brussels sprouts and iceberg lettuce! However her post-meal satiety would be short lived and an hour after eating the obsessive thoughts around her next scheduled meal would begin to haunt her.

Within weeks of leaving hospital, the fierce gain had affected her tiny immature joints. Walking became so painful she would cry from short walks to the shops. Escalating as quickly as her weight gain so did her pain – even walking across the living room, getting out of bed and the bath caused her to cry from pain. To add to the surreal and nightmarish quality of our daily existence she began hobbling and shuffling around like a little old woman, either crying or whispering *'ow ow ow'* with every little movement.

Bondi Junction was so convenient for access to medical personnel, pharmacies, food and clothes shops, but Hana was unable to even walk to buy food and so, after only a short time, so I could take care of the family, I decided to get her a wheelchair. I'd have used a stroller if she'd fit in one, but her weight gain meant that, even though she was still short in stature, she'd never fit in a stroller again. I was adamant that the wheelchair would not be seen as a negative thing but a positive aid to facilitating an easier life for us; less pain for Hana, less stress for me and Maryam.

My decision was immediately criticised by Hana's treating doctors. 'Why is she in this wheelchair?'

'I got the chair because she's in agony,' I said, trying to keep the defensive tone out of my voice. 'She cries with pain when walking! I can't bear the crying day after day – I need to be able to go to the shops to do simple things like get food for the family or her prescriptions from the pharmacy – no one else can do that for me.' Apart from my brother, who was in Australia for a few months, we were alone in Australia – no parents to help out, and a very small friendship network.

We actually named it the 'Sydney Curse' because, in our nine years in Australia, everyone we felt we connected with and with whom we wanted to pursue friendships, always ended up moving either interstate or abroad.

The doctor sat back in his chair, let out a deep breath as he nodded, '*We* tend to say that wheelchairs should only be used for, oh, I don't know, bigger trips, like going to the zoo.'

The zoo? I blinked and almost echoed him blankly. I couldn't fathom how disconnected he was from my daily hell if he could think for a single moment that Hana was well enough to go to the zoo.

'*We* don't encourage their use for local trips, like popping to the shops – things in the local community. Kids can get used to them, you know,' he continued knowingly. 'Then they use them more than, perhaps … they *should.*'

The early appointments with specialists; post-op appointments with a brain injury or rehab team and the endocrinologists who managed her hormones, had begun. I would outline the enormous issues we were facing with appetite disturbance and frightening weight gain, but there was a disconcerting inability to acknowledge the severity of our circumstances. Hana was on a nonstop fast train to rapid-onset morbid obesity, yet the precious time with specialists would be spent analysing hormone medications, which in our mind, were the easiest part of her brain injury and barely needed more than a ten minute analysis.

'She'll have to grow into her weight,' one dismissed. But how can anyone grow into a kilo a week?

And another: 'There's not much that can be done about the obesity. Unfortunately, it can happen with this tumour. *You'll just have to get used to it.*'

Then there was one that denied she even had a problem: 'She hasn't got hyperphagia – uncontrollable eating – unless she's picking food out of bins. This will settle down,' he said. 'It's normal to gain weight after surgery.'

But these long-awaited appointments were few and far between. The main reason we were told to see anyone was for hormone regulation – I would arrive at each appointment hopeful that we would actually formulate some sort of action plan, yet inconceivably no one was willing to attempt to fully address the hypothalamic obesity.

There had to be a way out of this. I couldn't stand the acute sense of disempowerment – it was torturous; if they wouldn't help us, I'd have to do it myself:

'There! Hypothalamic healing in rats with laser acupuncture,' I declared, pointing to the study on PubMed. I was on to something. 'Brain healing is possible!'

I had set out on my quest to heal Hana within days of getting her home. Clutching a wad of studies and papers in my hands, 'I'm going to find a way to heal Hana's brain,' I said fervently to Nour.

There wasn't any doubt in his eyes that I wouldn't when he whispered to me, 'I'm so glad I married you.'

We started with acupuncture, laser acupuncture, naturopathic regimes, and a variety of herbal remedies and drugs for both brain health and appetite control that I researched online.

I made 'The Promise' to Hana one morning as she walked out of my bedroom, the rays of sunlight streaming behind her, highlighting the blondest bits in her hair. She was sobbing with hunger, breakfast was over, but she'd forgotten she'd already eaten it and morning tea was hours away. I pulled her into my arms, this little girl that was my little girl and wasn't my little girl all at the same time.

'I will heal you,' I whispered fiercely, growling like a tiger. 'This will *not* last forever.' I believed it! I truly did. 'I will find a way to heal your brain.'

She looked up at me, clear blue-green eyes, although empty, were still a reflection of mine – she lisped her response, 'Yes, you will heal me, Mummy.'

Now there was no way I wouldn't succeed. It was done, contracted! I would dedicate my life to finding a cure until the day I died. I well knew that I would not find peace. When there is a raging war, there is no peace! I had declared war and the battles had only just began.

I would either succeed and make things right again or I would fail, but I would die trying.

Chapter Six

I was broken.

I was lying down on the carpet, amongst Maryam's scattered toys. We had just finished our evening game of dolls, and I was trying to muster the energy to give Hana her evening medications: hydrocortisone, Minirin and growth hormone before weighing her, brushing everyone's teeth, reading the bedtime story then tucking them both in. I always made sure Maryam and I had an evening game as it was the only time of the day that I could completely dedicate to her alone. I also felt I had to try and compensate for Hana's lack of interest in her now – Hana either ignored Maryam or snapped at her. In the same way I felt I had lost my daughter, I knew that Maryam was grieving for a lost sister.

I was looking up at the lights on the living-room ceiling. The familiar classical evening music that I put on every day at dusk was playing, lulling me out of my body. I pretended the light was the sun and that I was flying through space leaving this all behind. It was all over and I was so happy to die, even if it meant non-existence – not existing was better than the pain of living. The only time I could tolerate being here, being Naomi, was when I was about to fall asleep at night with Maryam curled up in my arms like a kitten or a coiled worm and the pain of being alive eased into oblivion for a few hours during sleep. But when the morning came, before I was even aware of who and where I was, sickness wormed its way into my stomach, warning me that I must remember that I didn't want to be here anymore and that I must be alive again that day.

For the first time since I'd chosen to be an atheist and faced the prospect of annihilation upon my death, I was grateful that I would not be able to live eternally. The thought that one day, when I died, I would not have to feel this pain anymore was blissful. It was looking at the stars at night that helped me. I identified with them: they were finite too, nothing was permanent. One day I would return to the nebulous dust that bore me – the whole of Planet Earth would return to dust as our Sun reached its dying days, scorching the planet and turning it to a cinder. Then it would all be over and the quiet that follows would be bliss.

I didn't know it was possible to feel so broken and still smile and carry on as if you hadn't disintegrated on the inside.

My beautiful fun-loving, strong, determined, hilarious, clown-like little girl had ballooned into a being that was unrecognisable. And it hurt to look at her – her suffering screamed with her size: she was now officially morbidly obese and days with her had separated me further from whatever 'normality' I thought I was ever close to achieving as a human. I had to update her wardrobe every few weeks as nothing would fit her for more than a couple of weeks at a time and finding shoes that fit her swollen, broad feet was getting impossible. For now she was living in the widest pair of sandals we could find, the Velcro straps only just touched each other to keep the sandal together.

When I pushed her in her wheelchair down the street, her white sandalled feet dangling below her, her belly ballooning in front of her like a pregnant mother, her little face upturned staring without emotion into the crowds, here but not here, *Mish Mawgood*, people stared at her then at me, then back to her.

And I would think, *I am not like you. I can't think like you think, I can't talk about the things you talk about, or laugh about, or care about. I am completely and utterly alone and I will never be like any of you ever again.*

'I've texted you a couple of times but didn't get a response—'

One day when walking back from Woolworths in Bondi Junction's bustling Westfield I bumped into a mum from Maryam's preschool. I hated bumping into people I knew because it meant I'd have to make conversation and maybe even smile at them. I blinked at her, slightly dazed in the sunlight and groggy from broken sleep. Hana's oral Minirin, her medication for her diabetes insipidus, just didn't seem to work effectively and I'd spent too many nights spontaneously waking up in shock only to find that she had literally peed out litres of fluid into her bed. The pull-up nappies we were using for this temporary night-time incontinence would weigh in at well over a 1kg on my Thermomix scales that I'd switch on in the eerie glow of the streetlamp-lit kitchen at 2 am. As well as this, her mattress and sheets would be drenched with unthinkable amounts of urine. Too many nights I'd had to drag her out of bed, sit her at the table and force her to down two litres of fluid before returning back to bed. I didn't ever dare to take her heart rate because I knew it would be sky high at the sudden fluid loss, simply placing my fingers over her pulse would be enough to frighten me out of any more sleep that night. I had been researching a new way of administering her medication intranasally – it was time to insist on a medication switch away from these useless tablets.

We stood in middle of the street, an island forking the stream of people.

'—It was about Ali's party, his birthday party.' She avoided my eyes, she was angry I could sense it, irritated that I may have ignored the party invite, how audacious of me.

My head spun with a response. My days are spent wracking my brains for a way to end Hana's suffering and a way to heal her. I count her pulse constantly because it helps me assess her hydration levels, thyroid levels or for when she needs a stress dose of steroids. I listen to her breathe in case she stops suddenly in her sleep, I monitor her shuffle on ankles to see how bad her pain is, I take note of the severity of her acid reflux, listen to her cry for food, and I try endlessly to keep her distracted from the monster hunger within. All the while I worry about the impact this is having on Maryam and I wonder if I'm doing a good enough job, and that I should be doing a better one.

But instead: 'P-party?' I said weakly. 'I'm not sure I got the text.' I turned away, I couldn't bear this conversation anymore. I couldn't even pretend to bear it. If I ever thought I was different before then I was an alien now. I wouldn't ever fit in anywhere ever again.

Ugly questions had begun to snake their way into my mind – was this a life worth living? If, knowing the fallout from this surgery, was the surgeon truly 'doing no harm' by saving her life? And the ugliest question of all – would *my* life be easier if she hadn't survived? If I could just grieve, then heal and move on. But now I was in a state of static grief whose best friend was terror – tightly knitted together, they created a whirlpool of despair.

These questions would swing by, replaced then with guilt. How could I ask myself these questions – I would reach out to take her pulse, and kiss her plump cheek – always slightly damp with sweat. I know I would die for her every day, over and over again.

Evening routine unfolded every night in the same fashion – playing with Maryam, a 200-piece space puzzle with Hana, meds, then time for the evening weight.

'Let's hop onto the scales before bed!' I'd call brightly, hiding the fear snaking its way through my stomach, knowing the numbers would go up, but hoping, always hoping for a miracle. Keeping that hope alive, however made it hurt even more each evening the weight would jump. It was the same every night, the digital numbers would flash 0:0 ... then the silence as it adjusted to get her weight, the heavy feeling of dread in those seconds until the flashing new weight screamed itself out at me. Oblivious, she would get off and head straight to the bedroom, sleep the only thing on her mind at that moment. And I would let out shuddery exhalation, close my eyes while resting my head against the cool white-tiled bathroom wall.

No, no, no. It can't be. It just can't be another kilo. This isn't real ...

I envied Nour for being able to escape our life by going to work – he never had to do the evening weighings and feel what I felt every day, inescapably face to face with Hana's suffering. If he was at home at weighing time, he'd walk by the bathroom door and he wouldn't even need to hear what I had to say because my face would say it all. But, in a monotone, I would declare the new weight, which was always impossibly higher than the day before. He would keep a straight face as I told him, because there is simply no expression for this. It's not like you can go, 'Oh shit, another kilo?' Not when this extra kilo was a kilo closer to taking your child's life away. It was such an absurd weight gain, so quick and so ferocious there was no expression your face can adopt when you see the scales go up. And the feeling of complete and utter powerlessness – there isn't even energy to speak.

My first medical breakthrough came on a Sunday afternoon while scrolling through my Facebook feed. I was sitting on the floor, leaning against the French windows, my background an endless blue sky, decorated with fluffy white clouds over Bondi.

One member of a Craniopharyngioma Facebook group posted an article on the 'love hormone' oxytocin, which she had found interesting because as a 'cranio' and new mum she was using intranasal oxytocin to facilitate the milk ejection reflex so she could breastfeed her newborn twins, without that hormone breastfeeding would have been impossible. Entranced, I opened the article and began to read – within seconds I couldn't believe that I had hadn't thought of this before.

The article outlined a myriad of ways that oxytocin was beneficial to the human body – way beyond the old fashioned concepts of it being solely a hormone for labour and lactation. There was documented benefits for social interaction, wound healing, bone integrity, muscle regeneration, feelings of wellbeing and reduced stress and anxiety. But two things struck, my heart began racing as I began exclaiming.

'Oh, my God ... this is amazing,'

Nour looked up from his computer at the dining-room table where he was working on a PowerPoint lecture he'd be presenting in Europe later in the year.

'This is ... I've found a missing link!' I said.

Oxytocin had been used in some clinical trials for obesity and appetite control! Because Hana's pituitary gland wasn't working, in theory, she should be unable to produce oxytocin as it was secreted from the posterior pituitary along with antidiuretic hormone for which she took her Minirin to substitute. Could aspects of her extreme hypothalamic damage be reduced by the administration of oxytocin? That is to say – could part of her weight issue be related to oxytocin deficiency as well her hypothalamic damage?

'I can't believe this! NOUR!' I shouted. 'Hana can't produce oxytocin, it's another hormone, right? She simply takes life-sustaining hormones – this one isn't necessary for keeping her alive but it may help her! In, oh loads of ways, but it has recently been shown to be useful in reducing appetite and in facilitating weight loss!'

Now I was pacing up and down the living room, my thoughts zooming through my head at a billion miles an hour. I tried to hold off talking, in this state I'd likely speak too loudly and quickly which Nour always said made me sound aggressive – although from my perspective it was just passion.

I knew that oxytocin was a 'safe' hormone – I had already come across clinical trials where it had been used safely in autistic children to improve social interaction and improve eye contact. I knew, in every ounce of my being, that Hana HAD to have this hormone. It had a myriad of bodily functions that could improve her overall health and longevity – and could likely improve her quality of life.

How would I get this medication? What sort of barriers would I have in front of me? My fists were literally balled and held ready for a fight. I did not have a single open-minded doctor that I could go to at that stage to even consider raising this issue. Trialling an untested hormone for the first time in this patient population in a *child*? No one would support this. Taking in a few deep breaths I sat down at my computer to conduct a search.

Within thirty minutes I'd successfully scoured the existing evidence base and could not find a single reference to oxytocin being used in the panhypopituitary population – that is to say, the patient population which had no pituitary function. My mind was completely boggling at this stage.

How on Earth could this incredibly well-known hormone never have been even trialled as a potential replacement therapy for those who could not produce it because of pituitary damage or failure? How sad, I thought, this had never been researched in populations of individuals whose quality of life were well documented to be poor.

Why and how could this hormone currently be utilised in clinical trials as a medication for disorders in many areas other than endocrinology (hormones) yet no one had even postulated that it might actually have some benefit for hormone 'patients', those who don't produce it at all? Had I really stumbled upon a concept that, if undertaken, would be a medical WORLD FIRST?

ME?

The enormity of what I had stumbled upon was so massive it kept hitting me in waves. I just didn't know what to do next – would anyone believe me? How could I disseminate this information to help Hana and wake up others to this? I wanted to yell it from the mountain tops.

My mother-in-law, who was a well-known, high profile paediatrician in Cairo, rang shortly afterwards to touch base with us and the girls via her weekly FaceTime call and I hurriedly explained my findings.

'I haven't heard of this,' she said, sounding confused.

'Yes, I know!' I sucked in some air and counted to five so that I didn't sound too passionate and impatient. 'I know you haven't heard of this, I'M THE FIRST person to suggest this, as far as I can see. The evidence base is totally devoid of any reference to oxytocin in the Panpit patient population yet it is a HORMONE that is USEFUL for the body!'

'I'll ask around,' she said, trying to be helpful. 'I'll see what my colleagues think.'

Blowing off an exasperated sigh into the spare room – sometimes my brain just galloped on ahead all by itself, and there was too much to say to even bother trying. When I was thinking like this I'd find the thought patterns of others too slow and gluey to even try to communicate. Especially when Nour would say something that I had ruled out light seconds ago – then I'd jut in too loudly and get accused of being aggressive. I surrendered my phone to Nour, there was no point in saying what I truly thought – that her colleagues wouldn't have considered this. No one had, yet it was so blindingly obvious, how can it have taken me three whole months to have missed this!? How stupid of me!

That afternoon I got typing. I started the series of blogs on oxytocin and got on to emailing whoever I could. The first doctor I emailed was based in Western Australia, he was a paediatric endocrinologist who specialised in obesity – someone I thought should be fascinated by this hormonal link to improving obesity. What did he know about oxytocin, I asked him. Could we study it to see if it could help children like Hana? I was willing to do a PhD on the topic! I was smugly convinced he'd be fascinated about this finding and be equally desperate to research the implications!

His reply was almost instant. *Interesting*, he said. *But not his area.*

I was dumbstruck! Hormones, obesity, yet not *his* area? Well then, whose area?

'I don't get it!' I exclaimed loudly at the screen of my lap top.

'I don't either,' Nour agreed. 'Endocrinology here in Australia just seems to be about diabetes – they aren't interested in anything else.'

My blog became my outlet – I sent out a plea for scientists worldwide to consider researching oxytocin for the panhypopit and hypothalamic obesity (HO) groups – my loyal followers were wonderful and the post had over reach of over 25,000 in three days, which, back in those days, was a huge audience for me. Then people from all over the world began to contact me, interested in this concept of oxytocin treatment. In a short time I'd become known as the 'go to' person for oxytocin for the pituitary and craniopharyngioma population.

But, what about getting it for Hana?

I was ready to jump on a plane or to procure it illegally – I was ready for anything, but as luck would have it, such dramatic actions weren't necessary.

The incredible barrier to getting a script for, and obtaining, oxytocin was something that I would, over the next few years, observe so many others face but, as pure luck would have it, there would be no barrier for me. Monday morning, through my own integrative compounding pharmacist, I was put in touch with John Hart, a progressive, integrative GP who had a clinic in the city, a few kilometres from our apartment. His passion was hormone regulation and brain health for ageing adults but, after hearing Hana's story through my pleading email, he agreed to see her. It has to be said that I fell a little bit in love with John; I had finally found a medical practitioner who I actually connected with and he was willing to work with me, welcoming my ideas and input, sharing potentially relevant information with me regularly. What an amazing find.

And so it happened that, within a week of discovering the 'hormone' gap in Hana's post-operative medication regime, oxytocin was sitting proudly in my fridge.

She was playing with her beads on the floor. I knelt down and squirted the medication up her nostril before leaning back onto my ankles. The house was filled with anticipation. Was this the cure to her uncontrollable weight gain? Would it take away her terrible hunger and transform our lives from today onwards?

The day unfolded pretty much as usual. Hana still wasn't back at school – she would only ever return part-time for a two-year period – and so I distracted her with some home schooling books, science experiments and reading books, there were snacks, puzzles, games ... but what was different, immediately from that first dose was Hana's sociability. That afternoon, after three months of literally cajoling her into the swimming pool for our afternoon swim, in the blink of an eye, she'd whipped off her towel, leapt into the pool and swam a width underwater ready for a game with her sister: Mums and Babies, the first game they'd played together since Hana's surgery. Spellbound, we watched dumbstruck as Hana emerged from the water in a splash, laughing her head off! This was the oxytocin: she was somehow happier, the happiness made her more motivated and this made her want to socialise.

The dramatic impact of the hormone during those initial days reduced a little as her body adjusted and after we lowered her dose due to its effect on her water retention; because oxytocin bears a very similar molecular structure to the antidiuretic hormone, both being secreted from the posterior pituitary. Hana's obsessive colouring-in and laying-out of pens, her OCD, had all but disappeared at the higher dose of oxytocin. We couldn't maintain that level, so it did return at the lower maintenance doses. However, one constant benefit stayed with us – her desire to do things with us again and, incredibly, the expression of love towards me and Nour, but mostly to Maryam. After the cold shoulder for three months, little Maryam began to get random hugs from Hana again, and 'I love my sister' … It would bring tears to my eyes. Darling Maryam deserved every cuddle and expression of affection. Weeks in, it was clear that oxytocin was not going to impact upon Hana's weight and appetite in the way I had hoped it would, however, because of the phenomenal social changes and dramatic improvement in quality of life, oxytocin was going to be a permanent aspect of her hormone regime.

Chapter Seven

In spite of the fact I had much-valued GP support behind Hana's oxytocin and had legally procured a prescription for it with ongoing guidance and input from John, there were still issues from Hana's specialists, including her current endocrinologist, for giving her medication that was not yet 'proven' by the mainstream.

'Oxytocin: NOT PRESCRIBED BY ME,' was one red flag she had written on a letter to Hana's paediatrician.

'You also altered Hana's thyroid hormones without doctor authorisation,' her paediatrician said, peering over his spectacles.

The world started spinning around me. Suddenly I knew what was going on: they were watching me for my over-involvement with Hana's care. I was definitely guilty – but also not guilty – I was desperately trying to keep my daughter alive where they were falling short!

'I HAD to decrease her thyroid because she was sweating like a … I don't know what, tachycardic and she couldn't sleep,' I protested passionately, feeling the backs of my legs begin to sweat against his leather couch. 'I can't wait six weeks for the next appointment to be told to lower her dose when it was clear her thyroid levels were too high! Literally two days after reducing her dose, her symptoms subsided. I called her, I emailed her suggesting we lower the dose due to these symptoms – but she wouldn't tell me to reduce the dose – what was I supposed to do?!' Tears sprung into my eyes.

'It's in my notes,' he said. This was a warning. But then things got worse.

I was actually there to see him to get help for Hana's obesity, her current endocrinologist had told her to 'watch what she ate' – painful advice considering it was well documented that HO, or hypothalamic obesity, was unaffected by strict dietary regimes. And we would wait weeks/months between appointments to see her. The inaction on her side was nothing but a prescription for an early death and so I had paid our paediatrician a visit asking that we transfer to someone at a different hospital who, I hoped, would be proactive in putting together a plan to tackle the weight. Upon seeing Hana, the paediatrician was really worried, thankfully, as worried as we were. So much so he picked up the phone and rang this new endocrinologist we wanted to see, in front of me.

The specialist on the end of the phone however how no idea that I was in the room.

'I'm REALLY worried about Hana,' our paed said. 'She's the patient transferring from—'

'Ah yes, I know of her,' the endo said, his voice muffled but audible. 'Her family have issues with *compliance*, and they discharged against medical advice—'

'Yes, I know. But there is something I can TELL YOU about that … the problem is, she needs to see you really urgently. She's already nearly doubled her weight and her parents say she is gasping for breath in her sleep so it looks like she's developed sleep apnoea—'

'Look, I'll have a look at her notes and send through some recommendations, but I don't know if—' he cut out, the paediatrician looked guiltily at me, '—and then we'll *see* about getting her into clinic sooner.'

After hanging up, the paediatrician pursed his lips. 'He is worried you won't *do what he says*.'

I felt my cheeks flush in instant indignation, my heart racing. Hana was sitting next to me on the fake leather couch, staring glumly into space. *Mish Mawgoud.*

'You must *do what he says*.'

Like a schoolgirl being told off by a teacher, my eyes welled up with tears. I worked so hard to educate myself to *know* as much as I possibly could! And now there was this terrible feeling creeping through me: Were they thinking of getting Social Services involved because I was giving Hana oxytocin and because I'd cut down her thyroid meds without permission? Then came guilt and shame – was *I* screwing up my daughter's care? With that thought self-doubt began to seep through me like ink.

'You've taken on too much,' he assured me. 'This is too much for you. You need to leave this up to the experts. Hormones are incredibly complex. She needs a specialist controlling this. Trust Rodney, he really knows what he is doing.'

I left the office giddy, my heart pounding loudly in my chest. With flushed cheeks and trembling hands, I steered Hana's wheelchair to the lifts – I was close to vomiting.

'Well, WE will decide if he is an expert when we see him.' Nour, bless him, instantly sided with me when I called him. He found it hard to answer his phone at work as he was usually back to back with patients. However, since Hana's surgery, he always made an effort to leave whatever he was doing now to answer my calls. My voice was subdued and sad – even our swim later that day hadn't erased my fury, guilt and nausea from the appointment with the paediatrician. But what was worse than all those feelings was my own sense of self-doubt, that somehow I was screwing up Hana's care.

'We haven't found a single "expert" in Australia after months of looking. And for God's sake, you don't need a degree in endocrinology to know when someone's *thyroid* dose is too high. It's like everyone deliberately freaks out about the word "endocrinology" like it's too complicated for anyone to even attempt to understand unless they are an endocrinologist,' he blew into the phone.

I was looking out the bedroom window, down at the courtyard, through the glass panes on the swimming pool roof. Someone had put a blue-and-white striped towel on one of the deckchairs. I felt a distracted wave of relief that the pool had been empty for our swim – I hated sharing the pool – and there was similar wave of relief that Nour supported me. What if he had begun to doubt me too? What if he had also thought that I was becoming the problem? He was leaving much of the research and planning for Hana up to me – believing that I could do it, but I wouldn't have been able to bear it if he'd thought I was going too far.

'Doctors are very proud and don't like to be questioned, Naomi. You really need to be more submissive.'

A medical relative had been reading through a long email I had put together for a genuine expert on HO, hypothalamic obesity and craniopharyngioma survivors based in Germany. He had published extensive research on the topic and had a huge cohort of craniopharyngioma survivors that he worked with – this was how one gained the title 'expert'! I had written frankly about our issues and the barriers we were facing to getting progressive help here in Australia.

'My friend didn't like the tone of your letter, Naomi. For Hana's sake you need to be more submissive because you will alienate her from getting the care she needs.'

After the appointment with the paediatrician, hearing this feedback made me feel even worse. The word *submissive* wasn't in my vocabulary! But could I be submissive for Hana's sake? But how would being submissive help Hana when Australian self-proclaimed 'experts' had no previous experience in caring for someone with her condition and equally weren't doing anything for her?

'The question is, will he bring forward Hana's appointment when he knows how worried the paed is and that she is gaining a kilo a week?' Nour asked.

'Not necessarily,' I said. 'But he *is* sending through some recommendations and one is to stop the oxytocin.'

'Oh really?' Nour said snidely. 'He can get stuffed with *that* recommendation.' I could see him shaking his head, disgusted, on the end of the phone. 'I had really hoped this one would be worth the wait but – far out – it isn't boding well, is it? If we wait until the end of August to see him that will be another eight kilos of weight gain.'

We didn't stop the oxytocin which would have decreased the quality of not only Hana's life but also ours and we *did* have to wait two months for the appointment, in spite of Hana's critical health issues. For the first time that year, Nour decided that he wouldn't leave me in the line of fire alone now, after seeing my self-confidence take a beating by the patronising accusations of having 'taken on too much'. He decided that, from now on, we would appear as a united front in how we approached Hana's care.

'I don't want you being bullied,' he'd said.

'I don't get bullied!' I protested loudly. 'No one bullies me! They're just …' I didn't have any words for it, but I would never see myself as a victim! As far as I was concerned no one would dare bully me. Yet … why did I feel so vulnerable?

Two months later and another eight kilos on Hana's tiny frame, we headed to another hospital's outpatient clinic to meet the new endocrinologist – the 'expert' who we must 'do what he says'. In Nour's backpack was a stack of medical papers on treatment options for extreme HO that can be tried in the most severe cases from Ritalin, a stimulant; to metformin, a drug for managing high insulin levels; an injectable drug called octreotride for severely high levels of insulin; surgical vagotomies, which involved cutting the vagus nerve; and lastly, bariatric surgery. It was the lap-band procedure among the bariatric procedures that interested us the most, and it was the German expert I'd written to who had conducted the most research in this area.

My heart was beating nervously in my chest. I desperately wanted to reveal the extent of my knowledge base so we could progress quickly and make some decisions, yet I knew it would be wrong to appear too confident and too knowledgeable in case he felt threatened and thought me overbearing.

Here's what I was dying to say:

As a first port of call, octreotide would be a good choice to reduce her hyperinsulinemia – which, as you most likely know, are commonly elevated to extreme levels with hypothalamic damage. The high levels of insulin alone contribute to the weight gain and appetite disturbance. Well, Lustig's studies have shown some promising results with weight control and appetite reduction. Although it is painful (two large subcutaneous injections a day) and it can have nasty side effects, such as life-threatening pancreatitis, it is, according to the research, generally very well tolerated.

I'm reluctant to try the Ritalin – I just don't see it as a good long-term option for her and the 'come-downs' may be an issue due to her moodiness. But, as I'm sure you're aware, the evidence suggests it may help compensate for decreased sympathetic nervous system 'tone' that can occur after craniopharyngioma. Enhancing this tone could, in theory, reduce her weight and appetite.

But what we are mostly interested in is the lap-band procedure. The studies have shown a significant decrease in 'food focus' in an adolescent patient sample who had the lap band with HO after craniopharyngioma which significantly improved their quality of life. But, I hear you ask, how would it work considering Hana doesn't overeat and the lap band is primarily prescribed for over-eaters? Well, it is postulated that the physical presence of the band over the vagus nerve provides a sort of 'functional vagotomy' – an alternative to the irreversible surgical vagotomy that Lustig has reported some successes with in studies on the hypothalamically obese population. Obviously we are in uncharted waters here as there are no case reports or studies to mention that refer to bariatrics in such a young age. But, considering this obesity is ultimately a life-threatening condition, we are prepared to lead the way with testing this treatment.

Instead, I sat there quietly, waiting for his first response: 'I've never heard of octreotide for this condition before.' He instantly dismissed this before we even had a chance to outline Lustig's extensive research in the area. I'd had been communicating with him personally in the USA by email a couple of weeks before.

'And bariatrics is completely contraindicated in this area,' he further advised poignantly before turning his attention to the hormones – as usual the only thing the endos wanted to focus on – the only aspect of Hana's health that we found easy to manage.

'I can't say that I'm happy with the oxytocin,' he said sternly, jotting down Hana's daily dose.

'She has had tremendous psychosocial improvements on it,' I spoke quietly and with respect so that I wouldn't come across as the non-compliant parent he believed I was.

'Hmm, *well.*' He then turned his attention to Hana's Minirin and water balance, and began to construct an incredibly complex equation where I would give Hana a tiny squirt of a different type of spray and see how long it lasted before phoning him to get told how much to give next time, even though we'd already changed to a spray that had finally begun to work for us. Nour and I smiled wanly, without even looking at each other we knew the show was over. Once again, the aspects of Hana's medical conditions we were aching to discuss, that were destroying her quality of life and reducing her life expectancy by the day, hadn't been discussed for more than a few minutes.

That night, Nour and I sat around the dining-room table, his laptop open and ready as we brainstormed how we would concoct our feedback about the long-awaited consult to the paediatrician.

'We have to be careful how we frame this,' I said. 'He already made it clear that he thinks he is an "expert" and that we must DO what he says!' We could be in hot water if we were now thought to be refusing to cooperate with this expert we'd been told was one of the best.

'What a joke of a specialist,' Nour snorted. 'He didn't have the decency to do any research on Hana's condition before we turned up and he had eight weeks to do so. It's just common sense – you know you're getting in a rare and complex case, you do your reading before they come in. In this day and age it's impossible to stay up to date with all the emerging research, studies, information shared at conferences and so on … You can't rely on what you were taught in medical school thirty years ago. Hang on, I've got an idea—'

He googled hypothalamic obesity, octreotide and bariatric surgery and took a screen shot of the first few pages of the search.

'I'll attach these images to the email. This is evidence that the treatment options we are proposing are evidence based AND to illustrate to him that this endo isn't the expert he thinks he is, not to mention highlighting how he didn't even take five minutes to update himself on the medical literature.'

'Great idea – he will then see for himself that even a simple Google search would have brought him up to date with the latest research and the things we've been suggesting.'

I then dictated a paragraph to highlight the endo's embarrassing confusion over bariatrics – bariatric surgeries such as lap bands were indeed contraindicated for HO that occurred as a result of a genetic condition called Prader-Willi syndrome, but not HO due to craniopharyngioma. These were two differing types of hypothalamic obesity and, since Hana didn't present with cognitive impairment and reduced impulse control, she wasn't at risk of 'eating herself to death' like someone suffering with Prader-Willi syndrome.

So, after months of anxious waiting to see this expert, we were back at square one and our support system here in Australia was dwindling – if we chose to pursue another endo because we didn't want to *'do what he says'*, we would most likely be further blacklisted as doctor shoppers.

Meanwhile I waited nervously for the reply from Germany. He now was our only hope for an intelligent, experienced 'expert' opinion on Hana. But my stomach twisted whenever I thought about it – *'she didn't like the tone'* – would he be insulted by my well-researched and frank portrayal of Hana's state and our struggles to her help? Was my extensive knowledge base going to insult him too? Should I have acted more dumb and clueless while appealing for his help? And would he be equally disdainful about the daring addition of oxytocin to her regime? If so, who could we turn to next for help?

Chapter Eight

'*WE* have a rule about drinking,' the nurse said, parading the offending object in her hands, spinning it around to highlight its transgression. It was a week after seeing the new endocrinologist we'd already crossed off our lists – yet, in order to appear compliant, as promised, I'd taken Hana into hospital to receive education on the intranasal spray the doctor was wanting us to switch to. Even though we had no intention of changing from a regime that had finally started working for us. '*WE* say water in normal drinking cups, *SPECIAL* drinks go in *SPECIAL* cups for *SPECIAL* occasions.'

'Yeah, well I—' my insides twisted with instant irritation, I felt like smashing my fist, no, better, my forehead into the table. *Here it comes, the pious, self-righteous lecture …*

She'd run out of things to say and, like a sniffer dog catching a glimpse of illicit drugs in someone's suitcase at the carousel, had caught a whiff of a slightly cloudy mixture in Hana's drinking bottle. Almost in slow motion I'd seen her reach out her hand. I felt like stretching out my arm, knocking her hand away – roaring 'NOOOOOO' in that deep, low sound voices make in slo-mo. Instead, only my eyes widened. She picked it up as if she owned it, gingerly gave it a little shake – oh she *knew* this was contraband! Her movements were possessive – as if it was the drinking bottle of her own child, not that of a total stranger she'd just met for the first time. Yep, I was totally sprung.

'Now, Hana.' She drew herself up tall as she took it upon herself to Reinforce The Law, then she stretched herself out over the desk to make a point to me, '*WE* say *SPECIAL* drinks go in *SPECIAL* cups for *SPECIAL* times, alright?' The 'alright' was drawn out and ended up in that slightly higher pitch, the end of a painfully patronising sentence.

'Yes,' Hana lisped, glancing up from her colouring, her eyes dark rimmed and sunken the way they go when she was really dehydrated and needed more fluid. She was also very tachycardic, the heat of the weekend had caught her (and me) out – the first time we'd had to really deal with her diabetes insipidus in the heat, and I was learning, rapidly, that she needed to drink a lot more on these hot days. A blood sodium taken the next day would reveal a sky-high number, a result that, if she had been in hospital, they'd have never have discharged her. And it would take me five whole days after that to get it down, measuring the impact of her continual sipping by her slowing pulse.

'Normally Hana will drink water, no problem, it's just I had to pick her up straight from school today and *I know* she's hypernatremic and I just wanted get to some quick fluid into her—' I started and I hated myself for feeling like I should justify the fact I was trying to keep my daughter hydrated by giving her the occasional diluted pear juice to sip as a change from the – literally – litres of water she had to gulp down every single day.

But the nurse wasn't listening. I'd committed the cardinal sin of giving my child FRUIT JUICE. No interest in the fact this 'fruit juice' was the tiniest piece of pureed pear mixed with freshly filtered alkaline water, no interest in the fact that this was the only source of fruit that Hana got because fruit is high carb. Or that I sometimes did give her diluted fruit juice to avoid a trip to ED for emergency IV fluids because her sense of thirst had been damaged by her tumour. Not to mention embracing the reality of looking after a child that has diabetes insipidus, the lived experience where 'theories' and 'rules' simply go to pot and you do what you need to do in order to survive and keep your daughter out of hospital and *alive.*

'Because this is part of the reason "we" are looking for treatment, isn't it?' She raised her eyebrows and I was being lectured to by an old school teacher, I'm twelve years old again and shifting in my uncomfortable black tie-up school shoes. 'This sort of thing would contribute, hmmm?'

'Well, she actually really loves water,' I blurt out like the twelve-year-old would and kick myself – if only I'd remembered to put water in her bottle for this appointment, screwed by one small slip …

At the same time I wanted to shout, 'How dare you speak to me like this? You know nothing about me, nothing about my educational background, my knowledge base and how I've devoted every waking second of my life to caring for my girls. Everything I do for them is for a well thought-out reason, highly analysed and critiqued a few times by my inner self and bounced off my equally critical husband – diluted pear juice is actually the result of one of these well thought-out, complex, critiqued analyses where we had to weigh immediate lifesaving intervention (hydration on a daily basis) versus increasing the severity of her hyperinsulinemia – something we'd been working hard at reducing through ensuring her snacks were healthy fat and protein-based rather than carbohydrates – hoping to avoid insulin spikes at morning and afternoon teatimes. This, we hoped, would slow (but not prevent) the inevitable progression of a different type of diabetes, diabetes mellitus Type 2 – sugar diabetes.'

'And how do you give the thyroid medication?' she asked suddenly, randomly changing the subject. I just want to tell her to piss off, I've been managing this completely alone for eight months now.

'Umm,' I say, giving myself time to think of the answer she may want to hear regardless of what I do … I shrug. What I do is perfect and well researched, so I say, 'I give it and wait 30 minutes before food.'

'Why?' The expression on her face says she finds that dumb.

'Because the absorption is better …' Not only does the thyroid consumer community support this, but it also says on the packet of synthetic thyroid pills that absorption is hindered with calcium-rich food. I have always wondered why in ICU they would give her thyroid medication at night, after her dinner when the packet clearly states that some food products hinder absorption.

She shrugged and shook her head violently, then tutted.

'But how do you *give* it to her?'

I want to groan, I know she is looking to rip whatever I say to shreds, but there is still a glimmer of hope that this time I'll get it right, so, twelve-year-old me really hoping to get some approval, declares confidently, 'I mix it in honey.'

New Zealand's best 16+ Manuka honey to be exact, almost $50 a go for a small tub. I justified the costs as I see it as a healthy valuable addition to her diet and an excellent way to strengthen her immune status.

She sighed.

'I worry about honey and teeth.' She opens her mouth and pointed to her teeth repeatedly to emphasise this. 'And then of course ... the reasons for wanting treatment?' She nodded as if I'm supposed to agree. 'Couldn't you just crush it and give it with water? What do *you* think, Hana?' She turned to my busy daughter, still mid-colouring a computer printout scene from *Frozen* I'd nabbed in the waiting room. 'Are you going to try taking your medicine with water? It's much better for you ...'

I want to scream, '*She is six years old for Christ's sake!* She's gone from never taking medication to being forced to take a hundred, absolutely disgusting tablets a day. *If she doesn't take them then she dies.* The fact she tolerates this pile of tablets a day, every frickin' day, is because the super high quality, healthy, Manuka honey makes them taste great.'

I stormed out of the hospital after smiling ever so sweetly and thanking her for her time. I walked so fast the wheels at the front of the wheelchair shuddered and wobbled, making a loud chuga-chuga-chuga noise on the squeaky, shining floors and everyone looked as I charged past, both my little girls squished in together: One blonde and obese, one dark and tiny, their mama bear pushing them with a face of thunder.

'Oh, for goodness sake,' I let erupt from my lips, it sounded almost like a growl.

'OH!' Another one slips out and I let my brows furrow and a mean look crosses my face as a volunteer for some charity tries to make meaningful eye contact, before asking for my generous donation. She quickly gets the vibe and steps back as I charge through the double doors.

I was trapped within this domineering, controlling, patriarchal system and there was no way out, *ever*. My daughter needed them watching over her to make sure she stayed alive and I had to just swallow that without Manuka honey to sweeten it.

This was one of the biggest, hardest pills I'd ever had to swallow and it was choking me.

In a bid to empower myself, I continued to delve deeper into my research beyond the mainstream … *Imagine if we never had to see another medical professional ever again because I could learn how to heal my girls naturally.* What an outrageous, outlandish thought for a registered nurse to have! Oh, and how they would crucify me on social media if I even hinted at such a preposterous thought! But it was there, I had thought it! *Imagine …*

We had ceased acupuncture after a few months – although I knew very well it had worked in other ways for countless others, it wasn't working for us at all. The selection of herbs and naturopathic supplements we had tried also had no impact on her weight and appetite, although I valued them as part of broader nutritional regime. We had tried a weekly hyperbaric oxygen chamber – which seemed promising in theory but in practice it was hard to organise getting there and occupying the girls in the small chamber for an hour a go wasn't easy. I also knew that we should really be getting daily treatments, which was too expensive and impossible to coordinate with Hana's appointments with the odd hour at school. It was time to turn my attention to something I'd only ever tried twice before, mainly for fun: homeopathy. Homeopathy was something I'd always found strange – I didn't understand how it would work, and therefore I questioned the very fact it could.

I feel I inherited my incredible dogmatism and arrogance over healing modalities like homeopathy and energy healing from a system that promoted an outright arrogance over the unknown and that which isn't (yet) 'scientifically proven' – 'I don't understand it therefore it's not real/doesn't exist/can't work.' I was beginning to extract myself from this inherited mindset – I kept hearing, or perhaps feeling, the words *Listen. Listen to what people are saying!* For two hundred years people had been using homeopathy and they say it works, why would they just make it up?

Excited by the prospect of learning something new, and exhilarated by the feeling of my mind opening in directions I'd never thought possible, I enrolled in a first aid homeopathy course with an English school of homeopathy. Here I was introduced to an incredible perspective on disease and illness that hadn't crossed my mind before: Symptoms were not something that should be eradicated but respected and listened to – they were the 'body doing the best it could under the circumstance', they were the signals of a deeper underlying problem, they weren't the problem itself!

I also loved the concept that all disease starts with *dis-ease* – that is, a precipitating factor that throws the body off balance momentarily and that allows for interference and illness to manifest. This could be something like a cold wind or an emotional phone call. Whatever it is, the body's balance is upset by this precipitating factor or 'change' to the energetic field. Thus, in finding the right remedy for an illness, the homeopath must not only look in detail at the symptoms but also at what was happening to the individual at the time the illness began to manifest.

I tried and tested first aid remedies on myself and my girls and, to my utter delight, truly found magic! Crazy improvements and transformations happened with insect bites, coughs, and a myriad of infections over the following weeks and months – so I had concrete proof that homeopathy worked when the correct remedy and the correct potency was found – but could it help heal Hana's brain? I found a brilliant homeopath, Karen, and I added her to my carefully assimilated team – me, John and, to my delight a new lovely GP who worked under our apartment building. He didn't think I was mad and admired what I was doing for Hana.

Karen was empowering – although brain healing was also unchartered territory for her, she was prepared to give it a go and supported my interest in organic remedies, 'sarcodes', for Hana's brain injury. We trialled some. The first that I had ordered from the USA was Brain 1M. Two doses of Brian 1M completely resolved Hana's OCD with regards to her colour coding and laying-out of pens – and I blogged about this phenomenal transformation, with photos to show the transition over a period of days, before surgery and after surgery pictures. After these doses of Brain 1M, Hana's pen-related OCD disappeared, never to return.

In many ways modern day science and the strict adherence to a 'scientific evidence-based truth' reminded me of the

Middle Ages: they had the Church and Kings; twenty-first century has scientists and a domineering medical paradigm.

In the Middle Ages, saying anything against the Church and King was heresy, which resulted in death. The twenty-first century approach to medical professionals who pursue something *'that is not scientifically proven'* is a little less barbaric but nevertheless, you were still a goner. In terms of credibility and professional reputation at least, you are pretty much a goner the moment you begin an open, non-biased conversation on something mainstream science has (currently) rejected or is continually striving to reject.

I had thought I was living in an era where free speech and freedom of expression were welcomed, but my eyes were slowly being opened to the fact that this wasn't the case – at least with regards to certain controversial issues in the fields of medicine because twenty-first century scientific mindset had become like a domineering, controlling religion, owning the minds, opinions and actions of the population. If you did try to hold a perspective in opposition to the mainstream, you might get called a quack', or 'woo-woo'. Discussing things such as the vaccines, homeopathy, food as medicine or natural cures for cancer, referring to 'big pharma' all have implications for the reputation of a healthcare professional.

Whereas healthcare professionals, particularly doctors, were seen as gods, there are people in the twenty-first century who are taking some control over their health and wellbeing by reading and researching. I felt that the 'doctor is god' perception had now died a death, at least in my generation and the ones to come. But this had left a gap in the consciousness of some people, paving the way to the birth of the Science Demi-God: a quest for *scientific proof* (which is different to *truth*), a new religion.

I could observe the Western world gripping on to science as if it was a god. *Science says … science doesn't say*, making us as narrow minded and timid in our thinking as the people of the royal court in the Middle Ages. Like the courtiers in Ancient Egypt and the Middle Ages who were forbidden to question the authority of the King and relevant gods, so, too, are healthcare professionals indirectly forcibly muted on issues that are of great importance to 'the people' (everyone else!). They risk their reputation by entering the conversation, or debate. 'Not science based' was a *terrible* condemnation for a healthcare professional.

Although excited and exhilarated by the discovery of new healing modalities, I also felt a sense of dread as I began to discover how amazing homeopathy was – the sheer effort at having to explain, justify and promote this incredible healing modality when so many people were so vehemently against the concept without knowing anything about it.

'*Disgusting,*' commented one individual on a Facebook post where I outlined the incredible permanent disappearance after only one dose of my exercise-induced asthma, my own constitutional remedy at that time.

Karen was based in the UK, so we communicated via Skype. 'I have dreams that I'm dancing ballet again, like I did as a child but when I take a leap into the air, I stay there suspended – I'm just too light for gravity to pull me down. Then I try and "grab" the air to pull me down, but it doesn't work.'

'This is very interesting,' was Karen's response, quickly jotting down notes as I described unusual aspects of my dreams and character that might reveal what remedy would best suit my constitution.

'Sometimes I feel this weird connection to … everyone,' I said, embarrassed.

Karen leaned towards the web cam. 'What is this connection like?'

I wrinkled my nose, I knew I would sound weird. 'Like … I'm giving out some energy or something. On those days people are most attracted to me – they stop and talk to me in the street, they look at me across the road. It's not to do with how I look … its more subtle, it's energy.'

'Yes, but what is that energy like?' Karen pushed, but I was reluctant to further cross-examine this weird aspect of myself.

'It's not like anything,' I dismissed. 'It just me … kind of feeling: *I AM HERE.*'

Karen nodded and went on to some other aspects. But the 'bingo' moment occurred later, once we'd hung up.

'Like a star,' I emailed her back. It was easier to be honest this way, as stupid and icky as it sounded, I sometimes did feel like a star.

When I opened my inbox the next morning, coffee in hand, an email from Karen whooshed in, my constitutional remedy … after all my years of being obsessed with space and stars, my remedy was the lightest, most basic element of the Universe, the stuff of Stars. *Of course* it would be hydrogen.

Upset by the venomous comment after sharing my success with homeopathic hydrogen, I asked myself, 'How could people feel so passionate about something they knew nothing about? Something they didn't understand and had no personal experience of?' I knew the answer to that question – because that was who I used to be. Thank goodness I had been given a chance to change – it was like a veil was being lifted from my eyes. For the first time I felt like I was beginning to see clearly.

And I was amazed to find that things were not as they had seemed.

'Thank you very much for the MRIs and the information about your daughter Hana. Your letter is certainly one of the most comprehensive parental reports I have ever received. I am also very impressed by your thoughts on potential treatment options, which reflect very high knowledge.'

The email from our German Guru finally arrived. Not only did he compliment my 'report', but he also outlined his great interest in my oxytocin treatment, declaring that he was interested in this area himself. My self-confidence was slowly beginning to rebuild itself – now we had the words of a true international expert on Hana's condition behind us – and he hadn't been offended by my knowledge base, my research and my 'tone'!

In a generously long and detailed email that would have taken him a fair amount of time and effort, particularly considering he was a specialist at the top of his field, he outlined a treatment program similar the one we had wanted to propose ourselves to the last endocrinologist, which included ruling out stimulants like Ritalin, the diabetes drug metformin, the insulin blocking drug octreotride, before coming back to him to discuss the option of a lap band. But now the very specialist we had been waiting months to see had already ruled out the very things we'd been wanting to try (and now had true 'expert' backing) who would we ask for help to undertake his plan?

I asked around and eventually found one more endo who was reluctantly willing to see us – not an easy feat considering our history of discharge against medical advice and our previous two changes of specialist – but the waiting list was a few months! This would be another *sixteen kilos* on Hana by the time we would get in to see him and he wasn't prepared to go out of his way to get us in early. So, during this wait, I sent out some desperate emails to a team of USA doctors with some experience – and therefore more expertise – with young people with hypothalamic obesity. Their generosity extended to a willingness to oversee our new and supportive GP prescribe some of these medications so we could 'strike' them off the list of things to try in attempt to curb Hana's obesity in our wait to see the new endo. And, in a phone call that they refused to charge us for, one of these doctors expressed his shock that Hana wasn't being seen as an urgent case by our local specialists, although he tried to be diplomatic.

'Um, over here we have a *triage* system – if someone is in need of urgent help, we get them in sooner …'

'All the specialists know of Hana's intractable weight gain and each time we've asked to see someone new they simply stick us on the wait list,' I explained. 'And, as you know, every week we wait is another kilo of weight.' A diplomatic yet baffled silence flowed along the crackly phone lines.

Although I had begun to feel a clear segregation from mainstream medical sciences, I still respected 'medicine' and science for how it was keeping my daughter alive. I decided to contribute to the medical evidence base myself: I would be audacious enough to write up Hana's oxytocin case report and submit it to a medical journal.

If science won't move for you, move science –

This became my motto. After all the blogging and huge international reach on my oxytocin blog posts, I still hadn't piqued the interest of any research centres, so I decided that my findings and Hana's experience would form the cornerstone for future research. I would embark on the journey of scientific publication – firstly to help others and secondly to help validate exactly what I was doing for Hana – for our own protection. If what I was doing was published, it would exist in the evidence base as a reference point for our own treatment.

I began writing and compiling my reference list. In the process, I contacted a couple of specialists in the USA I'd come across in my research who I thought might find the case interesting. One afternoon, after having towel-dried the girls on the poolside and opening the gate leading out of the swimming pool, hair still dripping with chlorine-scented water, I heard an email pop into my inbox:

I am very interested in your daughter's case and we would love to collaborate with you – help with write up and journal selection – if you like.

'Oh my gosh, oh my gosh!' I squealed, jumping up and down. 'They want to co-author with me! On my oxytocin case report!' The paper was in its second draft already with a full list of references completed. All I needed now was a hardcore medical editor and someone to put my references into 'EndNote' and then take the time to go about formatting and submitting it – these were the time-consuming aspects of preparing a paper for submission and something I was lacking.

'That is so awesome!' Nour agreed later that evening, before adding protectively, 'I still think you could do it alone. But sure, why not have some help with editing, formatting and references and things?'

So I excitedly sent my paper to my new, prestigious USA collaborators to edit, refine and prepare for the submission process. After a couple of months, another email popped into my inbox, after I'd badgered them for an updated edit for me to review:

Unfortunately, because the paper is about your daughter, it is unethical to list you as an author. I know this is not what you wanted to hear. I think in any other circumstance you have done as much or more than is necessary to be first or second author. It simply comes down to the ethics: having any patient's mother as an author of a case report on that patient makes any claim of clinical objectivity impossible. You would instead be the only person mentioned in the acknowledgements for your vital contributions.

There is not much to discuss about the matter. We cannot offer this for publication with a patient's mother as an author. It is simply an insurmountable conflict of interest. That is the unanimous opinion of our research group.

'WHAT?!' I gasped, 'What the *HELL*?' Acknowledged for my *'vital contributions'*? This was my paper! My research, my discovery, my battle, my fight, my hard work! Some high profile patronising git in the USA wanted to take this away from me? Just because I was Hana's mum?!

'NO. WAY.' Nour, furious, hissed down the phone, snatching two minutes between patients. 'You email him back right away and you tell him that this paper and research is YOUR copyright and you will proceed alone.'

He reflected for a minute. 'In science, sometimes it is the parents that have to trial and test things *on their own* in order to move things forwards in unique ways. This has always been the case! The fact that you are Hana's mum is a *strength* not a conflict of interest. What would you have to gain from fabricating this information? Nothing! There is no financial conflict of interests and ethically – what conflict is there? What is the *actual ethical problem*? I can't see it.'

'But what if I CAN'T get it published alone?' I whimpered, almost crying. Grateful for Nour's aggressive support and belief in me, but still feeling the onset of a pathetic weakness. 'Everyone else will lose out because I'm being selfish enough to claim this for myself. Isn't it about getting the information out there?'

I'd had feedback from some craniopharyngioma contacts. Some said that I should be grateful these doctors even wanted to take on my paper and had the drive to get it published, that I was being *selfish* to consider risking not getting published by refusing to take my own name off my paper. This severely dented my confidence – was I really being selfish? I couldn't tell! I desperately wanted to take full ownership for my contribution to science. Was this selfish of me or my right to claim it regardless?

'You WILL get it published,' Nour reassured me. 'It is well written as it is. Any reviewer with sense will see this is a great idea and that it needs to be disseminated. Come one! It is a CASE REPORT, it's saying this happened: we observed this – it was a surprise – further research is needed – The End. Tell him to fuck off or do you want me to tell him?'

'No, no!' I said, before hanging up, I could deal with this myself – and I reluctantly drafted an email affirming that I would no longer be collaborating with them. I sighed as the email whooshed out of my inbox – would I still be able to get my message out into the medical and scientific community without their help?

Chapter Nine

I was fifteen when I decided to stop eating. It was a Sunday morning. I was upset about something so I decided that I wouldn't eat that day. Or the day after. Then the evil whispery voice that haunted anorexic me made food a horrible thing, the concept of satisfying a hunger disgusted me. I wanted to suffer, to let my body ache and crave. It felt cleaner and purer to fade away to nothing – the non-physical. And when my ribs began to stick out as if I was a prisoner in a concentration camp, I felt relief, the ugliness of my inside was showing on the outside.

Once I'd decided I wouldn't eat, all the therapy in the world was just a waste of time, playing games with the psychologists and family therapists who really thought they were doing something to help me. I didn't know where my end would be. I didn't want to die – dying wasn't part of my plan, but I knew I wasn't ready to heal. I didn't want to heal, I wanted to suffer. And boy, did I think about food … all I could think about was food. I knew what it felt like to be hungry all the time.

I survived one term at school starving myself, throwing my lunch in the bin, leaving out empty breakfast cereal bowls carefully decorated with a trace of milk and cornflakes, as if I'd eaten something, and the weight fell off me. I began to get tired, my muscles screaming as I moved, then pins and needles all the time. I remember looking up at the top supermarket shelf and my face started prickling and stinging – pins and needles in my face. The summer holidays came and I was relieved to be able to rest, as much as I hated the fact I needed to rest, I found walking around too exhausting.

Food. It was all I could think about. I obsessed over meals, about how many calories I would eat, how I would try and run up and down the stairs afterward with my stick-thin, spindly legs to burn them off.

The family therapist at the Adolescent Unit overseeing our case would nod, fervently, whenever any of us spoke, like one of those nodding dogs on the dashboard of the car, except faster. Boing-boing-boing went his nodding head and my psychologist was gormless and so inexperienced, she bored me.

The unit was a dark depressing place, the smell of toast permanently wafting down the corridor. A stick-thin girl was always sitting at the end of the corridor where it joined the dining area, sitting in front of her unfinished meal. She would watch me push through the double doors from the waiting room on the way to the weighing room with black-rimmed eyes, her oversized knees jutting out of her black leggings.

Then one summer day, early in the holidays, they couldn't withdraw any blood from me at my weekly check-up. They let me go home, but rang my mum as soon as we were back, with a message from my overseeing doctor. I was sitting in the kitchen and saw the terror on her face as they ordered her to bring me urgently the next day. Now my weight loss was getting dangerous and I needed to become an inpatient. She tried to control the shaking of her hands as she placed the cordless phone back in the slot on the wall as she told me I was being admitted. My face was blank, impassive, empty. *Mish Mawgood*. There were few emotions with such a low body weight, something that I was grateful for, emotions were messy, sticky, physical things.

I counted my pulse before I slept that night, forty-eight beats a minute when it used to be ninety. Did that mean I might die in my sleep? My mum poked her head around my door, waiting to see if I was still breathing.

I'm not going to die! I thought, annoyed at her for thinking I would die. I wasn't going to die.

My head spinning and trying to hide my breathlessness due to the exertion – I insisted on carrying my own heavy suitcase from the car to the unit. I didn't need help, I wasn't vulnerable. I could do anything. I was shown to my room and put down my heavy bag, relieved to be there. Yes, they would make me eat, but it meant that I no longer had any say in the matter. The evil, whispery voice that forbade me from feeding myself wasn't allowed in there. In the unit I'd have no choice, the power was no longer mine.

My first meal there was toast and tenacious peanut butter that got stuck in my throat as I tried to swallow it. I sat and ate it dutifully under the close observation of the nurses, which I found extremely irritating and patronising. I hadn't realised they'd treat me like that, like a naughty child. I felt like telling them, 'I will eat. You don't have to stare at me!'

But of course I didn't say anything. I was a good, obedient anorexic patient. I was on fifteen-minute observations at the start. Wherever I was in the unit, a nurse would check on me every fifteen minutes to make sure I wasn't dying somewhere in the corner. I wasn't allowed to go to the toilet unaccompanied after eating in case I threw it up, which I'd never been able to do, although I had tried. I had to be weighed three times a week, naked except for my knickers after they watched me pee. They'd pull me out of bed early, still sleepy, hair messy, take me to the toilet and keep the door open while I peed in front of them.

On my second night, they made me eat moussaka. Aubergines make me vomit, I'd forgotten to put it on my 'Hate List' along with meat and butter – too late, I dutifully shoved it down, under the watchful eyes of the evening shift nurses. Of course they thought I was being a typical anorexic, fussing because the dish was high in calories. Then – with little warning, I dashed to the bathroom, a nurse chasing me down the corridor. I heaved over the loo with an angry nurse looking on at my disobedience. I ran back to my room and sobbed loudly for over an hour. A prim-lipped, unsympathetic night nurse sat at my side, totally fed up. After more howling, another nurse came in to see why I was making such a racket. I saw them raise their eyebrows at each other.

'You'll hate being in hospital. You'll hate the food,' Mum had said a few weeks before when my weight loss plummeted. *A nonstop steam train to self-destruction.* And now I was stuck there until I gained the ridiculous amount of weight they'd put on my giant weight chart that had been blu-tacked to my wall, opposite my bed, where I could track my kilo by kilo weight gain. I was a prisoner.

The first couple of weeks I was on chair-rest then, as I gained weight, I was allowed certain privileges that we'd written on my weight chart by certain weight targets. Each weight gain was plotted on that chart. Like a prisoner marking off the days in jail, I marked off each kilo that took me closer to getting out. First I was allowed a five-minute walk, then a fifteen-minute walk, then I was allowed to choose my own dessert and so on. The influences from the other kids there were toxic. Screaming girls being sedated and tube-fed, a young girl who would slash her arms and face to bits with crockery she'd steal from mealtimes then smash on the bathroom floor. If the nurses didn't get to her in time she'd emerge with blood dripping off her face.

Once, after everyone else had finished eating dinner, I was still picking my way through my dessert, a yoghurt and an apple. A small sliver of the apple fell on the floor. The hawk-eyed charge nurse scowled at me and promptly got me another apple to replace the tiny slice I seemingly had 'planned' to avoid eating. Which seemed really unjust, it was just a teeny sliver! I laughed at him.

'I don't need to eat that, it was just a small piece.'

'Cut a piece off the new one.'

'No!' Suddenly furious, I pushed my plate away. I was weeks into my stay at the unit – I had not once avoided a meal, and I was dutifully gaining weight, how dare he think I was being sneaky about one piece of apple that had no calories in it anyway. I got up and began to run down the corridor. He chased after me, reaching me in seconds as his legs were super long and he grabbed me by the arm. I shook him off, half hysterical with the absurdity of what was happening to me. Then I swung around and stalked back to the kitchen. He thought he had me! But I didn't stop at the table. Before he could stop me, I bombed out of the kitchen door and ran across the car park making my way to the adult mental hospital. The corridors there were twisty and full of loitering mad people – he'd never find me there.

It was my mum who 'tipped the scales' to get me out. 'The way I see it, you can eat loads while you're here, go back to the unit with a couple of extra kilos and get the heck out of there. Or you can go as slowly as you've been going and end up spending Christmas there.'

So I did it, on a weekend break I ate whatever I could and went back to the unit, proud to get on the scales at my target weight. Admittedly I did armour myself before that weighing session. I woke extra early and gulped back the two mugs I'd secretly filled with water the night before and hidden on my top shelf in my room: another sneaky 400 grams of insurance.

But that wasn't the end. Back at home, free to make my own decisions about nourishing myself, I sank into a deep depression. Without bones to display my sadness I had nothing. That was when I really wanted to die. My family would look at me, terrified, over the breakfast table as I stared in space. *Mish Mawgood*. I began to obsess over food more than before, cutting up my meals into tiny pieces, refusing to add salt in case it made it taste better and I might actually enjoy it. The weight began to drop off me again. I went to my weekly weigh-ins, where I was now allowed to be clothed, with my jeans pockets stuffed with anything heavy I could find in my room at home and as many mls of water in my stomach that I could knock back. I pretended to pee in the loo before being weighed. As I was an outpatient, they didn't stand by the door to watch me do it.

Being unhappy was horrible. I decided to get better three weeks after I started taking an antidepressant, Sertraline.

The grey haze suddenly lifted and I began to see the world in colour again. I remembered how to laugh! Just as clearly as I remember choosing not to eat, I remember choosing happiness. I was eating my dinner, my vegetarian sausages cut into teeny tiny pieces while watching *Home and Away* – the Australian actors looked so happy, fit and well, they were drinking smoothies at the diner and it seemed, even though I knew they were acting, that no one cared about eating. They could eat without agonising over every mouthful. How free, how liberated they must feel, I thought.

I chose to be happy, too! Just like that, I let go of my illness then, and it never returned, not because I didn't want to stay thin – I'd always wanted or *needed* to be slender – but because I chose happiness over misery.

Food took centre stage again when new-born Maryam was diagnosed with multiple food chemical sensitivities. We were lucky to even get a diagnosis, the only hospital at that time which practised this particular type of diet relating food to behaviour and other physical issues was in Sydney, and our paediatrician just happened to have worked there previously. With our medical backgrounds, the concept that food could affect mood was completely alien to Nour and me. However, I was so stressed and sleep deprived dealing with an unhappy, unwell baby and a severe temper-tantrum-prone three-year-old Hana, I caught on rapidly, doing hours of research, reading all that I could about this new pathway which would involve changing Hana's and my own diets.

We had been on the brink of taking Hana to a child psychologist at that point. She'd had very emotionally turbulent twos and the threes weren't improving in the slightest. Throw in an unwell baby who wouldn't sleep, night or day – I was desperate for a solution, and the answer to our troubles, it seemed, lay in our diet. I had already gone vegan while breastfeeding Maryam as her cow milk protein intolerance had been picked up very early on, but the concept that other food groups – healthy foods like fruit and many vegetables – were bad for us was too much for Nour to tolerate, at first.

'You are telling me that she will get a tantrum if she eats a tangerine?' he scoffed. I was sitting on the beanbag, girls finally put to sleep, wiped out from the lack of sleep and a whole new diet and cooking modality to learn.

'Just listen to yourself!' he raised his voice now. 'All you talk about is food! You're *obsessed*!'

I had no words. Yes, all I talked about was food, how each thing I'd fed my daughters that day may have affected their moods. I wondered if our marriage would begin to disintegrate over a tangerine. But I kept up the dietary changes and he slowly began to see how the dietary changes were life-transforming. Hana's tantrums and mood swings suddenly disappeared, only to rear their ugly heads when she ate fruit. Maryam stopped grizzling and began to sleep for the first time in her seven months of life. Nour began to 'get it' when he too began to re-evaluate his own sense of wellness in relation to what he was eating – with a sigh of relief a few months after watching the girls improve, he went gluten free and began to avoid foods high in glutamates and, once again, we were a united front in our approach to raising the girls.

This girl that couldn't stop thinking about food, was it really Hana? Or was it destined, always, to be me?

It was animal, the sound of her snores rackcting through the night, and every minute or so would be a 'whoop', a moment of silence as she stopped breathing, her apnoea was getting worse every night. I lay awake staring wide eyed into the darkness; like a child, I found night-times so much more terrifying than the blue days that streamed sunlight into our window-lined apartment. At night I could hear her life slipping away from me. Every moment she stopped breathing, my heart would race and I would wonder if that would be when she died. A little seven-year-old girl with Hana's condition had done that one night … just passed away in her sleep. Why wouldn't my little girl be next?

At times I wanted to scream at her across the room when she was snoring, 'Stop it! Stop doing this to me, stop hurting me!' Sometimes I picked up my duvet and pillow and slept in the lounge so I wouldn't hear her whooping and gasping for breath. Other nights I kept vigil by her bed, lying by her side just to make sure she wasn't dying. We had slotted her mattress on the floor at the bottom of our bed and I could fit in the narrow passage between the two if I lodged myself completely on my side. I could sleep better next to her there than two metres away in my own bed. Perhaps, if I was intertwined with her at night, my own life force would keep her alive.

Nour and I were adamant that the only thing we could try that actually might work was bariatric surgery – specifically, the lap band. We were still waiting to get in to see the new specialist and it was during this wait that Hana's plight had attracted national media interest due to my blog postings. We agreed to coverage almost as a sort of self-protective mechanism – we felt that if the story was properly understood by the general public, surely someone would come to our rescue if some pious healthcare professional wanted to call in Social Services due to the radical treatment we were proposing? Australia does not conduct bariatric procedures on children – in fact, when I emailed one bariatric surgeon carefully proposing a plan, he instantly emailed back, coldly stating, *Your daughter needs to be under the care of experts at the children's hospital.*

That 'expert' word again.

One day after an appearance on a national TV morning show where I was questioned on why I wanted a lap-band surgery for Hana and where I explained how it would most likely help her, I took Maryam to climb the rocks at Clovelly Beach. Hana was at school until lunch and so Maryam and I could just enjoy being together, marvelling at the crabs and waves – forgetting, for a while, Hana's hunger and pain. After an hour there, I checked my phone and saw I'd received a Facebook message from another cranio mum. Stunned, I read her message – her twenty-one year old son, a Facebook friend of mine, had died very suddenly the day before. He had been five when his tumour was removed and, like Hana, his weight had skyrocketed after his surgery.

One of his friends also messaged me: *I just wanted you to know what an impact you had on him. He saw you on TV and was so excited by it declaring, 'This woman is going to help change things for us!'*

I let my tears spill down my cheeks while I climbed the rocks, trying to hide them behind my sunglasses while Maryam hunted for crabs. This was Hana's future – except that I doubted she would make her twenty-first birthday, I doubted she'd even make her fifteenth, unless something was done about her weight, *now.*

A few weeks later it was Christmas and my parents-in-law flew out to visit us again. My mother-in-law suggested flying out to Egypt to get a lap-band procedure done there – she'd be able to organise the whole procedure easily with her contacts. My instinct was to pack up and go, and screw the system here. However, Nour, always more cautious and 'proper' than me, thought it would be better to 'do it the right way' by Australia. We had touched base with the new endocrinologist Dr Wong, who treated us with decency and respect but with an element of caution. He expressed that he'd rather not be Hana's endocrinologist, suggesting that she'd be better off under a large care team at a public hospital, but agreed, albeit notably with some reluctance, to work with us provided things were relatively stable.

'You need to let the experts do their work,' he explained. 'I know when it's my own kids I put aside all my *own* medical knowledge because it's impossible to be objective. You should stop taking an active role in Hana's care and hand over her responsibility to the team and just be the "*parents*".'

With his blessing and with the help of a colleague, once again we made yet another appointment and started waiting – this time we had booked in for a consult with one of Australia's top childhood obesity experts. We hoped he would see her dire health conditions and, because he worked in the world of 'obesity', would most likely be connected to some bariatric surgeons that would contemplate this medical world-first lap-band procedure. In Nour's eyes, seeing this team would be the most we could do here, before truly claiming we had thoroughly exhausted Australian help.

The long-awaited consult with the accompanying team of obesity specialists went like this:

'She needs to get out of the wheelchair. She needs more exercise.'

'She swims one kilometre a day. She can't walk because the of the weight on her tiny ankles and knees. The pain is simply excruciating for her,' I protested.

'But if she could get out of the wheelchair the increase in exercise might slow the gain.'

'If we could slow the gain, she might be able to walk again.' Me again.

Learning forwards, earnest about this: 'How about we try, *really* try and get her out of the wheelchair?'

Then: 'She's famished but she lives on salad, she is the most delicate and disciplined eater that I know. Particularly in light of her hunger.'

She scans Hana's immaculate diet sheet. 'You know we could admit her for a hospitalised stay for strict dietary observation, just to make sure that there are no *loopholes*.'

'Obviously, I'm sure you're aware the research states that hypothalamic obesity is notoriously resistant to strict exercise and dietary interventions …' I let some background knowledge slip out.

'What's she eating?'

'We are primarily organic vegan, high-vegetable, low-fruit intake – we are very healthy eaters. My children have never tasted junk food. They don't even know what the "sweets" are at the candy counter. There is no processed food in the house.'

'Well … what does she drink?'

'Filtered alkaline water.'

'Hmmm, well the diet sounds *OK*, but it might be worth seeing a dietician for, you know, any loopholes.'

So then we saw the dietician who scanned her organic, primarily vegan, high-vegetable diet:

'Well, the diet seems OK. I just wonder if there are a few things we can tweak, like the handful of walnuts for morning tea? They're very high in cholesterol, you know.'

The outcome of this appointment was a declaration that Hana needed more exercise and that she needed to 'get out of her wheelchair'. They couldn't, and wouldn't, recommend bariatrics simply because they would only do that if there was a centre that specialised in children's bariatrics. Because no such centre existed, they couldn't recommend any treatment.

Thus spoke the obesity 'experts'.

In Australia, Hana was doomed.

That night I sent out emails to our German Guru and also to the team in the USA we had been communicating with. I told them we had truly exhausted help here and had been forced to pursue bariatrics for Hana abroad – considering they had experience putting lap bands in adolescents, would they consider putting one in our little eight-year-old girl?

Chapter Ten

Light is streaming through the windows. You can see dust flurries floating in the shards that illuminate her hospital bed. I feel warm inside, and I recognise this feeling as peace, something I haven't felt in a long time. I am waiting next to Hana's bed, white sheets tousled after she left for surgery. She hasn't been gone long before she walks back into her room, her lap band in place, she is taller and slimmer than she ever was before – completely cured during her surgery.

The dream stayed with me for days. Of course, her lap-band surgery wouldn't cure her condition. At best it would be a treatment and even then we weren't sure how effective a treatment it would be in the long term. Meanwhile, emails were flying in from experts in Germany, Ireland and the USA and all of these forward-thinking individuals recommended that Hana receive bariatrics as a matter of urgency. One American specialist put me in touch with a colleague of his who happened to be in Australia. Hours after sending an email to this Australian bariatric surgeon I'd been hoping would help us, his reply came flying back:

'Let's talk.'

I literally whooped for joy. Maybe we could get help for Hana here after all! It seemed silly, but my thoughts then turned to her shoes! We were down to the final pair of shoes that we could find that fitted Hana, an exceptionally wide pair of trainers we'd found by chance in the sports shop in Westfield. The finding was an absolute godsend because we'd already visited a custom shoemaker who had promised to help only to ring back a week later saying that even his custom shoe sizes didn't come as large as Hana's feet. The trainers fitted perfectly and were now the only shoe she wore – it seemed such a small problem compared to her health status as a morbidly obese child but it was a question I would ask myself daily – what will she wear on her feet when she outgrows – in width – these shoes?

I paced up and down the kitchen in excitement, my bird's-eye view revealing the ocean at Bondi down to the airport where teeny planes landed and took off. Seeing these planes come and go was a daily reminder that we, too, had flown here. To my joy, he adamantly agreed that Hana should get a lap band – he also agreed that it was the best procedure for her, minimally invasive, removable and, besides, there wasn't a strong evidence base anyway to support that she undergo a more invasive irreversible procedure at her age. The lap band would hopefully improve things – at least a bit – and buy us time.

Appointments were set up with him, the anaesthetist and the hospital administration agreed, with no red tape issues. Was this really happening? My desperation began, for a moment, to fade with the intense hope that life would soon be changed for the better.

One week later we were in his office. 'Thank you so much for this,' I said. 'You have no idea how hard it has been to get here – finding people forward thinking enough to help has been very difficult.'

'That's OK,' he smiled. 'People sometimes get silly when it comes to children. It's quite clear that we need to try this. It's a minimally invasive procedure – she'll be in and out of theatre in under an hour and hopefully it'll help!'

'And the hospital agreed?' I asked, not believing my luck.

'I've had no issue with the hospital at all, and we already know my anaesthetist is keen to help. We just need an admitting paediatrician and a paediatric endocrinologist to oversee her hormones. Could her own doctors help?'

'I would have thought so ...' I nodded. Thinking of our new endocrinologist – would he agree to be involved in this highly controversial procedure? He didn't have prescribing rights at the hospital – but would he try and figure out a way to help?

'But, really, it is going to be very straightforward,' he continued.

I sighed and clutched my hands to my chest, looking at Hana who was doing her colouring-in on his desk, Maryam was engrossed in a game with her dolls under my chair. At least this time we'd remembered to bring her dolls to the appointment. I'd forgotten to pack her toys when we went to the last doctor and, after rummaging through my handbag for something, *anything,* to play with, she'd animatedly turned a bottle of Hana's steroids and my lipstick into walking, talking beings.

'So you swim one kilometre a day, Hana!' He laughed. 'That's more than I do!'

'She's pretty awesome', I agreed, although he had no idea of the tears we went through every day before and during the morning swim. Making her swim twice a day was no easy feat, I was exhausted being her constant motivational coach. Some mornings my smile wore thin and the old lady who floated on her noodle watching Hana plough up and down between bouts of sobs knew it.

'You are amazing,' she said, her double chin quivering with emotion, and her eyes wet with tears, as she paddled up the pool. 'What you do, how you cope with her.'

'When can you do it?' I asked excitedly. Just to think that maybe this time next week Hana could be relieved of her terrible hunger! To think she may be able to go a few hours without thinking of food! Oh, it would be such bliss. To think that she might have even lost some weight! The dream was golden, warm and made me fuzzy all over. We were so close now! After all the fighting, we were so close! Oh, how lucky we were!

'I'm going away for six weeks. I'll try and organise some things before I go, but it will have to be when I get back.'

The words slammed down on me like a sledgehammer. I bit the inside of my cheek. *Six weeks!* When we had waited so long and were so close, when six weeks was yet another six kilos of weight and six weeks of hunger, crying, misery and pain in between meals; six more weeks of torture!

'Are you sure it will definitely be as soon as you get back?' I said carefully, yet crestfallen, trying to hide my disappointment. 'It's just that if we have to wait any longer than that I will most likely take her to Egypt to do it ...' I trailed off. '... It's weight that she probably won't ever lose, you know, those extra six kilos.'

'You shouldn't have to go to Egypt for this,' he said confidently. 'As I said, people can get overly silly about procedures like this when it comes to kids, but we need to be

130

sensible about this – we certainly cannot NOT intervene and let things continue as they are!'

'Exactly,' I agreed. 'That's what my husband and I have been saying for so long and we have the international backing of HO experts behind us, so I'm grateful to have found someone as opened minded as you!'

Six weeks turned into I an agonising eight weeks. Hana had now *tripled* her weight in fourteen months and still cried daily from terrible hunger and relentless thoughts of food. I checked my emails obsessively while the surgeon was away in case he'd managed to organise something remotely. He stayed in contact, but no progress was made. Then, when he had been back from his travels for seven days and still no date had been suggested, I emailed him for the second time that week:

'Could you **please** let me know about the surgery? She is still gaining weight, of course. Do you have any contacts who would admit her and be willing to oversee her hormones?'

I received a blunt, angry reply: 'If you would simply ask my secretary then you would be up to speed on this. Your daughter's own specialists don't want to oversee this, which has slowed things down, but I am chipping away at it.'

What he didn't know is that I had rang his secretary multiple times only to be told there was no surgical date. What he also didn't know is that I had been told by Hana's own specialists that they personally couldn't be involved but were taking the time to ask colleagues at the participating hospital if *they* would contemplate being involved and it wasn't looking positive.

No one, except the surgeon, was willing to go out of their comfort zones to save my child. And, because the surgeon wasn't communicating with Hana's team personally, they weren't willing to participate or get temporary prescribing rights. After being so close, I was screaming into the void again.

The deal clincher came the following week at a medical appointment with the new endo – I asked whether his colleagues had finally agreed to help.

'They won't,' he said, looking slightly uncomfortable. 'I've already spoken to them about this matter and they have said that they won't be a part of this. You aren't going to have much luck here in Australia.'

As foul language directed at Australian healthcare professionals passed through my mind so too did the feeling of liberation: 'So we fly to Egypt then next week,' I declared, feeling something inside me unfold itself, almost like wings. 'I don't know how long we will be gone for, but it may be while until we see you again ...'

We spent the rest of the appointment filling out papers we needed for travel – Hana's emergency steroid injection that she needed on the plane and an enormous pile of prescriptions for her life-preserving hormones.

I called Nour at work as I walked through the Junction to get the scripts filled. 'Australia is a no-go,' I said. 'It's over here.'

'What?' he said. 'Maybe we should just wait and see wh—'

'No, Dr Wong just told me that he had spoken to both of the endos and one of the paediatricians that were going to be asked to help out at the surgery and he said they have all *refused* to be part of this.'

Nour swore quietly under his breath. 'OK, so it's Egypt then – but don't you want to wait a few weeks for me to organise time off work so I can come?'

'A few *weeks*? No!' I almost shouted but it was laced with mad laughter. 'We don't have time to wait! We've been waiting for eight fricken' weeks! We've been waiting almost a YEAR! I'm not waiting anymore. I'll go next week and I'll go alone.' I knew he'd agree. No matter how much he wanted to be there with us, he had a business to run, patients to see, while his own daughter was spiralling downwards every day. Of course he knew we had no time to spare – I would go alone.

Then I went to the pharmacy to fill the scripts. 'I'm leaving for some time,' I told them. There it was again, the feeling of wings further unfolding, getting ready for flight! We would soon be free.

'I want all you have in stock and can pick up the rest tomorrow if you need to order more.' I took the bags of medications home, worth hundreds of dollars and packed them into a large suitcase I'd brought up from the garage. The packing had begun.

That afternoon I FaceTimed my mother-in-law in Cairo. It was early morning there and she was sitting on her front porch feeding milk to the feral cats that sunbathed on the road of the compound she lived in. I could almost smell that dry, dusty, scented air of the desert through the phone. 'I'm coming,' I said. 'How quickly can you organise the surgery?'

'Just get on a plane and come,' she said, her face lighting up with excitement and pride. She would help save her granddaughter, in her own country that she was so proud of. 'Don't worry about anything. I will take care of it all. Book and come.'

By that evening she'd messaged back that she had a hospital bed, plus an ICU bed if needed, a paediatric endocrinologist and that the surgeon she had asked months ago if he would consider doing the unusual procedure had confirmed with her he was still willing to operate. Done. With the click of two determined fingers. How pathetic it made this civilised, First World country look with its proud healthcare system! The interminable skating around, the lousy excuses, umming and ahhing and the shrinking away from a simple, reversible sixty-minute procedure, that may just save a little girl's life.

We decided to keep the trip quiet, from my TV and newspapers contacts, who were following our progress and had asked to be kept updated for developments, and I obviously kept it off my blog and Facebook page. We were taking our daughter to a developing country for a procedure that the Australian system was refusing to undertake, a controversial medical world first − *if something went wrong* − how would we look? What if we were reported by some idiot and Social Services stopped me from taking her? I had crazy visions of Hana being taken away from me at the airport just as we were about the board the plane … No! We kept quiet about it and only told a few friends what we were planning. We would keep this a secret until we emerged triumphant.

'I'm hungry, Hana!' I made Hana's tummy speak in his loud, heavy voice that made her laugh when her hunger was bothering her.

'It's OK, tummy,' she soothed him. 'It'll be morning tea soon.'

'Pheweee!' said tummy. 'Sorry, Hana, sorry for being hungry.'

'Oh, tummy, I love you!' she chuckled.

'When do I get my hairband?' tummy asked.

'It's not a hairband, it's *lap* band!' Hana roared with laughter.

'But it goes on my head doesn't it, Hana? At the top, like a hair band?'

I had been making her tummy talk for a couple of months – my attempt to turn the darkness of the days into something lighter. Her hunger didn't seem so awful when we could laugh about it. I made conversations about the lap band funny and the laughter helped us get through the last few excruciating days before we would hop on that plane without a look back. I'd also been preparing her emotionally for the small liquid meals she'd need post surgery. We'd bought some cute tiny decorated tea cups for her 'soups' and cashew nut purees that she was becoming excited about using post op. I began to build her excitement for the procedure: the lap band was going to be her best friend.

'Bye, Daddy!' Hana said, waving from her wheelchair at the departure exit. I was smiling, but my throat was tight and tears welled up in my eyes as we said goodbye to Nour who looked small and frail as he stood alone at the exit, fighting his own tears. I popped Maryam into the wheelchair next to Hana, squidged in next to her, the arrangement both girls had both been happy with for the past year, even though it was uncomfortable for both of them.

'Bye bye, Daddy!' piped up Maryam's cartoon-like voice.

I stopped for one more wave before turning the corner, grateful that the girls were facing forwards in the wheelchair and couldn't see my tears. It was massive, travelling with both girls alone to do this. We had an incredible amount of luggage. Because of our food sensitivities, I'd had to pack certain things in large quantities that I didn't know when I'd be able to get again! Our low mould toxin cacao butter, certain organic oils, grass-fed ghee, enormous amounts of organic cashew nuts, which were a dietary staple for vegan butters, milks and creams – Maryam's buckwheat porridges, and organic maple syrups, and wheat and gluten-free cake mix which hadn't been available in Egypt up until then. Plus my organic cosmetics – shampoos and body creams for myself and the girls.

I also had my Thermomix as hand luggage in addition to a huge bag full of home-prepared meals and snacks – enough to last us a 14-hour flight. I had cooked and frozen in a ready-to-eat batch – lentil and vegetable soup so that when we landed in Dubai and arrived at my friend's house for a 48-hour stopover, we had a meal ready to go. Instructions had been sent to my mother-in-law to get red lentils, cabbage and celery in so I could whip up a fresh batch as soon as we landed in Cairo. Meals and snacks when travelling had been a constant source of stress until Hana's tumour was diagnosed. This time round, packing and planning food for four months of travel seemed like a piece of organic, vegan, gluten- and sugar-free cake.

Hana ate her pre-planned airport snack in the departure lounge as we watched our plane being prepared for the long trip ahead. As she snacked, Maryam and I had a glimpse in the newsagent opposite the lounge. Displayed in my full view was a book I'd had a niggling feeling I'd heard about before: *The Brain's Way of Healing* by Norman Doidge. The lap band was going to buy me time to find a way to heal her brain … My handbag was bursting to the brim with medications, food and travel details, but I bought the book and stuffed it in anyway. This would be post-lap band reading: the next steps!

'Hello!' A kind air steward came over to help us onto the plane. I pushed Hana's chair down the ramp without a glance back and made a vow: *When we come back here, she will walk off the plane.*

Night fell, the girls drifted off to sleep for a bit. I was completely wired – I knew that I wouldn't sleep a wink on this 14-hour flight. I put on some music and began to breathe deeply, trying to relax.

What if something happens? What if she dies during this surgery?

Nothing matters ... I am doing the right thing. There is nothing else to do.

You'll be judged by the whole of Australia when it gets out!

No one can judge a mother for trying to save her daughter's life. No one will judge me.

What if it doesn't work?

It WILL work. Whatever happens after this surgery it is going to be an improvement on the hell we are living now.

'I'm hungry, Mum!' Hana woke up suddenly and loudly uttered the most spoken words in her vocabulary. She looked around, confused by the dark cabin around her.

'Oh, Hana,' I sighed. 'It's sleeping time now. We can't eat anything we aren't due. You know I only have limited food anyway.' She began to cry.

Oh, my heart. How can it be torn like that every day and still beat?

'This is why we're going, love. This is the beginning of the end to your awful hunger. The lap band is going to be your friend. It's nearly over now.' The words comforted me as much as her and I tuned into my hope: *It's nearly over now!*

She nodded, eventually stopped crying and drifted back to sleep while the plane propelled us forwards, one mile at a time.

Chapter Eleven

The heat streamed through the dusty bus windows as we bumped along to the airport terminal. Maryam, my dark-skinned brunette, as delicate as a baby bird – her enormous brown eyes widened at being jostled about in a crowd of so many people. Then there was my blonde, Caucasian rosy-cheeked Hana, her obesity throwing her off balance, her face lined with pain at having to stand. Then me, sunken eyed with exhaustion, pale and underweight with stress, embracing my girls with my arms so they didn't fall at every bump and unpredictable swing of the bus. The heavy bulky Thermomix in one hand, two-wheeled hand luggage bags in the other and oversized, over-packed shoulder bag cutting into my skin.

We had landed after an exhausting stint in Dubai and upset getting to Cairo – they had wanted to separate me from the girls on this flight, and the woman who had been put in my seat was refusing to swap and let me sit with my girls because she felt it was against her religion to sit next to a man. By this point I hadn't slept more than three hours in 48 hours and I was extremely teary. I began to cry in front of all the passengers – protesting this woman's selfishness that she would separate me from both my girls who were also on the verge of tears. Someone eventually stepped in and made everything alright, but it was the last thing I needed – it was so ludicrous, it felt surreal.

Then we were being met off the bus by one of my mother-in-law's airport contacts – I breathed out a sigh of relief. As usual, he organised our visas and personally took us through passport control. I was one lucky woman to be married to such a well-connected family. And there was my mother-in-law, sitting alone in the airport café – the entire arrivals gate had been vacated due to security risks after a spate of bombing in the city, but she was there, privileged access due to her contacts. Both Nour's grandfathers had been high profile politicians – one a prime minister – during a happier political time in the country. His family weren't just respected for their previous role in Egyptian politics but for their influence as well-known doctors in Cairo and, more importantly, for their kind-hearted generosity. My in-laws were smart, well-connected, good, open- minded people who had never abused their positions of power in a system that was rife with self-serving corruption. As a family they were well liked, well known and highly respected. My mother-in-law was waiting with the grinning family driver – what a sight for sore eyes.

'Let Nanna take care of everything!' she declared proudly as we stepped into the blinding sunlight, moved through the teeming hordes of people crowding outside the arrivals gate and got in the car. 'You don't have to worry about a thing here, in Egypt – Nanna takes care of everything.' I sank gratefully into the plastic-lined seat of her new car – Egyptians were always reluctant to make the final decision to remove the plastic off a new car because of the merciless desert dust – and I exhaled the stress of travel: I knew we were safe in the hands of my mother-in-law.

Years before, during my early months in Egypt, before anyone had really 'known' me, she had been driven to help me find work, took me under her wing when I had appendicitis and needed emergency abdominal surgery, offered me a room in their house when I had awoken to an intruder at the window of my first apartment. It had been the first hot night in my ramshackle cockroach-infested pit of a home and so, scantily clad that night, I'd opened the windows and shutters only to awaken in the early hours to find a boy at my window spying on me while I'd been sleeping. In his hand was an enormous rod, multiple sticks tied together with a spike at the end, stretched throughout my entire bedroom, with which he'd been tapping at my pink Nokia mobile phone that was lying on the rag-rugged floor next to my bed. I had sensed during those early months that she had a slight unease with me – after all, who was this strange foreign girl who insisted on living in Egypt yet initially had no job and very little money to support herself! Why was she here? At the same time, I saw her bending over backwards to help me … it was as if she knew somehow I would become a permanent part of their lives. As time progressed and my relationship with Nour was slowly revealed to the family, some extended family members piped up their concern at Nour's plans to marry a foreigner and a family rift followed. She and my father-in-law stood by us and refused to partake in any negative talk regarding the relationship between Nour and me, which within the tightly knit family circles of Egyptian culture, was a huge deal.

We set out on to the traffic-jammed roads that I had travelled down so many times for nearly 15 years now: A student venturing here on her first Egyptian backpacking adventure, a returning lover of the country then after that, drawn here intuitively – knowing that this was where my future would unfold – then, time after time, feeling semi-Egyptian, engaged to an Egyptian man. Once, at the airport my visa had expired, but they just let me in because I told them I was engaged to an Egyptian – they didn't even stamp my passport.

'Masraya keda,' the man had chuckled. 'Like an Egyptian'.

Familiar hot air blasted out of the air conditioner. It always took Egyptian cars a good fifteen minutes to get some sort of air conditioning working in summer time. I remembered with a smile how the many taxi drivers I'd been with had wound down their windows declaring natural 'teekeef' (air conditioning) from the hot, dusty desert winds – it often worked better than beaten-up old car air con anyway. We drove through Misr Gedida, where I'd become a qualified English teacher, studying for my English Teaching Certificate or 'CELTA', in the day, frequenting the local restaurants at night with Nour, then through Zamalek, an island of affluence in the middle of the Nile – where I'd lived for four years – those dirt-lined streets had been my home. Then we drove through Mohandasseen where I'd held private tutoring classes in glamourous cafés, gone clothes shopping and met expat friends for super sweet, caramel syrup lattes and chocolate cheesecake (yes, I used to eat like a normal human back then) and then crossing the bridge to the Mehwar – the desert road out to 6 October city, where many Cairenes had begun to build a quieter life for themselves in the desert, villas in beautiful compounds away from the pollution and chaos of downtown Cairo.

Coming back to my in-laws' house was always like coming back to a home of sorts. Over the years I had stayed there for a period of months – post-appendectomy, post-tonsillectomy, in between rental properties or just when I wasn't feeling well! It was in between rental places, in Nour's family home when we had begun to fall in love ... our first kiss had been in the family kitchen quite unexpectedly one evening after a long drive back from a camping trip on the Red Sea in the mountains of Sinai. A goodnight hug that suddenly became the kind of kiss when you hear a whole orchestra or heavenly choir joining in! And it was there a year or two after that kiss that he chose to propose to me – one evening, the entire kitchen covered in tea light candles his sister had set up while we'd were driving back from Agouza. I'd been working at the British Council all day – in charge of looking after a celebrity singer as part of a huge event on the Nile River in front of the building to celebrate a new program we were launching. Nour and I emerged from the kitchen out to the living area where his mum and sister were already waiting with a chocolate sponge cake –

'Did she say yes?' his mum asked, and when I laughed away her question she repeated it, just to be sure. 'Did you say yes?'

After two days attempting to recover from jet lag and a good few hours shopping at the swish local mall for new Egyptian cotton pyjamas and boxes of craft activities to do in hospital, we were ready for Hana's surgery.

'What's happening today, Hana?' I asked a sleepy little girl, set upon devouring her cashew nut 'cream' for breakfast.

'I'm having my lap band!' she smiled. We had discussed the fact she would be on a liquid diet for a week post-surgery and I was ready with thin lentil soup and cashew nut milk sprinkled with carob powder that I had packed into a freezer bag ready for the hospital.

The nerves started in the car ride there, then hit with a vengeance once we were settled in our room. We had the largest suite in the hospital – it had a living area separate to the bedroom, a large bathroom and sleeping area. A friend and colleague of my mother-in-law, a paediatric endocrinologist joined us in the suite – and stayed by our sides the whole day.

'Don't you think a sleeve gastrectomy would be a better option?' she quizzed me.

'No – the physical presence of the lap band over the vagus nerve is speculated to confer some interruption to vagal stimulation and it is this that is thought to reduce the food focus. In addition, the fact that there is an eating routine with the band – that is to say, one bite every minute means that the oesophagus must repeatedly send "I'm full" messages to the brain. These messages come from oesophageal contractions. So, whereas one bite usually leads to one direct contraction for us, for a lap-band wearer there will be many more contractions per bite and this increases early onset satiety.'

She nodded. 'Very impressive. I think you know more about this subject than any doctor.'

'That's because I have higher stakes at play than any doctor I've met,' I said with a hint of sadness.

Hana was fasting – something she found unbearable with her extreme hunger. The tears started around midday – when we were already one hour later for her anaesthesia – apparently the hospital staff were ready for the procedure but the lap band itself was stuck in traffic, being transported from the adult hospital to the paediatric. I could just imagine whoever it was clutching the precious lap-band container, sweating under the pressure with the hundreds of cars beeping and tooting while he made his way over to us.

'Hasn't she gone in yet?' Nour FaceTimed us as usual once he finished work, although it was now late in Sydney, but he was waiting for her to 'go under' before falling asleep.

'No,' I smiled ruefully. 'Everyone here is ready but … the lap band is stuck in traffic.'

'What the?' He shook his head in disbelief, Cairo!

Eventually the anaesthetist arrived. He gave Hana a large shot of the sedative midazolam which made her sob with fear and confusion as she began to lose her sense of orientation. I escorted her to the operating rooms where they completed the induction. Then she was whisked off to theatre … Gone.

I made my way back down to the suite. Maryam had curled up on the sofa, her blanky over her – she had been chilly in the air conditioning. I sat next to her, stroking her, staring into space. My eyes filled with tears, but I was too shell-shocked to let them spill and start crying. My mother-in-law looked at me and nodded.

'It will all be OK, Nounou.' Then she gave me some space and went to sit with the paediatric endocrinologist in the sitting room of our suite. I focused on feeling nothing at all in tune with the rattle of the noisy air conditioner that bumped and spluttered on the wall above me. For while I wanted to be *Mish Mawgoud*.

A couple of hours went by … I began clock watching. This was supposed to be a short procedure. What was taking so long?

Above: This picture was taken on Bondi Beach, Christmas Day 2013. As we were skipping towards the camera I had a fleeting feeling this picture would be significant and iconic to us in a way I didn't yet understand.

Right: Hana just before her surgery, aged 5 January 2014.

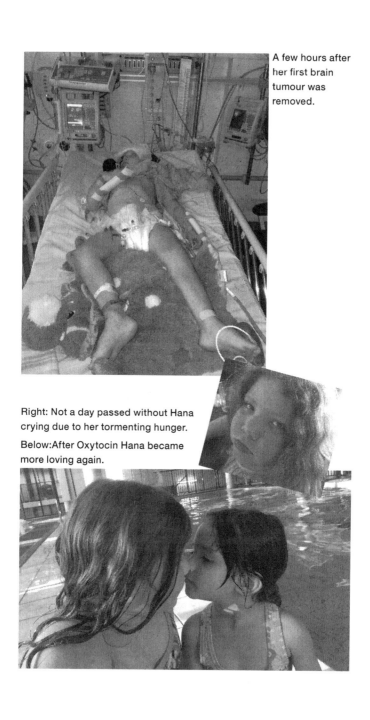

A few hours after her first brain tumour was removed.

Right: Not a day passed without Hana crying due to her tormenting hunger.

Below: After Oxytocin Hana became more loving again.

Left: Front page of the *Sunday Telegraph*, note they were wrong in claiming she couldn't stop eating, her weight gain was due to metabolic dysfunction however she was always hungry.

Below: Hana's rapid onset weight gain left her wheelchair bound within a few months.

SHE EATS, BUT IS NEVER FULL
Meet the little girl with a condition that piles on weight

sunrise

BRI
29°

DOCKERS: 'BANNED DRUG WAS IN A PAINKILLER'

8:24

Above: We appeared in a news program for Cure Brain Cancer and Hana met Charlie Teo. On Channel 7's Sunrise – asking for help.

Below: I spent many an hour home-schooling Hana for two years post op as she was too fragile to attend full time.

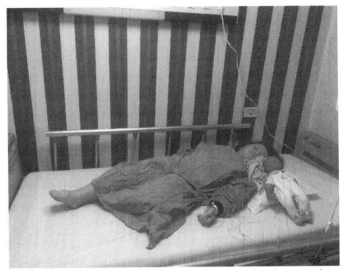

Above: In Cairo, Egypt, June 2015, just before her lap band surgery, jet lagged, fasting and nervous.

Below: In the UK a few weeks after Hana's lap band surgery, looking forward to the future.

Above: In Toronto for Brain Healing with Fred Kahn, the film crew we travelled with took this family shot.

Left: Hana having Low Level Laser Therapy.

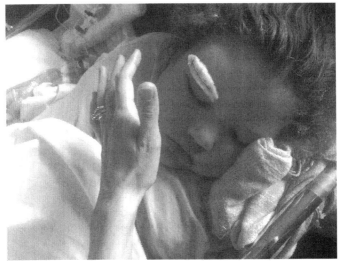

Above: Giving Reiki to Hana in ICU after her second tumour was removed, May 2016.

Below: Giving Reiki to Hana felt so instinctive: it was an honour to help her in this way.

Right: Nour and I, in spite of our hell, somehow still in love!

Above: Hana experiencing severe headaches post surgery, she wanted to 'go back to the angel world'.

Left: A rare family photo in our new home, July 2017.

Maybe she died.

Oh stop it!

What if they gave her a sleeve gastrectomy instead?

Enough!

Another hour went by and the message came she was coming round. Like a rabbit, I leapt up the stairs, but with a sinking feeling in my gut – I could hear screams before I'd reached the top step. Loud, animal screams: they were hers.

The double doors were locked. I bunched my fists and banged against them like a mad woman, no other thought except a wild instinctive feeling that I had to get to my child! There was a strange large gap between the bottom of the door and the floor – to this day I have no idea why this door was seemingly 'unfinished'. I began sizing it up – I could definitely fit under the door! Just as I was about to bend over and crawl under the door on my hands and knees, it swung open. Hana was writhing in her narrow trolley bed in front the door. Her face red, spittle flying out of her mouth, eyes glazed and unfocused.

'MUUUUUUUUMMY!' she screamed. I grabbed her,

'Baby! It's OK. I'm here. You did it. I'm here!'

She continued to roar as the medical team apologetically told me they wanted a blood sample to check her sodium levels so we could plan for the afternoon's IV fluid replacement. Due to her medication that stopped her from peeing, fluid overload from IVs was a death risk – too much would led to fatal brain swelling. But Hana's veins had collapsed from being under anaesthesia and her cannula IV had fluids running through which would give a false reading if the sample was taken from there so they needed to 'stab' her with a needle. She swung out her arms and refused to let them grab her as they forced her wrists down.

'I'm going to have to give more anaesthesia,' the anaesthetist said.

Shit, shit, shit, why? Why so much drama? I held my breath as he shot a volume of thick white fluid into her cannula.

Within seconds she went dusky blue, eyes rolling back in her head as she slipped into unconsciousness again.

'Does she need some oxygen?' I panicked as she gurgled, her tongue slipping back over her airway.

Oh dear baby girl. How have our lives come to this? You here — screaming like a tortured animal on a hospital trolley, stabbed with needles, filled with drugs, your tiny body exploded with obesity and mutilated by surgeon's knives and instruments. Your face dusky blue as you slip so easily away from me.

How did this happen? How did we travel this far?

'No, this will only last a few minutes,' he assured me. He was right, within a few minutes she was more aware, the rage and screaming stopped, but continued moaning as we wheeled her back to the rooms. The extra dose of anaesthesia knocked her out all afternoon. After another three hours had passed, I looked at the endocrinologist who, bless her heart, was still by our sides. She looked concerned, as did my mother-in-law: Hana needed to wake up now.

'I'll use a homeopathic remedy,' I whispered. 'Phosphorous is excellent at reversing anaesthesia.'

I crushed the pillule and mixed it some water then dabbed Hana's lips. She licked them in response, and seconds later, began to rouse.

'You are a magician!' my mother-in-law beamed.

'I'm just glad that you understand that this stuff actually works!' I laughed as Hana began trying to sit up in bed. 'Once you get the right remedy, it truly works like magic. Thank goodness you are open minded too.'

'I too was desperate once to help my father as he was passing away from cancer and explored everything I could to help his pain,' she murmured as Hana began stirring. 'Homeopathy helped him a lot.'

I stroked Hana's forehead. 'Hello darling!' I murmured.

'Mum,' Hana croaked. 'Mum.' she began to cry:

'I'm **hungry**.'

Please, no. Please don't tell me it didn't work and that we must go straight back to the hell we thought we'd left behind?

The endocrinologist caught my eye and we shared a moment of fear.

I drew myself up straight. 'Of course you are, darling! You've been fasting since this morning. Let's get you some lentil soup. Would you like that?' I tenderly fed her three teaspoons of the semi-warm soup.

'That's enough,' she said. Three teaspoons?! My heart stopped fluttering so painfully.

It was all going to be OK.

My mother-in-law and the endocrinologist left late in the evening. Hana was sleeping – amazingly without any need for morphine and Maryam was curled up next to me on a large sofa near Hana's bed. I was wrecked – during the trip over I'd had only the few hours of sleep and over the last couple of days I'd found jet lag had been pretty full-on, combined with the nervousness around the surgery. Now the monster day was over and my stress levels were even higher than ever. Hana had IV fluids trickling through which always worried me from a sodium perspective but, as she hadn't been drinking, she needed them. Then I focused on my other worry – her hydrocortisone coverage. Was she dosed enough to prevent an adrenal crisis? Then, how bad would her pain be in the morning? And, *would she be hungry?*

My phone beeped, it was Nour waking up in Sydney – I rang him for a quiet, quick chat and filled him in on the day in a low voice. Then I lay there wide awake for hours. At midnight, one of the surgical registrars came in, so I moved into the sitting room.

'How is she?'

'She's great,' I said. 'Minimal pain, sleeping well.'

'It took a little longer than expected as she is small. As you know, we are only used to doing this on adults,' he said. 'So she will need a liquid diet for a week and then soft foods – I believe you know the protocol?'

'Yes, thanks. I have books and instructions on the topic from a high-profile doctor in Australia – they are very detailed.'

'The band is deflated now but we will fill it a little bit in a few weeks once the swelling around the oesophagus has subsided. By the way, one thing we were discussing in the surgery was the efficacy of the lap band for her condition. We weren't really sure how you were thinking this would work, because bariatric surgery is rarely recommended for this condition and when it is, it is usually the sleeve or gastric bypass.'

I went on to explain the potential neuro-hormonal impact as postulated by the German research and he nodded, impressed with the postulated effects. Then I went back to lie down with Maryam, feeling too exhausted now to sleep. I was going to need some seriously good coffee in the morning.

Chapter Twelve

'Chop chop! Get your shoes on and we'll walk through the woods before bed.'

'Okay,' Hana said, grabbing a basket. 'Can I collect some flowers?' The words slipped out so easily but I didn't forget for a second to relish every single syllable. *Going for a walk! Before bed!*

It was a month later and we were in Oxford, in the UK. We had spent two weeks recovering in the compound in Sheikh Zayad post op – swimming twice daily at a beautiful outdoor resort, walking around the compound at sunset as the local mosque echoed out the evening call to prayer. Days were spent roaming around the air-conditioned malls and homeschooling around the dining-room table. Thanks to our pre-op emotional preparation Hana had been amazing with her post-op meal plan, consuming thin soups and cashew nut milks and creams for the first full seven days. Her pain was controlled mainly with homeopathic arnica, which has incredible pain-relieving abilities. That week, I weighed her every day and, for the first time in a year and a half, I witnessed the scales go down. By the end of the week she had dropped four kilos. I nearly yelled with jubilation.

But … the most amazing aspect of her lap-band experience was indeed a reduced food obsession. Yes, she still got hungry at mealtimes, but the constant thoughts of food had reduced dramatically. I was beginning to thank my lucky stars.

The heat was too much for us to stay in Cairo and I was running short of ways to keep both girls entertained during the heat of the day so I booked us flights to England – I was desperate for some English countryside and to catch up with my mum, dad and brothers whom I hadn't seen for ages. During our years in Australia we'd tried to travel back to both Egypt and the UK once a year: the last time we'd been was as proud triathletes competing at the ITU Triathlon World Championships in London only five months before Hana had been diagnosed. Nour had trained me up to racing standard and I'd done so well at my qualifying races that I was on the Australian team and got to wear the green and gold suit in London. Nour had decided to race on the Egyptian team so we'd both packed our racing bikes and gear for our UK trip followed by two weeks on the Red Sea in Egypt after the race.

Hana, Maryam and I shared a giant mattress on the floor of my mum's spare room and I began to blog about our adventures – I was ready to share now that Hana was safely post op and benefiting from the procedure. We did a little filming for an Australian news program who were keen to share the updates in our journey. The channel had a film crew based in London who came up to Oxford for the day to interview me and film Hana. We filled our days with parks and short walks. Little by little I was easing Hana out of the wheelchair – she was soon able to do a twenty-minute walk through the woods every evening before bed without tears from the pain in her ankles.

Hope tasted as fresh as the English air and looked as triumphant as the masses of tall proud wild flowers Hana picked every time we went for a walk.

And then came the time for the lap-band fills! An old friend of Nour's who happened to be working as a bariatric surgeon in London offered to help out with band fills, a beautiful example of how things were finally going our way! We made arrangements to see his wonderful nurse almost weekly on a Saturday morning in London for fills. She was also training me to be able to adjust the band. We took it slowly each week as filling the band too quickly could impact on Hana's ability to consume fluids – with diabetes insipidus this would be dangerous.

So I would wake the girls at 4.30 am every Saturday, hop in a taxi to Oxford station for our trips to London, English fields – *home* – rolling by as the train sped on. The needle to put saline into the port to fill the band was a biggie, and the port access was below skin level, deep in subcutaneous tissue. Fortunately, the surgeon had considered ease of access over 'visibility' and aesthetics due to Hana's age and he had placed the port close to the surface of skin so it protruded out from under the skin. This caused considerable discomfort for about three months post op, but eventually the irritation ceased and we enjoyed the fact her port was easy to access every time we had to fill the band. Of course, the port was given the affectionate name of 'Porty'!

Every Saturday morning I placed a local anaesthetic cream (Emla) over the port area while we were still on the train, one hour before the band fill so she that she would have minimal pain. Then, after filling 0.5–1ml of saline, Hana would 'test' the band for tightness by having a drink. If the water passed through easily then we were fit to go! So into a taxi to Paddington station and back off to Oxford, usually just in time for a Saturday afternoon swim at a friend's house.

At that point I was keeping Hana on a strictly ketogenic diet, measuring ketones on her urine every day. I also followed that diet with her for moral support. There were several reasons for such a diet. The first was that ketones were thought to confer neuroprotective properties and possibly played a role in neurogeneration, so, from a brain healing perspective, it was important to try this diet. Secondly, there was an increasing number of success stories about very high-fat, low-carb diets, demonstrating appetite reduction and weight loss for many patients. This meant very minimal carbs! Since we were already low carb in that we weren't eating bread, pasta or rice, this meant further restricting the carb content in certain vegetables and nuts too. Hana was able to stay in ketosis with the occasional portion of lentil soup, but being vegetarian (and for myself, vegan), food choices were limited. With lap-band food restrictions thrown in, it took a huge amount of dedication and discipline. She lived on salad, creamy broccoli soup, omelettes and easy-to-chew and swallow vegetables.

'Can you SMELL that!' I declared. The English countryside was whizzing by as I drove into the Cotswolds.

'It's stinks!' protested Maryam. 'What is that smell?'

'That, my dears, is the smell of the countryside! That's horse pooh – manure. It's used to keep the vegetables growing nicely.'

'Euuuuh.' She screwed up her face.

I need this, I need to be in the countryside – this was a nagging feeling that was growing so much stronger by the month. The thought of returning to our bustling Bondi Junction high-rise apartment, which by now was surrounded on every side by massive developments, and the ever-present noise made me feel sick. I had loved our early years there but now things had changed and even thinking about it made me feel claustrophobic. But how to do this? We couldn't leave Australia for England with Nour's clinic now in full swing …

'When will you come back?' We were FaceTiming Nour right before he went to bed one morning.

'I'm just not ready yet,' I said. 'I want to return completely triumphant − without the wheelchair, healed from the surgery with no shadow of a doubt in anyone's minds that we did the right thing. And … after all we've been through, I'm just not ready to come yet.' I felt like the walls in our apartment would contain the memories of our dark suffering − I couldn't bear to reconnect with those feelings.

He understood and wanted the girls to stay away as long as possible so that they could 'heal' on an emotional level surrounded by family − particularly Maryam, who was beginning to open like a flower. 'I'll fly out then, in August for two weeks then we can go back together,' he agreed. So we planned a family holiday on the Red Sea in our honeymoon resort as the last 'hit out' before returning back home.

'Ten years ago we were here just newly weds,' Nour reminisced as we walked along the promenade at sunset, salty wind blowing in our faces.

'We were kids,' I said quietly, wondering how I would have reacted all those years ago if anyone had told me what we had in store for us. I turned around to look at Hana and Maryam who were pointing at a stingray nestled in the shallow waters below us.

'Has she lost any more weight?' he asked.

'No … she's plateaued,' I said nervously. Hana had lost only a few kilos with the band and, according to the studies, the greatest weight loss occurred in the first six months followed by a regain and then stabilisation. 'But it doesn't matter, all we want is stability and the transformation on her appetite—'

'She's so much happier,' Nour agreed. 'It's like she's free to be a kid again.' We walked on in silence – in agreement that we weren't expecting miracle weight loss with the band, just time to catch our breath after the relentless weight gain and hunger. Even though we both felt this, there was a question mark hanging over our heads – how long would this honeymoon period last? Would we have to return to the dark days of endless weight gain in the future?

I inhaled the warm air, always tangy with a peppery plant in the evening, reminding me of our honeymoon here. The sky was turning the sea and mountains across the waters pink. This hotel had witnessed our holiday as newly weds and trips here with happy, healthy children who spent hours running around on the sand, playing in the enormous pool, and who adored our ritual of walks in the dark at night where we'd marvel at the hazy band of the Milky Way above us.

Although Hana would come to the beach and pool, it was with reluctance, just like at home. She preferred to stay inside colouring-in. She found it too hot and bright to be on the beach with everyone else, and without the wheelchair – which we'd left in Cairo – she chose to walk only short distances because of her ankle pain. Glancing out the balcony, I could see Maryam was playing happily on the beach with her cousins and my mother-in-law. Nour had gone for a bike ride, so I picked up *The Brain's Way of Healing*, the book I'd bought on the spur of the moment in the airport three months ago.

A few chapters in, I found the answer to my question on the next steps to take in healing Hana's brain: the story of an amazing man called Fred Kahn and *Low Level Laser Therapy*, or LLLT. Just as I finished reading the chapter, Nour came back, hot, sweaty and dehydrated from his ride. I pounced on him.

'It's the next step!' I hissed quietly as Hana had just fallen asleep. 'Low level laser therapy. It can have incredible results for brain healing – I need to email this Kahn guy. This is huge!'

'Laser? That sounds dangerous,' he said.

'Oh, shush!' I brushed him aside, raising my voice slightly, cross that the first thing he'd say was negative when I'd had ants in my pants for an hour, itching to tell him my most awesome find yet. I wanted him to be as ecstatic as I was. 'It's *cold* laser!'

'Stop shouting!'

'I'm not shouting, I'm whispering, Hana is asleep if you haven't noticed,' I retorted, now my amazing discovery was leading to an argument! This was the problem when I was excited and passionate about something – I'd raise my voice and he always took it the wrong way. Also, I had a sense of hyperactive optimism – in contrast to his cautiousness and tendency to critique new ideas. My rose-tinted glasses meant that I got more disappointed by people and circumstances than he did when the 'amazing' things I discovered turned out to not be so amazing after all. Then I'd had to admit that 'he was right', which I didn't enjoy at all. If I was being honest with myself, I'd say we balanced each other out. But I was stubborn, so, instead, I preferred to moan at him for being negative.

'Calm down. You don't need to be defensive about the laser. I'm entitled to ask these questions, aren't I?'

'If you are interested, you can read all about it here! It has been done many times – there are stories of miracles after brain injuries being healed here – so no, it's not dangerous!'

I offered him the book but, since reading wasn't really his thing, he decided to accept my word for it and didn't criticise my finding any further. I smugly felt that I'd won our little argument and knew, anyway, that he would always support me and my wild schemes – I was lucky to have his steadfast trust.

Once Hana had woken up, we walked down to the beach for the late afternoon swim and sandcastles. I couldn't contain my excitement at having found this lead for my next step and fervently tried to explain all I had discovered to my relatives – my father-in-law, my sister-in-law, who were trying to rest on the sun lounges. It struck me, as I watched Hana collect sea snails, giggling at how they curled around on her hands, how important 'hope' was. So long as there is hope, it is always possible to keep going and stay positive. Being without hope? That must be the darkest place a human can ever go.

We arrived back in Australia at the beginning of September, without the wheelchair. I let myself feel that triumph as we stalked through the airport to baggage collection: I had accomplished all I had set out to do. Hana went straight back to school, coping extremely well with her lap band. There were occasions when it would block during a mealtime and I would sit with her while she vomited it up. Sometimes I would stick my fingers towards the back of her mouth to activate her gag reflex. During these moments, I almost felt like I was standing out of my body watching a different mum and little girl. It was hard to believe I was here, doing this, making my daughter vomit, encouraging her to stick her fingers down her throat. How ludicrous it was.

But I never felt sorry for myself or her. I felt gratitude. We were lucky to have this band – it had given Hana back an aspect of her childhood. Not a day went by that I didn't think about her life being saved daily by the lap band that was saving her life by stabilising her weight.

The first day Hana went back to school I found Fred Kahn's email address online and I sent him a long, descriptive email pleading for help. I had been lucky enough to have been given time to heal my daughter's brain while her dangerous condition was under control. Now I needed his help to continue with my quest to cure her condition before my luck ran out again.

Would he reply? He was now famous after Norman Doidge's book – perhaps he was inundated with emails from desperate parents or individuals like me and my plea would go unnoticed.

A few mornings later, I emerged bleary-eyed at five o'clock with Hana, her usual wake-up time. We got her thyroid meds and her water from the fridge and the Nespresso machine was just warming up when I opened my inbox. I gasped in excitement, heart racing, before I'd had a chance to sip my double espresso.

We would be pleased to attempt to assist you in your daughter's therapy. It is possible that we might bring significant benefit to her status but in medicine, as you well know, there are no guarantees.

The only way to determine if she can be helped is to try perhaps 10–20 treatments over a course of 2–3 weeks.

Sincerely, Fred Kahn

I raced over to the bedroom,

'Nour!' I called out, 'Sorry to wake you, but this is AWESOME! He replied, he replied!'

'Who replied?' a disgruntled, crumpled Nour mumbled from under the bedclothes, clearly very unimpressed.

'Fred Kahn!' I laughed. 'Oh, hurry up and get up! We're going to Toronto!'

Chapter Thirteen

Five weeks later I looked at the drip coffee machine the others were using so enthusiastically and wrinkled my nose – I needed something better than this – but there wasn't a café in sight here either.

'We only landed a few hours ago from Australia,' I explained to the man behind me in the coffee queue. We had found our Airbnb in the dead of the night and put the girls to bed around one a.m. 'I think I only had an hour's sleep before my alarm went off!'

I grabbed a paper cup and pressed 'go' for something that neither looked nor smelt like coffee, it is common knowledge that living in Sydney induced a life long coffee-snobbishness. It was 8 am and we were at Meditech, Fred Kahn's company headquarters, a company that produced LLLT machines and devices as well as treated patients in clinic. We were getting ready for Dr Kahn's practitioner course in low level laser therapy for healthcare professionals run by Meditech so that I would be qualified to practice LLLT myself. Nour and I had planned for Hana to have an intensive course of treatments for three weeks in Toronto before returning home with a machine of our own to continue working with.

We had flown over with an Australian news and current affairs program film crew who were shadowing our trip. I had popped over to the clinic next door to say hi before leaving them to set up ready for the day's filming. I rushed back to my course, still grieving the lack of Sydney quality coffee in this part of town – the Meditech offices were situated in a quite industrial area without a single funky-looking café or trendy coffee bar in sight. I was so desperate for strong coffee even a Starbucks would have done the job. But, once the lectures started, my adrenalin kept me going: the theory and studies on the success of Fred's treatment protocols were blowing my mind. I just knew this would help Hana!

I learnt that LLLT had been around for a long time and was used primarily to treat soft tissue injuries; it wasn't a 'new' therapy. However, using it for treating brain injury was relatively new and had really been brought to public attention through *The Brain's Way of Healing*. I discovered that there were more than 4000 scientific publications on LLLT with over 400 double blind studies published on the topic. Although it was not considered mainstream medical practice, with such a large, established evidence base, I thought it jolly well should be!

Dr Kahn's clinic delivered LLLT in the form of 'array' placements on damaged body areas. The array was a large, flat device with lots of tiny light bulbs on the undersurface that delivered red light for a few minutes and then switched to infra-red light for a few more minutes. The array was then removed and followed by a placement of two laser probes for more direct, piercing light therapy, of both red and infra-red lights, which moved in sequence over damaged areas.

On a cellular level, these lights, in the form of photons, 'spoke' to light-sensitive components in the cell, causing a biochemical reaction: *photobiomodulation*. For example, photon receptors in the mitochondria within our cells, once stimulated, can activate energy production, facilitating renewal and repair. The photons were also thought to help reduce chronic, painful inflammation through improving the immune response of white blood cells. Photons ultimately reduce the actions of inflammatory neutrophils, instead stimulating the actions of macrophages – large phagocytic cells that then travel to the area and gobble up the debris that contributes to persistent inflammation – a cause of chronic pain.

Although I was taught that the impact of LLLT on soft tissue injuries had been well documented, documentation on the impact on traumatic brain injury (TBI) was still growing. However, the theory was the same – that by placing 'lights' on the cranial and spinal areas, the cerebrospinal fluids and blood vessels would be flooded with photons that would travel to damaged cells stimulating cellular renewal and regeneration – which of course, *could* equate to brain healing.

My hand aching from my fervent note taking, I put down my pen and gathered up my stuff mid morning,

'I'll slip out now to meet Dr Kahn as it's Hana's appointment,' I told one of the clinicians. I was so excited about meeting Dr Kahn. We'd exchanged many emails and he had a good idea of my passionate quest to heal Hana. We got 'mic'ed-up' for the camera crew to record our first meeting with Dr Kahn, a man with sparkling blue eyes and shock of white hair. He was in his eighties, worked full-time and was agile, slender and strong, living proof of the anti-ageing properties of his machines and protocols!

When Hana received her first treatments, the arrays placed on her spinal areas, she started bawling almost immediately, 'I want to go home!'

'Tired, you're just tired,' I soothed her and held her hand.

I snuck back to my course once she had settled and later heard from Nour that, due to the endorphin-releasing effect of the laser, she had gone so hyper and jovial at the end of her session, she had burst into fits of giggles trying to hide from Dr Kahn under his desk. Relieved the girls had gone back to the condo, I settled back into my course. By the end of the day, I was so sleep deprived, I felt like I was hallucinating.

'You're going to have to drive here,' Nour declared that night as I started unpacking the girls clothes. 'I'll hire a car for you.' He was staying with us for only a few days before returning to Sydney – we couldn't afford for him to take any longer off work.

'There's no way I'm driving here, it's the wrong side of the road. I can't flip my brain over like that. And look,' I protested, pointing out the window to the most enormous freeway I'd ever seen – the monster was about six lanes wide. We were staying on the 24th floor in a small but every elegant and swish condo in Etobicoke, way too far to walk to our appointments, and in between appointments we would be stuck without a car – what would I do for two weeks alone here with the girls?

'You have to,' Nour decided firmly. 'We'll find some back roads to get to the clinic so you can avoid that ...' He beckoned to the window. 'Look, if you can drive in Sydney, you'll be fine here.'

The idea of staying alone with the girls for two weeks seemed scary – I hated driving on unfamiliar roads back home, let alone in a busy city like Toronto in a car I wasn't familiar with, not to mention if the first snows came.

Then, feeling like the biggest wuss, I said meekly, 'Maybe I should just come back with you, now I've done the course and we are buying the machine!'

'Don't be silly,' Nour said. 'We'll practise driving to the mall, the clinic and Loblaws.' (Loblaws was a huge supermarket nearby with, much to my delight, a huge range of fresh vegetables and organic food.) 'You'll be fine.'

Apart from being a total chicken and leaving Toronto with Nour because I was too afraid to drive, I couldn't find a better solution than to agree to hiring a car. At the end of the first week, we farewelled the film crew who were flying back now they had sufficient footage of Hana's treatments. Then it was Nour's turn to go – two weeks of occupying the girls alone in a strange city in winter loomed in front of me. We would be limited by where I had confidence to drive and how far Hana was able to walk without ankle pain, which was really only a few minutes. I reluctantly kissed Nour goodbye at the door to our condo and sighed as he stepped into the lift. Alone in a strange country with two kids to take care of …

Being a grown-up sucked sometimes.

'I really admire you,' Dr Kahn said, a couple of days later. I had survived the first few drives to the clinic and back without crashing or getting lost. His office, like the clinic, was simply and functionally set out. There was a minimalistic layout of a desk, bed, a couple of chairs and some posters on the wall. 'What you are doing for your daughter, it is to be admired.'

Uh oh. I felt a balloon of emotion rising in my chest – I would not cry! Then to my horror, tears began forming in my eyes and, before I knew it, they were pouring down my cheeks – most likely in black mascara rivulets.

'You have no idea what we've been through,' I managed to say, my throat and voice tight as I wiped away my tears, the back of my hand stained black. I was clearly going to emerge from his room looking very Gothic.

'I can imagine,' he said quietly, resting his eyes – bluer than blue in contrast to his white shock of hair – on me. Both girls were also looking at me, uncomfortable and worried that I was crying.

'Thank you.' I focused on pulling myself together – I wasn't used to unravelling spontaneously like that. 'It means a lot to me.' Something warm was settling in my stomach in this clinic. The grey wintery sky and grey buildings stark along a wide concrete road, surrounded by other industrial developments … the lack of local 'niceties,' greenery and sun didn't matter, the staff and clinicians, along with Dr Kahn were bright enough for us.

I gave Dr Kahn a huge hug. Apart from John Hart and our wonderful GP who believed in me – it was pretty much the first time since Hana had been diagnosed that I felt respected and validated for my efforts to fight for her. How grateful I was to have met this man and to be here with him. His staff were equally passionate about their work – it was just wonderful to be surrounded by open-minded healthcare professionals after experiencing the closed-minded, apathetic rigidity and negative mindsets back home. There was hope for Hana, and these people believed it just as much as I did.

'Keep up the good work,' he smiled, hugging tightly back.

'We need more people like you in this world,' I declared, smiling as Maryam looked up to check if I was still crying.

'I think we need more people like *you*,' he smiled back.

We took our spot in our usual treatment room: Hana in her cosy armchair and Maryam playing between the table and bed. They settled down to some colouring-in. The clinic staff had bent over backwards to welcome us and today someone had bought the girls a bag of colouring-in books and pens, only days after Dr Kahn had organised a huge bag of Christmas gifts for them. We were being spoilt ... we were there for Hana's wounds to heal, yet, surrounded by the positivity and optimism of the staff at Meditech, I could feel my own wounds beginning to close.

My ongoing struggle – unifying the mainstream with my new perspective continued. The word 'patient' had been bugging me for a long time. I found the term derogatory, patronising and belittling. Patience in itself was not relevant to the state an individual should find themselves in when controlling their health and wellness and I found it extremely antiquated that we still referred to people who used the healthcare system as 'patients'. This implied we must 'wait for what the doctor orders, or prescribes for us to do'.

'You must do what he says, Naomi.'

While guidance from an experienced and qualified individual was valuable and potentially lifesaving, the implication of inaction on the part of the recipient, the *patient* wasn't. This is an era in which an increasing number of people want to take an active role in their healthcare – educating themselves via the internet and presenting with treatment options to their healthcare providers who may not be aware of the latest developments. Consumers of healthcare should feel their empowerment via their access to reliable knowledge. But this then threw up issues of 'truth'.

The thing is – once I started thinking about it, the very concept of truth now appeared very differently to me. *What is truth?* Is it what science dictates or is it what people are saying? If something is a truth to you, would you change your belief if science discredited it? Scientific truths, proofs – these were not TRUTH! Scientific proofs were 'working' truths relevant to the context within which they had been procured, and these contexts were usually artificial, necessary for the stringent 'Randomized Controlled Trial' guidelines. They were often 'lab' truths, not real world truths and the problem was, they were often not long-lasting truths! One moment science declared one thing about a certain drug and the next year it said the opposite. This changing of truth reveals how transient scientific 'truths' are – they are not permanent and they change with their context.

Having had an obsession with truth and meaning since my teens, I could definitely concur that exploring concepts to prove or disprove them was an awesome thing we'd done as humans. However, I had begun to feel we needed to be really cautious before saying or believing 'science has officially proven/disproven' anything. Everything occurs within a context, that includes inference of results and understanding of 'truths'. As a society, we are *all* familiar with the chopping and changing of scientific truths – fat is bad, fat is good, fat is OK but … Yet many of us are still suckers for media headlines that play this tug-of-war with our belief systems and paradigms. I agree that science is good, but feel so strongly that we mustn't forget that understanding is limited to context and current thinking.

But the problem isn't just a misunderstanding of 'truth' – it is in the very way modern day science is utilised – I could see some parallels between science and philosophy. I had thought that science was about keeping an open mind in the pursuit of understanding while acknowledging that, at any point in time, an accepted truth can change with another discovery. Yet, on my own quest to push the boundaries of science to find a way to heal my daughter, I had encountered a completely different notion of science – I called it 'closed-minded science'. I could see this closed mindedness permeating my Facebook feed as articles from science blogs, medical newsletters emanating the same 'closed by what I know' vibe – 'science has disproved that' or 'science has proven this' – as a means to ridicule or rule out what others may be saying about something. What was wrong with saying, 'This phenomena exists, but we just have no fricken idea what it means yet? We still don't understand it.'

I was thoroughly disappointed by the scientific closed mindedness I had encountered in my quest to save my daughter's life. I had thought more of 21st-century approaches to scientific problems. I had expected more passion, more curiosity, more courage to tackle, explore and discover ways to solve this apparently unsolvable problem, this untreatable condition. Instead, my husband and I had led this two-man crusade for a long, long while, fruitlessly challenging the rigidity of scientific minds that were so closed by the science they knew, they couldn't, for a moment, entertain any notion of a science they hadn't yet encountered. (And that's a truth).

Now here I was, in Toronto, surrounded by an optimistic, scientifically open-minded team of medical professionals. I felt I was finding 'people like me' and, for the first time, I began to worry about my girls and their understanding of 'truth' as well as their ability to understand the limitations of current scientific mindsets. I wanted my girls to question purported truths as rigorously as I did, but how could I raise them that way when the education system and society they were growing up in so strongly dictated what we must believe or disregard? I began to research alternative schooling methods, becoming particularly interested in the Montessori teaching style. That, with my increasing desire to be in the countryside, made me feel I was about to precipitate a huge life change.

'I'm thinking of bad things,' Maryam whispered from the back of the car.

'It's OK, baby. Let's try and put some nice thoughts there now shall we?' I called back before murmuring to my second cousin, 'It's her way of processing everything she's witnessed over the past two years. She's seen things and felt things most children and many adults don't get to experience.'

We had visited relatives who lived a few hours outside of Toronto for the weekend. Now we were being driven back to the city ready for our next week of appointments. Maryam was continuing to heal too – but, for her, the healing involved visiting dark feelings and places she'd been hoarding in her subconscious mind for nearly two years.

'I want to go back home,' Hana piped up.

'Not long now. Just one more week to go, darlings,' I said, also aching to be home again and not living out of a suitcase.

We were all yearning for something that resembled a normal life – a routine of school instead of travelling around the world. *Normal* … what would that be like? We were so close now.

We spent our mornings in the clinic with Hana getting treatments and me trying out our new machine, familiarising myself with how to operate it. In the afternoons we'd go for a walk to a nearby park before swimming in the pool at our apartment block. Due to the heavy influx of light particles, Hana was literally 'glowing' with health. There had been an instant improvement in how nourished she seemed after sleep as well as a rapid improvement in her memory. Although this had improved from the early post-operative days of muddled chaos, she was still forgetful and needed frequent reassurance and reminders. Yet, in Toronto and in the weeks that followed, she began reminding *me* about what I had to do and began to recall situations more accurately that I did. To my concern her daily headaches continued to persist even though in Dr Kahn's case reports on TBI, headaches were usually found to improve rapidly with treatment.

'What's the time, Mister Wolf?' I yelled out to Maryam across the park, turning back to look at Hana sitting sullenly on the bench behind me. Her head was hurting and that gave me a strange feeling in my tummy. 'You sure don't want to join in, Hon? It's pretty cold sitting still in this!'

'Nah,' she said, shaking her head. I felt a pang of sadness for her and felt frustrated. I wished she *wanted* to join in and have fun – I had come so far to put things right, but I still had a long way to go.

177

Apparently it was a very mild early December for Toronto as so far there'd been no snow, but we were bundled up in thick coats, with layers of long sleeves and jumpers, scarves, hats and gloves. After I'd forced Maryam to expend some energy in the playground, pink cheeked, we made our way back to our condo – it was late afternoon but already twilight. We usually had an early dinner and popped down to the pool before playing board games to finish off the day. Sometimes, on a day off from therapy, I'd drive the girls to a local shopping mall where we invested in beautiful moccasins for Hana and a pile of trainers – (they actually fit her, so I invested in no less than five pairs) – a triumphant celebration that we finally could find shoes that fit. Then, after counting off every day until we could go home, two weeks later it was time to say goodbye.

'Thank you so, so much for having us,' I hugged Dr Kahn after Hana's last treatment session. 'I'm going to really miss you – your energy, the energy of your staff.'

'We will keep in touch,' he said as we posed for pictures. 'Any questions, send them our way, it has been a pleasure meeting you.'

Because we were excited to get back home, the mammoth journey back to Sydney was tolerable – we had travelled so much that year, what was another 30 hours of travel? I had grown up longing to travel and explore the world – now I was over it. I'd happily never board another plane as long as I lived and my kids, at their young ages were already over it too!

After flying from Toronto to Dallas, we boarded for the final leg to Sydney, 16 hours straight, the longest flight in the world. We settled into our seats, the girls on either side of me and they were fast asleep before we'd even taken off.

I went over the plans Nour and I had tentatively been formulating via FaceTime: we'd move away from Bondi Junction and enrol the girls in a Montessori school.

'I told you years ago we should move north over the bridge,' Nour had said, surprised but excited by my proposal, 'but you always said no!'

'I know,' I agreed, 'but I'm ready to change our lives now, I wasn't then. I'm ready for a new adventure – brain healing, cancer prevention and health for Hana, a new schooling style that will suit free-spirited Maryam as well as Hana's unique needs. Let's move somewhere more ... bushy!'

I'd told the girls about the potential change of school and they loved the idea of having more freedom in the classroom than in a mainstream school. Although we weren't planning to move somewhere rural, we still talked about moving to 'the bush' because anywhere green outside of Bondi Junction felt like 'bush' to us. We were about to embark on a huge life change – a new family adventure – and we were all excited about it.

And guinea pigs, there were definitely guinea pigs in our future ... and perhaps a mini donkey one day too.

I yawned and slumped in my seat, trying to get comfortable as I dozily congratulated myself: I was so glad I had this chance to have my mind opened by circumstances, even though these circumstances had been painful. I wouldn't want to go back to who I used to be ... now I questioned things I used to take for granted, now I LISTENED to people.

'Oh no you don't,' said a little nagging voice in the back of my mind. Startled, I sat straight up in my chair and listened to what this voice had to say for itself. It continued, 'How about religion? People say it's true yet you won't entertain that as a truth.' I began to pout in the darkness of the cabin, the hum of the engines a constant background noise. *Yeah, well that's because I've been there, done that.* I glanced sideways, feeling slightly guilty.

Hmmm. What *about* the spiritual? Why couldn't I entertain the notion of a spiritual dimension? Maybe I wasn't as open minded as I had thought myself to be. Maybe there still was little difference between me and the closed-minded followers of the mainstream I felt I had left forever behind.

'People *say* they see ghosts, people *say* they experience God, people *say* prayer works – if you reckon you are listening to people then why not listen to that?'

I crossed my arms and declared loudly to my self, 'Fine, if there IS a spiritual dimension then it better show itself, even if I have to see ghosts or hear the voice of God himself. Spiritual stuff I won't believe unless I see it for myself.'

After that declaration to my inner self, I closed my eyes and snuggled up next to Maryam and slept.

Chapter Fourteen

'Wait until you see her,' I said proudly. 'You won't believe it!'

'She looks AMAZING!' The mums at the school gate were flabbergasted with Hana's glowing looks, slimmer post-lap-band body as, wheelchair-less she strode proudly out of school. We had made it back from Toronto for the end of the school year so she could say goodbye to her friends and teachers – next year she would be a Montessori student on the Sydney's North Shore.

I did this! I saved my daughter!

We walked to the car, just like the other normal kids without a wheelchair and drove home. It had been Hana's first full day of school for months – she'd managed only a handful of full days at school since her surgery nearly two years ago. I proudly posted a picture on my Facebook page declaring: 'I don't pray for miracles. I hunt them down.'

I was winning this battle, I was winning the war even! Hana was stable and we were on our way to brain healing. I had a clear vision in mind that the laser would help to regenerate her pituitary, eventually eliminating her need for hormone replacement therapy and, of course, fully regenerating her hypothalamus, so that one day we could take out the lap band. I was creating our futures – and everything was happening as I had intended it would, just as I felt I had engineered much of my life so far. My power was returning.

'We all want bobs!' I declared at the hairdressers. On the first day of the Christmas holidays, we would sever all links with the past, and that meant long hair was out! Maryam and I had waist-length hair – mine had been long since I was a child and Hana hadn't had hers cut for nearly three years because the tumour had stopped her hair growth and we had been afraid that if it was cut it wouldn't grow back. But today we weren't afraid of anything!

'Bobs and fringes for me and Maryam and Hana will just have a bob,' I said We began to squeal as the floor filled up with our long locks. We emerged brand-new, laughing at how our newly short hair flicked out in the wind as we walked through the bustling pre-Christmas craziness in the Junction back to our apartment.

We had secured a place at a Montessori school on the North Shore for the girls and we began house hunting on the weekends – my yearning for nature was growing rapidly in intensity, Hana's thirst began to mirror mine. She craved green space and peace. And I knew this was the healthier thing to do. Now we were healing and stable, I also needed to work on preventing tumour regrowth, which meant and avoiding excessive EMFs (electromagnetic frequencies) from the hundreds of wi-fi signals we were exposed to living in a high-rise in the city. I had found a building biologist who would thoroughly check our new house for dirty electricity, wi-fi signals, mould and moisture levels so that we knew that our new house would be healthy.

I'd chosen guinea pigs from three different breeders – a chocolate brown rex agouti for Hana, a white American crested for Maryam and I simply could not resist getting a Peruvian (OK, two Peruvians) for myself. I arranged to pick them up two days before Christmas and kept them hidden in the spare room for two days. Whenever they started wheeking for food I'd say, 'Oh goodness, there go those lorikeets again. They must have nested near our balcony.'

We had decided to have a Christmas without toys. The girls had received so many presents over the two years that we had more toys than furniture – our two-bed apartment was cluttered with them. The girls, similarly feeling the lack of space at home, had readily agreed to no toys for Christmas, thinking they would get a plant each or a couple of books. Instead, I filled their stockings with hay, combs and guinea pig treats before blindfolding them and carrying out their piggies in a snuggle bag, and placing them on their laps. It was beautiful having these gorgeous creatures in our house to cuddle and stroke whenever we wanted and it was glorious to see Hana's maternal instinct with the little things – mummying them so well!

But, after crafting things so carefully together, things began to go wrong.

Just after Christmas I noticed that Hana had gained some weight. The scales began to clock in this weight gain – unbelievably, we were back to a kilo a week. At the same time, she began to get quieter and more sullen, her headaches were now more than a daily occurrence and had begun to really impact on her quality of life.

'Let's try metformin again,' I said to Nour.

'Why not the octreotide?' he asked. 'We still have that huge stock in the fridge, it's worth thousands of dollars.' He was referring to a desperate impulse purchase of vials of octreotide we had bought during a national shortage. Our initial trials of octreotide had led to a small decrease in weight gain and so, once hearing about the shortage, we had purchased as many boxes as we could in case we had truly found a medication that helped Hana's HO. However, after six weeks of treatment, Hana had developed abdominal pain – an indication that her pancreas was becoming inflamed. Because a side effect octreotide was life-threatening pancreatitis, we'd ceased treatment immediately.

'I know, but the metformin is less invasive with fewer side effects. I don't WANT her on it, I don't want her on any medication like that! But this weight gain ...' I had no words. Neither did he. The last time we had felt this, there had been hope that the lap band would end it – for longer than this at least.

'Have we had our honeymoon period then?' he reflected. 'Well, it's been six months, hasn't it? If she follows the pattern of those in the study, she may end up stabilising again ... OK, let's try the metformin.'

This time round Hana tolerated the metformin very well, unlike two years before when there had been no positive impact on her weight and her appetite had actually increased. She'd also become very unwell on it – her fingers had swelled up like sausages and she'd been unable to focus on anything. This time, her appetite, although weakened by the lap band, decreased again with the metformin and, due to its ability to reduce insulin levels, the weight gain slowed down, enough to stop us from spiralling into sheer panic. But her headaches persisted. I was continuing with the LLLT with ongoing excellent results on her memory, but I was still hoping it would eventually reduce her head pain.

Then, two weeks before we were due to start part of our new lives at the new school, Hana had her yearly MRI.

'Has she had surgery before?' the radiographer asked, popping back into the room to get Hana ready for the contrast injection.

'Oh yeah, she's had enormous surgery,' I explained. 'She had a brain tumour.'

She nodded. 'Was it over the pituitary?'

'Yep,' I said, my voice much lighter than the suspicions now forming in my own head. *What the hell had she found above the pituitary?* I exhaled.

Two days later the results were sitting on Hana's neurosurgeon's desk. The receptionist had told me he would look at the results that day and then she would call with an action plan.

'Action plan?' I had relayed to Nour over the phone that morning. 'What action plan? The plan was that *he'd* call us with the results because, if it's clear, he said we won't have to go in again!'

'I'm still waiting for the secretary to phone me with your results, darling,' I told Hana later that day. 'But let's pop out to Smiggles anyway.' The girls had seen school bags they wanted for their new uniform-less school.

We walked through the busy Junction. There were huge advantages to living in the city – we could pop out whenever we wanted to get whatever we wanted! It had certainly been an amazing experience, living in the thick of things, on the doorstep of a giant, bustling, happening Westfield, but I was excited at the thought of soon being able to leave it all behind, once we'd found a house – actually, once I'd found a *garden* that had a house I wanted to live in! It was a warm day, so we stuck to the shade as we walked through the bustling streets. Everyone else was out getting ready in 'back to school' mode. The girls happily chose their bags, blue and fluffy, and we took a different route home to get away from the crowds in Westfield.

I prided myself in how I described medical procedures to the girls. I could make them sound almost fun – like MRIs, for example. I once recorded the sounds of the play therapy MRI machine and then proceeded to make up this dance to the whoosh-whoosh, beeps, bangs and booms. It's something like techno crossed with robotic moves with a dash of heavy metal head banging thrown in for good measure. I called it 'the MRI Dance'. I found it hilarious and so did the girls at the time, although Hana never let me do it in public.

But this was a day that I would screw up.

My phone rang. I'd put it in my back pocket so I would feel it vibrate as the noise from all the construction in the Junction made it impossible to hear a mobile phone.

'It's about your MRI,' I hushed the girls as I quickly answered it. They silenced quickly, used to important phone calls. The only sounds left were the cars racing down the road and the gaggle of international students, mostly Brazilian, leaving their English classes for the day – the English Language Centre I had been a teacher at for our first two years here in Sydney. The last time I'd taught there I'd been heavily pregnant with Hana.

I held my breath. *Please be clear.*

'Hi, it's Kate,' the receptionist said.

I didn't like that … that wasn't a good start, surely *she* couldn't give us the all-clear over the phone?

'We need you to come in tomorrow to discuss the results.'

My stomach flopped and my legs instantly went weak, a weird coolness spread over my forehead. Before I got to ask why she continued, 'Because, yeah, they found *something* in the scan.'

So it's back.

It's back after only two years and after paying such an enormous price for the aggressive surgery that was *supposed* to reduce the chances of it reoccurring. Severe hypothalamic obesity, lifelong, life-threatening obesity for only two years without cancer?

I dimly made arrangements to go in the next day as the girls looked at me questioningly. The world was beginning to slip away from me. The future with the blue fluffy school bags, a house on the edge of the bush, health and wellness, brain healing, were all beginning to spin and spiral away, sucked up into the sky, out of my reach. The happy things I'd felt like I'd *earnt*. The sickening feeling of despair and despair's twin sister – stone-cold loneliness – began to descend. No amount of Australian sunlight could brighten up the darkness these siblings bring.

I hung up.

I couldn't make light of it. I couldn't even pretend that this was going to be OK. Everything was being snatched away from us just when we were *so close* to having a better life. Both girls looked at me – Hana showing her worry already; she was developing the art of reading my phone calls.

'What, Mum?' she asked, uplifting her beautiful little round face, blue-green eyes – my eyes – reflecting her concern.

187

'I'm sorry, baby.' I drew her to me, my mouth and face twisted with the bitterness at having to tell her. 'I'm so sorry. But they found something on your MRI.'

'Found what, Mum?' Her voice was strained – she knew.

'Well … your tumour might have come back.'

Then *her* face screwed up. 'But I don't want my brain tumour back,' she began to cry instantly. And I knew that I'd messed up. I should have played it down and said in a light, funny voice, 'Mmm, they've spotted something in your scan – we better head in tomorrow to make sure it's not a sneaky cashew nut hiding in your brain (because you eat so many of them, hahaha).'

'Look,' I squeezed her tight, trying to make it up, 'we're going in tomorrow to see what it is. It *might* not be anything we need to worry about …'

Oh dear God, it was too late for that. Why hadn't I just thought before I'd said, 'I'm so sorry?'. Of all the stupid ways to break bad news to an eight-year-old, you don't say, 'I'm so sorry, baby.'

Stupid. Stupid.

And then Maryam started bawling loudly, 'But tomorrow is horse riding!' She'd been looking forward to that all week and now she'd have to miss out, again, because of yet another medical appointment.

'It's OK, sweetie, I know.' My heart now aching for her and the life she'd had to live because of her sick sister. 'We'll make horse riding another day.' Then I added, 'Don't worry about Hana, sweetie. She's going to be fine.' It was typical of Maryam to hide her fears for her sister by pretending she was upset about something else.

'I'm NOT worried about Hana,' she protested, bawling even more loudly. 'I just want to go h-h-HORSE riding!'

Both girls were sobbing as we waited at the traffic lights, my useless, helpless arms around them both. A couple of women were at the crossing next to us, glancing over as I felt the disconnection return. Once again we existed on a different plane to everyone else around us, a bubble of suffering that set us apart. After the lap band I'd finally felt myself reintegrating with humans around me, making eye contact on the street, caring about people I spoke to, but the disconnection was already back, like a switch had been flipped. I avoided eye contact with them.

I'm not like you. My world has been turned upside down again.

'What *will* happen if my tumour is back?' Hana wiped away tears, trying to be brave as we walked the last one hundred metres home.

'I don't know yet, but maybe radiation, baby,' I said, my thoughts racing to the Proton Beam Center in Florida that all the other cranios were so keen on. The Proton Beam Radiation program would take months. My chest felt impossibly tight at the thought of spending another year abroad and an even worse thought: the fallout of something so toxic it *caused* cancer … after radiation, how could she ever be healthy again?

'But I don't want to miss any school!' she protested loudly. 'I will do radiation but maybe in one year, or in *two* years after I've gone to school for a while—' She burst into a fresh fit of sobs. I scooped tear-soaked Maryam into one arm and placed the other around Hana's shoulders: The Comforter, when all I wanted to do was collapse on the ground and wail with them.

My phone went again in the lobby. It was Nour who had been trying to chase up the scan results that morning:

'I haven't had chance—' he began.

'—Habibi.'

'—to ring yet. Lunch was—'

'Habibi!' I said louder this time.

'—so busy and—'

'LISTEN!' I raised my voice almost to the point of shouting and he finally quietened. Someone got out of the lift and walked past us out of the doors, looking at us all the while.

'I've spoken to Katie. They have found something on the scan and we need to go in tomorrow.'

'So, we've got regrowth then?' he said finally.

Chapter Fifteen

I woke at 4.30 again, a dull grey heaviness weighing down my stomach; the nausea that comes with waking up in a state of fear. Nour was awake, too, sitting in the darkness at the dining-room table, his face ghostly, lit up with the screen of his iPhone as he absent-mindedly scrolled through his newsfeed on Facebook. I sat next to him, my hands cupping my coffee mug, staring into nothingness.

We were back in hell. It was even worse this time because we had barely had time to close our wounds since the last trip down there. We avoided looking into the mirror of one another's eyes: to do so would connect us with a pain we were holding deep inside and we were not prepared to do that yet.

It had been two weeks since finding the regrowth and we had been busy – we had contacted over fifteen international specialists all over the world. Dr Kahn had facilitated contact with oncologists and radiologists in Canada; family friends had put us in touch with specialists in the USA; there were Egyptian experts; contact with German oncologists and radiologists facilitated by our German expert. We had the luxury of multiple opinions on what to do, but those were equally split between conventional radiation and surgery.

'Yeah, we can see the regrowth here, just in the pituitary,' Hana's surgeon had said, unblinking, on the day we were supposed to have gone horse riding. He didn't seem to have any recollection of his smug face two years before, grinning at the doors to Recovery where we'd lost the Hana we'd known. 'A little bit of radiation will fix that up. If you start it next week, you could squeeze in a few treatments before the school year starts.'

Squeeze in just a little bit of radiation. He said it like it was a nothing, like we were talking about a graze on her leg 'an itsy bitzy little bandaid will fix that up … you'll be better in no time.'

Oh, how much better did we know two years on that there was no '*little bit of this or that'* when it came down to the brain. Radiation was so incredibly toxic to all tissues, the healthy and diseased, it ultimately put receivers at high risk of developing further tumours and cancers. How could he speak of it as it was a quick and easy fix? And that was the late fallout, whereas immediately post-radiation individuals were frequently exhausted with severe brain fog that could go on for months. How on Earth he could be thinking of sending Hana to school immediately post-radiation?

'We are quite interested in investigating options for Proton Beam,' Nour explained. 'There is a cohort of cranios taking part in a study in the USA and we've heard there may be less collateral damage with it.'

He looked surprised. 'I've sent kids for proton in the USA before,' he said, 'but this tumour is surrounded by fluid. There is plenty of space for conventional radiation to get in and target the tumour without damaging local structures.'

'And you wouldn't recommend surgery?' Nour asked.

'Nah,' he shook his head. 'It's so small I think it would suit radiation.'

After that first appointment we had gone home and researched how radiation targeted tumours in the brain: The *entire* brain was infiltrated with toxic rays – with both entrance and exit points. The Google image showed uncountable crisscrossed lines passing in and out of a skull.

Then we got our second opinion:

'I would absolutely under NO circumstances recommend radiation,' the neurosurgeon said, looking horrified and a little disgusted by what we had been advised.

'Radiation would, ultimately, be a death threat. With radiation you are hitting healthy tissues at the same time – it is unavoidable. I highly recommend keyhole surgery, through the right eyebrow. Why would you irradiate a child's entire brain and put them at lifelong risk of fallout – which is pretty much guaranteed – when the tumour is so small and so easily accessible? I use an endoscopic approach. It is minimally invasive surgery and I am very good at what I do.'

'We are frightened about this because we had a terrible experience with surgery last time,' I explained.

'Yes, I can see that,' he said, flicking Hana a sideways glance. 'But you might change your mind on surgical approaches this time – especially if she is in and out of hospital in three days.'

Three days! Wow, that was a different scenario to the two weeks of hell we'd spent in ICU last time.

'You have been given advice that is the complete opposite to my recommendations, so you need to go and think about it,' he said.

The more research Nour and I did on radiation, the more we began to see that it was the wrong option: Hana's tumour was small and very accessible from the eyebrow region. There seemed absolutely no need to completely and repeatedly infiltrate her young, immature brain with radiation waves, which were so toxic they were ultimately carcinogenic, over a six-week period.

I also began to research the history of radiation online where I found a resource called 'The Truth About Cancer'. I was amazed at the incredible research Ty Bollinger had conducted in his quest for truth about natural cancer cures around the world. He visited countless individuals and medical professionals, both mainstream and alternative, but, naturally, the proponents of the mainstream completely slated his statements.

'You hit a cancer-prone body with cancer-causing agents like chemo and radiation and hope for long-term wellness?' Ty challenged.

Ty's mission was to share these stories of hope to awaken us to the possibilities of treating cancer beyond the mainstream's standard of chemo and radiation.

Listen. The little voice again … *Listen to what people are saying.* Ty was right, the concepts of using cancer-causing agents to 'cure' cancer was ludicrous! Where had we gone so wrong in treating cancer? And, more importantly, why hadn't this occurred to me before? Once again, I was quietly thankful for being shown this and the ability to see alternative truths about our health and wellbeing – but were we in a position where we could utilise this knowledge safely in our own child?

'Just listen to this.' It was dark, late one evening when I'd been watching one of Ty's documentaries on the history of radiation and chemotherapy on my iPhone in bed. 'Radiation, it's … you just need to see this!' Nour quietly watched the show and nodded gravely, equally subdued by the frightening side effects of these 'cancer treatments that caused cancer'. I breathed in deeply, filled with gratitude once again that he was open minded and smart enough to question what so many of our colleagues and friends would see as quackery.

'So what do we do then?' Nour finally asked. 'The thought of surgery again, with all its risks …' Stroke, brain haemorrhage, blindness, further hypothalamic damage … the risks sat heavily unspoken in the air around us.

'Let's watch and wait,' I said. 'I'll check that the new neuro team are happy with that. It's taken a year to reach this size, surely it won't suddenly get enormous over the next couple of months. We'll try some natural "cancer treatments" to try and stabilise it and review it in eight weeks – you never know, it could stabilise anyway. Some tumours do that. What do you think?'

Nour agreed, leaving it up to me to research the natural cancer treatments. There was so much that I wanted to try, but I would be limited by first what I could access easily and second could trial safely in a little girl with co-morbid health issues. I would have to tread very carefully – any intervention, be it natural or pharmaceutical, was still an intervention that could have side effects of some kind. We tend to see 'natural' things as safe, whereas they may not be! After all, many drugs have natural origins: morphine from poppies and atropine from the deadly belladonna.

I started Hana with frankincense oil, the Banerji Homeopathic Protocol, Craniosacral Therapy, a vitamin regime including Theracumin, Ubiquniol, high-dose vitamin C and …

'I'm going to do something that you will know nothing about,' I said to Nour. 'If I get arrested, you know nothing about this, OK?'

'Nounou …' Nour warned, but then proceeded to ignore me completely – walking out of the room, as I placed two tubes of sticky brown illegal cannabis CBD oil in the fridge under an old medication box where no one would see them. It had taken a couple of emails and phone calls and as a mama bear on a mission, I'd soon found a local dealer of CBD oil who supported its use for medicinal purposes.

'You need the RSO,' he said, handing over the tubes of CBD in his kitchen in front of his mum and two kids, his excited dog repeatedly jumping up on me leaving wet patches on my thighs from his tongue. He was referring to Rick Simpson Oil, a type of cannabis oil high in the psychoactive component 'THC'. 'This won't clear a tumour.'

'I would be keen to try it,' I explained, 'but I don't want her to get "high" – she goes to school! I am also concerned about the increase of appetite that can occur with RSO cannabis.'

The CBD oil did not contain the psychoactive components that RSO did. In effect, it was simply a 'hemp' oil, containing nutritional substances that people in the natural cancer community were benefiting from – how could I not source and try this on Hana, even though it was illegal? Surely at the worst I could be arrested and Nour would take custody of the children considering he was wholly ignorant of my actions? So long as he had custody of them, it would all be OK.

'If I get arrested, you just tell them you know nothing and that you've been increasingly concerned about *my* interest in the *woo-woo* since Hana's brain tumour. You can even exclaim with utter disgust, "She's started studying homeopathy, for Christ's sake!"' I called out to Nour as I closed the fridge door.

I didn't care if I was arrested for sourcing natural cures for my daughter – all that mattered was Hana's health. However, I was now inundated with ideas – there was so much to try and it was tough balancing the range of 'natural treatments'. For her safety, I was starting very low and going very slow, but I was aware that they may not have a chance to get to work in the very short time frame I required. Her tumour was cystic in nature, which meant it could quickly grow simply by absorbing more fluid. Would these treatments even work on a cystic tumour? There were heaps more things that I wanted to try – this made me feel panicky and incompetent.

Then, whenever Hana's headaches increased in severity, I'd blame one of my natural treatments and cut back or stop then re-start – helpless in what I was doing. After six weeks, she was well established on the vitamin regime. I'd scrapped the Banerji Protocol as it clearly made her headaches worse and I didn't feel I have the expert support I needed to continue as the creators of this regime were in India. I regularly infused frankincense oil and had started the Craniosacral Therapy. I was disillusioned with the CBD oil – she was starting so low and slow and without the RSO I didn't feel it could possibly do enough.

'This guys says that proton beam hasn't been proven as better than standard radiation – so that we're better off going with standard,' Nour read out an email from a specialist in the USA.

'But this is very short-sighted thinking!' I complained. 'Just because it hasn't been proven yet? I hate this mentality! But it doesn't matter anyway, we've decided that we will go for surgery again, right? When we have the choice between surgery and radiation, how could we opt for a *cancer-causing treatment* in a child who is innately prone to issues with cellular proliferation and differentiation?'

My research was further extending into cancer, its causes and natural treatments. There were true miracles reported around the world that did not include chemo, surgery or radiation … I knew I was once again drifting further and further away from all that I thought I knew.

People often asked me, 'Do they know what causes this tumour?' and I'd feel like laughing because now it was so obvious to me!

Don't you know? What causes any state of ill-health or disease? Clearly a body that is not 'well' and harmonious in some shape or form – some energetic problem! Because you can blame 'cancer' on an unhealthy diet, yet this isn't absolute as there are many poor eaters who do not get cancer. In the same way, why do some smokers get cancer while others live into their nineties? The picture is so much bigger than the diet, lifestyle, environment and genes … the ultimate cause of cancer in my opinion lay in our electromagnetic spectrums or energetic fields.

That night I kissed both girls to sleep, holding Maryam as she drifted off, then turned to watch Hana. Glad no one was watching and feeling like an idiot, I was suddenly compelled to hold my hands over her. I watched them, useless, over her – if only I could heal her with my hands or with my love! My love for her was so strong, surely it should be able to eradicate that tumour? Why couldn't *I HEAL HER?*

Am I going to lose you, baby girl?

It was a question that kept creeping up on me, at any given point every day. Will you soon be gone from my life? I then had pictures of an empty dining-room table in the mornings, a quietness as we got home from being out just me and Maryam taking off our shoes at the front door … Life without Hana would feel so empty, but I felt it was close by.

Feeling sick of being in my own skin, I walked out into the living room where Nour was sitting in the darkness watching TV.

'Just turn it off,' I muttered. I hated TV. I hadn't watched it in nearly eight years now and the more time went on, the more I felt an intense sense of irritation whenever it was on. He obediently flicked it off.

I let out loud sigh. He looked up surprised to see me and to observe that I wasn't holding it together – he could sense something was coming.

'I just have a scary feeling our time with her is limited … that we will lose her.' I burst into tears.

He sighed, 'I feel it too.'

The room was very dark without the TV on, but still, with Bondi Junction light pollution from the street lights eleven floors below, there was enough light to illuminate the lounge with an eerie glow.

'I'm haunted by something I've never told you.' Now I was really crying, like I hadn't cried since Hana was first diagnosed. I felt the emotion boiling up in my stomach. 'I just couldn't tell you.'

I felt him brace himself.

'You know that she had a terrible time going under the anaesthesia? She fought it, but she also screamed something. She screamed, "*God help me*" right before she went under.' I sobbed, 'It's like she knew her life was going to be destroyed after that, and I betrayed her by allowing it to happen.'

He began sobbing too. Both of us, useless, heartbroken specimens of humans who put smiles on their faces in the day. Me, acting as if nothing was wrong in front of the kids and him, putting braces on other people's kids who moaned and complained about the discomfort, their parents ohhing and ahhing over them – the image in his head all the while, of his own broken little girl at home who had endured more discomfort then these individuals could ever fathom.

We didn't touch one another, we didn't look at one another, we just cried side by side in the darkness, this hell we were living that would never end.

Chapter Sixteen

'We have another battle on our hands.' 'We're going to fight this together.'

The words slip out automatically. It's the cancer lingo, jargon everyone uses to talk about cancer or chronic illness. The implication is that illness is the foreign body, the enemy inside, something to be battled, fought, rallied against and … hated.

I'd used these words with Hana, in front of Hana, for Hana. She'd heard the lingo people say, 'Good job you're a fighter sweetie!' And it's true − she had battled daily for anything resembling a normal existence. And it's true that when we appeared to conquer one aspect of her morbidities, something else cropped up for us to push for, fight for, fight against, rally our resources. Life had been a battle for the whole family unit.

Over the past two years, somewhere deep inside I'd began to develop an itch about using war jargon about her morbidities in front of her, but I didn't know what the itch was until one Saturday morning a few weeks after we found out her tumour had come back. Hana, Maryam and I were sitting on the couch in our Bondi Junction apartment, overlooking the blue ocean at Bondi to our right and the green bush of the North Shore over the bridge. Hana was hungry.

'Why am I hungry, Mum?'

'I'm not sure, baby. You're not usually hungry for morning tea this early.' I felt unsettled. The word 'hungry' triggered me in a way no other word could.

'I wish I wasn't hungry. I don't like being hungry.' She began to cry. I felt my unease grow, I hated being triggered by a word that should be associated with nourishment, not illness.

'Oh, sweetie.' I pulled her to me. 'I know. I don't like you being hungry either. It's awful for you.'

Why for the life of me *couldn't I make this right?* After all that I done, I had still failed because, today, at this moment, my daughter was unhappy.

Out of sheer frustration, she began to sob loudly. She had tried so hard to overcome this; the youngest child with hypothalamic obesity in the world to get a lap band, keeping busy, the highly restrictive no-carb ketogenic diet, painful injections, horrid medication, keeping busy again. But today, for some unknown reason she was hungry before morning tea and that ache in her belly brought back dark, dark memories of 18 months of endless hunger and suffering.

'It's not your fault, sweetie.' My eyes filled with tears. 'It's not your fault. This is your condition, because you have a brain tumour …'

That was the point when everything changed:

'I know,' she mouthed the words, barely about to speak from crying. But then she blurted out forcefully, loud enough to shock Maryam who instantly crawled next to me for comfort, a little frightened mouse.

'I WISH I DIDN'T HAVE A BRAIN TUMOUR!'

Bondi Junction froze in motion – the construction sites, the traffic, the car horns, the excited babble of people walking down Waverley Street went silent.

The realisation dawned on me, crystal clear.

I wouldn't have my daughter wishing her life was different – even though up until that point I knew I had been guilty of similar thoughts countless times. I couldn't have my beautiful girl wishing for a different life from such a young age. No! This was not helpful or healthy for her. I needed to change this – now.

I stroked her forehead, carefully thinking how to phrase it to turn things around; turn around *all* of our perspectives on everything we were experiencing.

It was during this pause that the words began to come to me: 'But you do,' I said quietly. 'And this is *your* body ... this is *your* tumour ... this is *who you are*. This tumour is part of *you*, baby girl.' I didn't have to explain any further because she instantly understood what I was saying: *Love yourself, cherish yourself, and that includes your tumour.*

'I know,' she managed to utter, heartbroken, the tears spilling were now sad, not enraged. She intuitively cherished and respected herself too much to be filled with 'hate' at the tumour inside. In the same way, she accepted and loved her ballooning belly, 'tummy'. She hadn't learnt self-hatred yet, and I wasn't about to let her develop it – or teach it to her.

I would not have my daughter filled with *hate* for an invisible enemy stuck inside her body that she was unable to control and felt she must fight because this was expected of her. I could now see the power in the words we chose to describe her conditions – how we spoke about her conditions had the ability to mould her perception of herself!

She began to calm down and I continued to speak quietly, 'Your tumour is your body saying, *"Hello, Hana! Something's not quite right in here and that's why I'm growing like this!"* and together we will try and figure out what it is. It's not your fault, it's not your body's fault and it's *not* your tumour's fault.'

I had learnt through my early research into homeopathy that Hana's tumour was her body reacting in the best possible way it could – under the circumstances. How *I* could seek to change those circumstances that supported disorderly and inappropriate tissue growth however, may well be my lifelong project, along with healing her brain.

She nodded, tears beginning to dry up while Maryam's had started – a little empathic sponge, sharing Hana's suffering. I held Maryam still and encouraged her cry it out while Hana pulled herself together, and sat up straight beside me to stroke her sister.

I had had an epiphany that afternoon about *love*, not hate. We, I, had been guilty of hate! Hating Hana's tumour, her conditions, her suffering. But we *loved* Hana, and Hana must love herself and this love must include her tumour and all her health conditions. Faced with the concept of living in either hate or love, I just couldn't see how she could ever heal or hope to be cancer free if she started carrying around a hatred at such a young age. She must love and respect herself and honour her body for 'doing the best it can – under the circumstances' and we must too.

This was the 'love shift' and it was key to how everything afterwards unfolded … yet I still faced another question over finding peace.

I had wrestled for two years – *fighting* – to restore health and wellbeing to Hana. I had made the contract – that commitment to heal her – and I thought I had surrendered the option of peace in the process. But now I felt love, not hate, so I was able to ask myself the question again, 'Will I ever be at peace? Can a parent ever have peace when their child is suffering?'

How could a parent ever be at peace when their child was being tortured in front of their eyes every single day, their condition 'incurable'? I had thought that the only way to live with that suffering was to fight it, to conquer and kill it, and there to find peace.

And I had been close to that – I had sought and facilitated two medical world firsts in 12 months, I had facilitated treatment options her doctors weren't aware of, brought about weight stabilisation with the lap band and started an intensive, exciting journey to brain healing. I had travelled the world. But after the 'love shift', something strange began to happen.

As my love grew, so did my gratitude, and I was slowly becoming aware that I no longer felt the downwards pull of longing and sadness when I observed the simple, happy-go-lucky lives of those around me. I also realised I was no longer looking at old photos of Hana pre-tumour diagnosis with a heartbreaking ache for the past. As my feelings towards our situation and my internal landscape were radically shifting, I became aware that, with that change of outlook, something else was happening too.

Peace was beginning to find me.

But, one great difficultly still remained. I just couldn't see how, on a practical level, I could come face to face with Hana's suffering it in its rawest form in my daily dealings with her and not suffer with her. Practically speaking, this seemed impossible, her suffering caused physical, biochemical reactions in me that I could not control. How could I not hurt and suffer with her for as long as she suffered? I threw this question out to the universe and weeks later an answer I never expected came in a form I never would have anticipated – but before then something amazing happened.

I was in the kitchen chopping up some cucumber for Hana's salad – she had insisted on having another salad for dinner, even though she'd had one for lunch and dinner the past three days in a row. Cucumber, heaps of iceberg lettuce, a handful of kidney beans, a smattering of walnuts dotted with cheddar cheese cubes. Then she came into the kitchen and grinned at me, I stopped suddenly – there was something different about her …

I looked deeply into her eyes: I could SEE her again! The essence of her that I hadn't been able to see and connect with since she woke up empty eyed after her surgery – it was there! Hana was back.

'Oh, baby!' I exclaimed, dropping the knife onto the pile of cucumber chunks and ran over to her, trying to angle myself to get an even deeper look in her eyes. 'I can *see* you in there! You look happy! Are you happy in there?'

'Yes,' she said, lisping as always, a little bemused by my intense reaction. My heart fluttering with joy, I went back to chopping the cucumber. In spite of it all, in spite of the recent weeks having been so dark with fear over her regrowth, it was crazy to imagine that somehow things were changing for the better.

'This is perfect!' I sighed wistfully as I looked around the house. It was in a blue ribbon district in North Turramurra, an exquisitely green and bushy area. Although we had been tempted, we had ruled out living more remotely somewhere on acreage so we could be close to school and after-school activities. I also wanted to be able to pick Hana up quickly if she wasn't feeling well, leaving Maryam to live her life more independently from Hana's needs.

Outside an enormous tree-lined garden stretched so far down, I could barely see the end. *Could I fit a mini donkey there?* I wondered. A large turquoise pool scattered dancing lights over the kitchen ceiling and trees filtered green light through the windows upstairs.

After months of looking for the perfect house, we'd finally found it! It had such an English feel to it, that it had felt like home the moment we walked in. It was two minutes from the girl's new school, two minutes from an organic supermarket, minutes from bushwalks and we had an actual, real live Australian creek running alongside the whole garden – the perfect tropical bushy backdrop.

My building biologist came out to take a look and, after testing walls and the atmospheres with her fancy gadgets, declared it fit for health – soon afterwards we secured it at auction. We couldn't believe that it was going to be ours! Hana was over the moon that she'd soon be surrounded by nature and the quiet and Maryam couldn't wait to run up and down the big garden. We were literally counting down the weeks until we could move in – Bondi Junction seemed noisier, more polluted and busier than it had ever been.

Chapter Seventeen

'Come on,' Hana hurried me, laughing as she led the way through the sunny courtyard out of our building. It was still midsummer and hot, but a warm dusty wind, reminiscent of Cairo, blew in between the two buildings that made up our complex. We were heading to a Crystal Workshop for her eighth birthday celebration, just me and her, to learn all about crystals.

I'd popped into the crystal shop in the mall only metres away from our busy urban apartment a few times over the previous few weeks. Initially I had been researching the best crystals to help reduce the impact of surgical pain or to counteract the effects of radiation when we'd been trying to figure out the best treatment option for Hana's regrowth. But Hana was developing a 'thing' for them … and so was I! The weird thing is the first time I'd gone in, I'd nearly vomited. The moment I stepped inside, I'd been hit with a very dizzy, car-sick sensation. I had ignored it and began browsing over the shelves of fantastic sparkly stones when the room began spinning and I broke into a sweat. I felt wretched for the two hours that followed, even after I'd got home. Random fits of vertigo and light-headedness just didn't happen to me, so I was perplexed and interested in what that might mean: it was clearly something to do with 'energy' – but what exactly?

When the same thing happened a second time, I was even more intrigued and so I became just as keen to learn about the energy of crystals as Hana was, so we booked in for an education session on her birthday.

We sat in a small group around one of the dining tables in the food court of the Westfield shopping mall while our instructor guided us on how to feel the energy of crystals: 'Place your hand over it, change the distance if you need to. And look out for any sensation on your body, tingles, burning, tickling – it can occur anywhere in your body, not just your hands.'

I randomly grabbed a stone and held my hand over it. *Probably won't feel anything*, I thought.

It was as if a button was pressed.

Instantly, there was a painful sensation in the centre of my right palm, the one I was holding over the crystal, but not only that palm! My left hand was nestled in my lap and at the same time, the centre of that palm also began to burn and ache.

'Woah!' Shocked I pulled my hand off the small tumblestone. 'It's the centre of both of my hands!' I exclaimed loudly. 'Right there!' I pointed to each palm in turn.

'That's where you hand chakra is,' the instructor explained.

'But I wasn't even holding this hand over the crystal!'

'It's the crystal energy in your energy centres – you must be very sensitive,' she said.

It was only as I put the tumblestone back into the pile to try with another crystal, that I realised the significance of my first choice in what had appeared to awaken such a strong sensitivity to energy in my hands – it had been an amethyst, Hana's birthstone.

Further exercises followed, but I found the feeling in the palms of my hands wouldn't go away, and the more I *thought* about crystals, the more intense the feeling became. My heart rate picked up in excitement and anticipation for what would come next.

We went into the shop to buy a crystal each once the workshop was over. Hana chose a lovely smooth Rose Quartz finger. I held a large Herkimer diamond in one hand and a piece of Apophyllite in the other – and I gasped, the sensation was out of this world. The energy from both crystals was reverberating up my arms, a real force! The Herkimer diamond was literally vibrating in my hand. I put them down, a little frightened now. What was this whole new world I'd stumbled onto? The ache and burn in my hands, my 'chakras' as they were called, were hurting me, yet I suddenly felt a sense of limitless possibility dawning on me. This was new … this was exciting, but what did it mean?

Walking home, I felt elated. I *knew* I had discovered something that would lead me in a different direction – where and what, I had no idea. At home I tested out my sudden and new-found sensitivity to everything! I found I could sense energy in everything – whatever I held my hand up against, the ache and burn would increase. As the feeling developed, I felt a sense of something pouring out of my hands, like a release would occur after it built up!

'Ow ow ow!' I shook my hand viciously over my coffee cup the next morning – even the energy of coffee was hurting me. Nour looked over his coffee mug at me and shook his head.

'Why can't you feel it too?' I asked him, pushing a piece of black obsidian his way.

He closed his eyes and focused really hard then suddenly yelled out, 'ARGHHHH…' Then he stopped. 'Only joking. I can't feel a thing. You're making it up.'

'Hana feels it in her arms. Don't you Hana?' I persisted. 'But not like I've got it, I'm in serious pain here! I can't control it! I feel like I could MOVE something with this …'

'Are you a witch or what?' Nour asked, between further sips, ultimately disinterested in this drama unfolding in my life that I was beginning to suspect was going to change everything!

'Yes, I think that might be case,' I said deliberately nonchalantly, heading over to a hanging wind charm. I guided my hands around it and let the flow of energy discharge from my hands. 'I reckon I could do telekinesis with this …'

'The day I see you move something without touching it, I'll be impressed,' he said. 'And now I have to go to work.'

Driving the girls to school that day hurt – my palms were radiating on the steering wheel and while they might calm down for a minute, it would only take a random thought for them to charge up painfully again. The pain in my hands also entered my dreams. I'd feel the bulge of energy there and wake up needing to flap my hands around to attempt to discharge and disperse the pain. I didn't know what the hell was happening to me. Was this a sign I was supposed to conduct telekinesis? Was this a sign I was supposed to be a hands-on healer?

I began to google 'telekinesis'. The static coming out of my hands had successfully spun a Psi Spinner, but I could tell this was electromagnetic charge being dispersed through the air, not true telekinesis, which would involve moving something with the mind. After wading through a few websites on telekinesis 'how to' videos, I got taken to another site on Energy Mastery, AEMI, set up by a cool, normal, non-hippie-looking guy called Michael Monk.

'Energetic gifts like telekinesis and clairvoyance are awesome, but it is helpful to put them into a context,' Michael said. Suddenly I was riveted, *listen!* 'We need to look at the context of what and who we are in order to develop and refine these gifts.'

That resonated so deeply, the rest of the truth began to dawn.

If I could *feel* energy pouring through my hands. It must mean that I was so much more than just my physical body. Yes, I already knew that we also existed on an electromagnetic spectrum, but what if we consisted primarily of an electromagnetic or spiritual spectrum, *what if we were more energy than we were physical*? I would have to rethink my entire understanding of what and who I was ... I'd been more interested in my hands and telekinesis, but the fact was, I needed a deeper understanding of 'who' I was – and perhaps once understanding that, I'd truly be able to master the energetic gifts my hands were signalling I possessed.

I signed up for the online course – if I had been wrong in understanding myself as a being, then I needed to begin to educate myself on the truth. The premise of this course was that we were primarily energetic matter or spiritual beings and, due to this, put forward the belief that all humans had psychic or energetic abilities that were simply latent until activated or practised, as I was now practising mine. I was guided through basic exercises to activate my sensation of energy, including the ability to see energy – clairvoyance – as well as other energetic gifts, like the telekinesis that had drawn me to the site in the first place.

'Just stare at yourself in the mirror, but don't look at yourself, look at your entire body outline at the same time. When you do that you'll be able to see your aura.'

And he was right. I had dashed all the way back over the bridge from the North Shore where the girls were settling into their new Montessori school. Today, rather than 'camping' at Nour's clinic in Chatswood to do some Nurse Naomi blogs, I had wanted to do more of my course in privacy. This exercise was to practise 'clairvoyance' – seeing energy. I found going into clairvoyance so natural! I realised that I had been switching my brain into this mode for years. For me it was a sensation of 'meshing' both hemispheres, and switching off all focus. I'd stare into space and simply take 'time out' in a place that was free from pain because it was free from thought. Almost *Mish Mawgoud*.

My eyes stung as I focused on the outside of my body, but Michael was right, within a couple of minutes, I could see a bluish-silvery, candle flame-like halo around my entire body. I started laughing with joy, this was incredible! And, as I laughed the dynamic aura around me billowed out and in as if it were laughing too.

I maintained the non-focused stare that was activating this ability and glanced over the room – I was surprised to see what looked like my aura hanging off the girls' toy stroller. I returned my eyes to a normal visual focus and I realised that the blue aura was surrounding a T-shirt of mine that I'd forgotten I'd thrown there a week ago. My energetic imprint was still hovering around it!

'Far out,' I murmured.

Then Michael instructed us to look at ourselves in the mirror, but to focus on both eyes at the same time with the relaxed stare needed for clairvoyance. Before he could go on to explain what would happen next, I freaked out. My face had changed to the face of someone else! It was an older woman's face, one I didn't recognise. I pulled back out of the clairvoyance, my heart racing – did this mean some evil entity was in the room? But I didn't believe in evil entities, did I?

'And you will see that your face begins to take on a multitude of other faces in succession. These are other energies that you are – past lives or energetic imprints you contain. Don't be afraid of them, just integrate them and accept them as you.'

I drew in a deep breath, comforted by this and let further faces flicker and flash on to mine. As I relaxed into it and let them come, I could see more details on some, then suddenly, I couldn't even see my body anymore! In the mirror was a plump, pompous, prim-lipped condescending-looking woman with short brown hair. She was so intense I pushed the image away, but the moment I relaxed, she sprang back into the mirror. I completely freaked out again and pulled out of clairvoyance.

I was initially rather frightened by these strong images and so I communicated with some other students in my course who advised me to 'integrate' all that I'd seen as simply 'me':

We are all energy – everything you see is you and your creation. There is nothing else other than that.

This felt very level-headed and grounded – very useful advice for a beginner embarking on this completely alien and bizarre exploration I had thrown myself into. So very early on, rather than freaking out about evil spirits and negative entities, I held on to that very precious early advice that all I see and feel is a projection off me – I wasn't a victim to my reality. Over time I began to see how incredibly essential and useful this initial 'pointer' was to me – for months that followed I saw and read much superstition surrounding 'Spirituality' which I found incredibly off-putting. As a young Christian growing up, I had been taught to avoid superstition because 'God' would take care of everything, for a born-again Christian, God is understood and known to be more powerful than any 'negative' entity or belief system. Then, as an atheist – limited in how I perceived myself as a physical being, I believed in the 'power of the mind' but not of anything beyond that. During my years in Egypt, I witnessed individuals who were terrified of the Evil Eye – a superstition that is true for so many I'd met and as far as I could see the Evil Eye was true for those who *believed* it was true. I'd been so careful with these 'fragile' belief systems, I'd sometimes found it hard to know what to say:

'Look! Rania's had her baby!' Nour once dragged me over to an old family friend who passed near our table where we were having a toasted cheese sandwich lunch in Zamalek's upper-class hangout, the Gezirah Club. I stuttered and started, staring at the positively enormous, drooling baby boy lolling about in its pram as Rania, her mother, and Nour all looked at me, waiting for me to say something nice. I knew there was some 'protective' word I was supposed to say whenever I gave a compliment – *something something allah.*

Instead, to the dismay of everyone listening I blurted out the worst thing I could say, 'Wow, he's really ... *big*!'

'Mashallah, mashallah!' Everyone responded quickly and the baby was immediately shielded from my sight like I'd just given him a curse.

Over time I would find that other spiritual teachers were adamant about using 'white light' or even better super strength 'gold light' (because, I was once poignantly advised, white light simply wasn't 'strong enough') when meditating or when using psychic abilities. This simply did not resonate with me – if I am being completely honest, I found this superstition repellant because I simply *'knew'* to the very core of my being that I was always safe regardless of the colour of light surrounding me and whether I choose to mentally cloak myself with light or not. Why would I need to protect myself with white or gold light when I felt that white light was of my entire essence anyway? Preferences like this helped me decipher and discern which teachers to listen to, and which to ignore, as I continued to explore my energetic form.

I was addicted to my course. I was so hungry to know more and experience more – I was suddenly so greedy to discover myself and develop my extrasensory abilities. The following weekend I woke early to do some further work on my clairvoyance by expanding my energetic self out into the living room. When it was time to go for my run, I was still mulling over the feelings I'd had that morning and I decided to test myself when I heard a car behind me, without looking I asked myself: *What colour is it?*

Immediately an image of a very distinct matt purple-blue old car appeared in my mind. *Yeah, right,* I mocked myself. Of course I wouldn't get it right, especially with a weird colour like that! It was probably a brand-new white four-wheel drive, knowing the taste of most drivers in the Eastern Suburbs of Sydney. So I glanced over my shoulder to prove myself how wrong I was and there it was: an old strangely coloured matt, purple-blue car. I burst out laughing.

'Does Nour know how much this is affecting you?' It was late evening and I was snatching a five-minute private FaceTime with my mum inside my walk-in wardrobe, the only place I could get privacy in our apartment – and I was bawling my eyes out.

'Not yet, but he'll see it soon, Mum. It's changing everything,' I sniffed. 'I swear I'm not sad! These are tears of release … or relief – I don't know which,' I explained. 'It's just so sudden! And intense.' I began flapping my hands in the air – hot energy was pouring out of them.

'If it was anyone else saying this stuff I'd think they were nuts,' she said, 'but to hear it from you, *YOU*! You are the least spiritual person I know,' she laughed. 'This is … huge!'

My mum was 'spiritual'. She was no longer the religious Christian mum I'd grown up with. Soon after I'd become an atheist, both my parents had stopped going to church, too. My dad, because he didn't believe in God anymore; my mum, because she disliked the 'religion' that overrode what she felt was the essence of spirituality. Only she, my dad, Nour and perhaps my brothers knew how hardcore atheist and 'anti-spiritual' I had been for my last twenty years. But I'd kept my non-spiritual beliefs to myself once Nour and I had committed to marriage.

'If you are a believer, the Quran says it's OK to get married,' he explained. 'And Islam recognises Christians as being believers. But if you are a public atheist, this is a

218

problem as our marriage can't be recognised by the Law of the Land.'

I had mulled over this, alone in my Zamalek apartment, lying on the thin, hard mattress on my bed in the weeks before we got engaged. I was a philosopher, ripping apart ideas, theories and exploring concepts, discussion and the analysis of truth made me feel alive! If I was going to commit to marrying Nour, then to protect our marriage, I'd have to commit to never speaking publicly about my non-spiritual beliefs again. Could I deny that aspect of myself for him?

As an eleven-year-old child I had read the Bible from cover to cover – as an adult in Egypt I had also read an English version of the Quran from cover to cover … I deeply respected the belief systems of others and so it was a passage in the Bible that helped me make my decision. It is stated that, if there are others with a 'weaker faith' or, in other words, a more fragile belief system than you, you must 'protect' them by shielding them where necessary. Nour and I knew that being a good, moral, kind person was more important than whether I believed in God, so I agreed to keep quiet on my beliefs so as not to unnecessarily 'upset' and stir those who believed otherwise.

'This is huge, Naomi,' my mum exhaled, her expressive brown eyes wide with shock at all I had been telling her. It was rare that we could get privacy to talk, which was why I had been pouring it all out to her beneath my winter coat and in between bags of my old triathlon clothes. But now I could hear Maryam stomp into the bedroom and, not finding me there, began pummeling on the wardrobe door. I hastily wiped the black-stained tears off my face,

'I know … Let's see where it leads. What am I supposed to do with these gifts? But I can say this already – it has changed everything.'

Later that night, once the girls were asleep, I turned off the pink Himalayan salt lamp to see if I was able to 'see' energy more clearly in the dark. According to Michael, shards of energy come off our fingertips. I hadn't been able to see this in daylight at all but, as I held up my hands in front of me, the room still dimly lit from the streetlamps below, there they were: shards of energy shooting out of my fingertips endlessly into the air around me. I smiled at the beauty of my discovery in the darkness, there was something quite Edward Scissorhands about it!

I played with my fingers, watching the long shards move with my fingers, then I held my fingers away from my body before moving them around pointing them in the direction of my arm. In the quiet darkness I was able to feel the tickle and of energy reach my flesh. Then I placed my hands together, pushing energy in and stretching it out, before bouncing an invisible ball of energy from one hand to another. I held my hands apart in the darkness and shoved energy across the space one to the other. The other hand would 'receive' the ball of energy almost immediately after I pushed it.

'Energy catch!'

That night I became aware of another developing sensation emerging beyond my control – the same tickly burning feeling of energy building up and pouring out of my feet. I googled it – there was another chakra that I hadn't known existed.

Only days into the opening of my hand chakras and energy course, while I was typing up a blog post in the kitchen at Nour's clinic, one of his staff members recommended a book to me on reincarnation: *Many Lives, Many Masters* by Brian Weiss. The concept of reincarnation was something I would have sneered at until only a matter of days ago. I *did not* believe in reincarnation and past lives! But this time, thanks to the burning in my hands and on the soles of my feet reminding me of all that I truly did not know – my mind was ready to consider exploring what other people were saying!

Both girls nestled up next to me as, in the pink-orange light of the Himalayan salt lamp, I began reading. Two chapters in and I felt as if the rest of my entire reality had crumbled around me:

So it's true? There is more than this?

With that realisation I drove back from school for the second time that week in order to fully surrender my old belief system, and open myself to whatever was unfolding in and around me. My intention, ultimately was to pray.

I'd barely closed the front door, slipped off my shoes before flinging myself down on the floor, ready to surrender and allow whatever I needed to know to come to me.

OK! I whispered, admitting defeat, feeling my walls crumple and fall around me. 'I was wrong. There IS more … I'm ready to listen now.'

I felt my energetic form rise a little above my physical body, like I was experiencing the onset of an out-of-body experience, something we were practising in the energy course. But then, much to my disappointment, I started shaking all over, which fully drew me back into my body. I was glad that no one was around because I knew that it would look like I was having a seizure. I wasn't perturbed by it as it reminded me of Tremor Release Technique or TRE, an energy-healing modality that brings on fine tremors and shaking to stimulate healing – I'd taken a course in it once to see if it could help Hana. But this time, rather than fatiguing the muscles to bring on tremors, I wasn't doing anything to stimulate the shaking which came in waves, up and down my body in bouts of intensity and it went on for an hour.

Eventually I became exhausted, I pulled myself out of the meditative state and rolled onto my side, too spent to pull myself up. There was a burning sensation on my hand – was there something there? Another energetic being? It felt like something was with me and it was emanating unconditional love. Tears welled up and began to pour down my face, I was brimming with sadness and intense empathy – for *myself!* It was coming both from me and this energy was with me.

'Why does it have to be so hard?' I asked this energy. 'Why did I have to suffer so intensely to get here?'

More empathy was pushed towards me, I or we both knew the answer. The suffering I experienced meant I could be here today, shaking on the floor, my old belief systems, walls and ego finally surrendering, LISTENING, truly for the first time in my life.

After this meditation, I was intensely cold, even though it was a boiling hot and humid day and I hadn't bothered to turn on the air conditioning when I'd returned home. Yet I found myself grabbing a pink rug from the girls wardrobe and wrapped it around myself, completely stunned at the intensity of the past hour. I sat and looked at my washed-out, tear-streaked face in their mirror. The experiences of the last couple of weeks were so intense and fast moving – but of course they had to be. I wouldn't have 'listened' had it been any other way.

Then, within a few hours, I could feel it pour down like silver rain – I had a vague memory of an anonymous Valentine's card I'd received at university mid philosophy degree, a simple card with beautiful words that have stayed with me ever since:

You Pour Down Like Silver.

Now peace had begun to pour down on me like silver rain – my entire body felt quietened, warm, in a state of immutable wellbeing that I knew nothing could shake. This was peace.

I had no idea what happened to me that day – the shaking, the cold, the crying – until a week later I'd come across the term 'Kundalini Awakening' when researching Spiritual Awakenings. Kundalini is an Eastern Philosophical term but there are reports of intense 'Kundalini Awakenings' occurring in a similar fashion to this – the shaking, the crying and extremes of temperatures.

But what next?

My mind, continually greedy for more, wouldn't stop searching and asking questions: What was I supposed to do next? I felt a strong sense of purpose arising from this 'Awakening' I had apparently experienced, but where would this sense of purpose lead me? Was I supposed to work as a healer? But I didn't want to work as a healer, I just wanted to heal Hana!

A non-spiritual gift of mine is the ability to read so fast there is something Darth Vader-esque about it (it's also expensive!). My readings by Brian Weiss, quickly lead to other researchers and authors on past life regression hypnosis such as Michael Newton and Dolores Cannon.

'You sound religious.' It was an accusation – Nour just didn't know who I was anymore – what crazy stuff would I be prattling on about next? Hands pouring with energy, souls, karmic lessons, peace ... He looked at me strangely across the red couch as I positively beamed love and happiness back at him.

'I know,' I admitted, feeling peace pouring through me to him. 'But this isn't religion, it's spirituality. From what I can understand, we are souls who have chosen to be here in these bodies and roles in order to learn certain things ... about our*selves*.' Then I added carefully and quietly, 'Hana's tumour and the fallout would have been our choice ...'

He stiffened. He was so incredibly open minded, but he wasn't ready to accept that yet. So I drew his attention back to my readings.

'Doesn't it just make you want to see your own past lives?' I quizzed him – I'd just briefed him on *Many Lives, Many Masters*. After devouring this myriad of theories on spiritual and physical realms and this concept of reincarnation, I could see no other pathway than to start researching my own past lives. If people were saying they could learn more about their true spiritual selves by doing this, how could I possibly not try it for myself? If people were saying they experienced instantaneous healings through this healing modality, could this help my little girl?

'Um, I don't really know,' he said, intrigued by some of the evidence on reincarnation that I'd shared, but also not yet convinced by all I was spewing on him.

'I just HAVE to know,' I told him. 'Can I book an evening hypnotic regression one day if you can get home from work early?' I licked my lips – my curiosity was insatiable.

'Sure,' he said shrugging a little, losing interest in our conversation as he started planning how he'd reschedule clients on that day.

'Thanks, Habibi,' I whispered, butterflies of excitement fluttering in my tummy.

Chapter Eighteen

'Take a deep breath and go even deeper.'

A few weeks later I breathed in, out, and then let myself sink further into a completely relaxed hypnotic state. My body was limp, my breathing slow and steady, although my heart was still fluttering nervously in my chest. This was my first-ever attempt at being hypnotised and, not only was I nervous about what that might feel like, but I was actually doing this to 'see' *truths* about who I was, who I'd been and where I'd come from. Most of all, I was desperately hoping to find some clues for how I could help heal Hana!

I was lying on a comfortable massage table, a sheet pulled up around me. A slight waft of clary sage and burning candlewick met my nostrils as I focused on my breathing. There were noises on the street outside – cyclists ringing their bells, cars zooming by, the chatter of people walking home from work; the world carrying on around me as I was determined to take these steps into a different place in space and time – a different reality.

'Imagine you can see a—'

'White flower!' I laughed, quietly interrupting her. I had been able to smell the white lily before she'd even given me the suggestion that I would see a flower in front of me.

'That's good, that means we are on the same wavelength,' she continued. 'Now imagine a beam of light all around you … then I want you to drift up into that light and travel to a time and place that is relevant to the things we've discussed today.'

I continued to breathe slowly in and out through my nose. I was travelling with this light, but would I see anything? Would I be able to truly SEE a past life like Dolores Cannon, Brian Weiss and Michael Newton's subjects did? I ached to know more! To get closer to the *truth* behind it all …

'What can you see?'

For a second I panicked. Nothing! This wasn't going to work. But, then in my mind's eye I saw a …

'Picnic rug?' I whispered, disappointed. Of all the boring and stupid things to see!

'OK, good!' said my hypnotherapist, warmly. 'What else?'

'Apple trees?' I wrinkled my nose. 'There are really red shiny apples. We are in a meadow having a picnic.' Urgh! Boring!

'Who is there?'

'Well me … and Hana!'

Hana's face flashed in front of me; I knew that we weren't in this lifetime because of the location. She felt different – older, nine or twelve years old maybe, but the expression on her face was the happy-go-lucky, energetic hard-to-tame three-year-old she had been before her tumour was diagnosed. She was carefree, running around the meadow.

'Where are you?'

'This isn't Planet Earth,' I whispered. 'The colour of the sun on us is different here. This place is very … golden.

Nearby there are fields of crops, wheat? It's all very ... golden.'

'How many suns are there?'

Without a beat, I answered, 'Two.' There had been no question in my mind, it was a binary star system.

Suddenly I surprised myself by gasping for breath, a horrible feeling was growing in my stomach, it was unmistakably the feeling of dread.

'Hana!' I gasped.

'What's happening now?'

But my face was already scrunched up, and tears were pouring uncontrollably down my face. My gut ached – my body clearly didn't want me to look any further, it was going to hurt me too much! But urged on by my hypnotherapist, I began to let myself see more.

'I'm looking for her, shouting for her. She was playing in the meadow and went off to explore. Now she's gone.'

'Where is she?'

'She's gone, she isn't *here* anymore. She's ... gone.'

'What do you mean by that?'

I didn't want to say the words but I dragged them up from the ancient place I was revisiting.

'Dead. I know it, I can't *feel* her anymore, her presence – she's just ... gone.'

'Do you want to see what happened to her?' she asked me.

At that point I wanted to say no! I didn't want see or re-live anything as horrid as that feeling my tummy was warning me it was. I was holding onto horrors.

'Yes,' I breathed in and out quickly, not sure if I meant it. The tears still pouring. 'I can see my dad now,' I said. 'He's a farmer in the neighbouring field.'

'Your dad from this life?' she asked.

'Yes, but here he watches over me sometimes, our tiny cottage is close to his farmhouse.' Suddenly I saw myself have a memory in that past life – wandering around this farmer's house – the bright fields golden outside. I was walking down the stairs, looking at oil paintings on the wall. But then I was back to the first scene – 'He is helping me find her. She's …'

My stomach seized up again as I experienced a racing of images showing a long search through a field of waist-high crops, all golden yellow. The light from the two suns shone down with a much richer golden sheen than Planet Earth. Then scenes began to unfold – I didn't have to 'look' for what happened next, it began to flow.

'She's face down in the stream. I pull her up. Her face is cold and wet … *screaming*.' I mouthed the words because I couldn't say them out loud: 'I'm screaming.' There was a sudden pained silence from my hypnotherapist. I could feel her energy fields ache with mine while I simultaneously watched myself howl to the sky, my dad the farmer man standing helplessly beside me.

'Now we load her onto a wagon to go the village, a morgue? A place for the dead. We put her on a table there. She's dead. There's nothing we can do. We leave her there.'

'How did this happen?' she asked.

'Killed,' I said, the images in my mind of a burly hairy chest, and thick muscular arms. His hands around her neck. I could see her face as he'd done this. It was the face I'd witnessed as she'd been forced to undergo her anaesthesia for her brain tumour in this life.

GOD HELP ME.

'Why?'

'Because I loved her so much, there was no place in my heart for him.'

'Is he someone you know?'

'Not in this life … in that life he was a villager. He thought he loved me.' Then more images flooded through my mind. 'I'm now coming home in the wagon with my dad – the farmer man.' Scenes began to unfold with a faster pace like I was watching a movie and I spoke quickly to get my hypnotherapist up to speed with what I was witnessing. 'The man who murdered Hana is at the window. He says he has heard about Hana. He is coming in to make me a hot drink and we sit down on small wooden stools. He is trying to be a comfort to me.'

'What happens next?'

'I am … broken. Completely broken. There is no reason to "be" anymore.'

'And what happens with this man?'

'He tries to make himself useful to me, trying to get into my heart until —' I began gagging – my body was reliving my memories ahead of my brain and mind. I quickly tried to explain what I was experiencing as my brain began to catch up with the closing of my windpipe, my voice husky.

'I can't give him what he wants the most.' My heart, I couldn't give him my heart.

'It's evening, he's in my cottage, furious.' I was opening closing my mouth between words to try and escape the sensation. 'But I am empty – there is nothing left in me. I'm so empty. He strangles me—'

I heard my voice rasp as my throat finally closed over. But then, and very quickly as I died in that lifetime, I left the scene, shooting up rapidly above that little golden world, my small cottage with its windows lit with the orange flames of candlelight or some small lanterns. The dragging emotional torment from that life completely dissolved in to cooling, blue-white light. I was free …

'Ah, this place.' I breathed, already swimming in peaceful bliss.

The typical 'life review' that some hypnotherapists help subjects conduct after experiencing a past life memory was tough for me. I didn't feel deep enough in hypnosis to gain true clarity and meaning on the horror of that life. I couldn't 'see' the fine details on the spiritual dimension as clearly as Newton's subjects, all I could see was blue-and-white light around me. In honesty, I didn't *want* to have conversations with souls I was 'presented' with via hypnotic instruction and suggestion. Maybe this form of spiritual insight wasn't a 'truth' for me? I *wanted* it to be so … yet I was also cautious of taking on concepts by hypnotic suggestion, if I didn't 'see' a panel of souls around me, I wasn't keen to create them because I'd been told that's what I would see. So we struggled through this part of the session and then I slowly came out of the hypnotic state, feeling rather dazed and exhausted.

Regardless of the 'truths' on theories of reincarnation – whether past lives truly exist in purported sequential order as represented in Weiss's and Newton's research or whether we were simply tapping into a Universal Consciousness, an Omniscience of all that has ever been and all that ever will be didn't matter. In hypnosis people usually saw something that was relevant and ultimately healing for them. So what could *I* learn from witnessing this life?

I had been so utterly and painfully broken at losing Hana. There had been no reason to continue living. Then I began to realise that, until I had found peace, my quest to heal Hana had been one fueled by fear. Fear at losing her and ultimately fear at being broken by her loss. It was as if my unconscious self remembered what that had felt like and wanted to do all it could – at the expense of being at peace – to avoid that terrible broken feeling again.

But now I was no longer afraid, now that I knew there was more than this physical dimension. I didn't think I could ever be broken like that again – now that I knew there was more, or perhaps knowing that 'I was more' than this simple physical embodiment I was currently experiencing.

Unsatisfied with this first session alone, greedy as always to see more, to know more, I booked in for another session with a different hypnotherapist. In this session I experienced a primordial meeting with group of relatively formless spiritual beings who were all me – at least they all had my face. I couldn't recount anything about this memory except that there was a feeling of origin, a beginning, an anticipation and a sense of duty or responsibility between me and all the beings there who were also me.

I then had memories being a male scribe in Ancient Egypt, obsessed with the *truth* and the stars. My first 'feeling' was the flickering heat of naked flame near my own bare leg and the smell of 'cooking resin'. In my mind's eye – at the time, the smell was familiar to me. I was ambitious, working in Pharaoh's palace but got caught one day exploring the entrance to a famous tomb at night – looking for the truth about something in the hieroglyphics. My death was an accident, killed by a wound to my head by a palace guard in a celebration of some sort, but the wound was in the exact spot of Hana's first craniotomy.

'Is Naomi fully incarnated?' The new hypnotherapist utilised Quantum Healing, a different form of past life regression created by Dolores Cannon. Her technique didn't maintain the same understanding of the almost regimented spiritual realm as that described by Michael Newton. Her focus was on past lives, but she also had a keen interest in extraterrestrial truths and information – she sought subjects with 'missing' time they couldn't explain. In Cannon's approach, the aim of post-past life experience was to connect to the 'super-consciousness' or higher self after passing through the death scene which seemed to work better for me than seeing a panel of souls and having a post-incarnation debrief.

'She ... doesn't want to be here,' I whispered. And I heard a 'yet' but didn't share it. Although we were bypassing my conscious mind, I felt 'rational' me understand – being in this body, seeing the horrors that happen on Planet Earth, the stupidity and suffering of humans, the suffering of animals, the focus on physical pleasures. On some level being in a 'skin' had never felt ... normal. I had searched for a place here to be normal, yet I had never felt I 'fit in' no matter what I did or where I went. And I ached so desperately for the stars.

'Is it right for Naomi to be sharing her experiences via her writings and her blog?'

I felt amused laughter billow around me, then I spoke in a low, powerful, even voice that came from my belly – 'This is *why* she is here.'

'And what can you tell Naomi about boundaries that she must be aware of when sharing aspects of her story?' my hypnotherapist asked. When we had chatted before the hypnotic induction she seemed very unsettled about my story being in the public domain.

There was quiet and then a strong energy coursed through me like electricity and I – or my 'higher self' – retorted bluntly, 'Boundaries are for humans.'

'Right,' she responded. Her question had been answered but also left unanswered at the same time. There was no time to explore what my superconscious had meant by that because we were running overtime. She brought me back to full conscious awareness, my eyes still wide and pupils dilated as I sat up on the bed, blinking. Although the journey had been fascinating I still had no answers, still no clues …

I walked home quickly through Bondi Junction, mulling over all I had seen before phoning Nour. He was cross.

'I was under hypnosis so I wasn't gonna exactly call you to say I was running half an hour late was I?' I sighed. 'I'll be home in five anyway.'

What did all I'd seen mean? And, I had to ask the question: Did it really mean anything at all?

I'd had no real lightbulb moments like Weiss and Newton's subjects seemed to get and I hadn't reached the somnambulistic stage that Cannon's subjects achieved – a very deep state of hypnosis where subjects are unable to remember anything afterwards, which I thought sounded absolutely awesome. My hypnotherapist thought I was close to achieving this rare depth of hypnosis – perhaps I could accomplish this in the future. Surely if I reached the somnambulistic stage, would I find deeper 'truths' there?

Could I trust myself that anything I could see, remember, report so far, was my 'truth'? Hana's tumour was still there, so was her brain injury … no answers for how to save and heal her had yet been revealed via my quests through space and time. What was the point of remembering that I was a scribe in Ancient Egypt who died of a head wound where Hana's craniotomy was? Or my spiritual memory of an 'origin' of some sort being surrounded by light beings who were all 'me' with something important to do? How could any of that help my daughter?

I opened the front door, slipped off my shoes and straightaway went to wash my hands, a hygiene routine I'd drilled into my girls as well. Nour looked up from his iPhone as he sat on the couch in the semi-darkness of the lounge.

'So?' He looked at me strangely, there was nervousness there, he was worried about what I may have seen and confront him with. My heart ached for him, he really had nothing to fear, we were partners in this … he was still just unaware of his role in it.

'I don't know,' I said. 'It was interesting but … I need to further understand more about myself and Hana to see if remembering more will help her. I know that our souls are very intertwined. You know,' I pondered, 'I've always felt that Maryam is my baby, but Hana … more like a part of ME. When she was born I was …' I closed my eyes to remember the jolt of surprise that had shot through me as I laid hands on her to pull her to my belly – before I'd even laid eyes on her, I'd felt it. I'd thought … I don't KNOW what I'd thought. Nevertheless, Hana felt more like a *limb* to me than a baby. Then I let out a sigh. 'But what to do next? I need to wait and see.'

I went to bed, closed my eyes and defiantly whispered out into the darkness, *I want to know! I want to know who I am, who*

Hana is. I want to know about humans ... why are we doing this? Why are we here?

My gut told me that the truth was bigger, broader and more incomprehensible that Newton and Weiss's subjects portrayed it with souls choosing lives, living then dying, reviewing and progressing up the levels to higher vibrations and frequencies. Yes, this must be an aspect of Truth ... but there was more. The very fact that I could conceive of there being more to our Truth and Existence meant that had to be simply because I could conceive it. How could I find the 'more'? Where was the rest of the Truth?

How can I cure Hana? How can I heal her?'

All that knowledge was locked inside me – it was there! But I was blind and deaf to it. I was stuck in a state of being only half awake – knowing that I simply didn't know! Knowing where the truth may lie – but not being able to reach it.

Was further hypnosis the key? Or did I need to embark on discovering what and who I was, alone? I envied those who seemed so confident in knowing exactly who they were and why there were here ... Psychics who could see and hear their guides as if they were really in the room! Spiritual gurus who had it all sussed out – the whole of creation, spiritual hierarchies, planes of existence and their raison d'etre mapped out in complicated spiritual theories – some encompassing extraterrestrial histories and involvement, wars of good versus evil – duality, ascended masters and angels.

Could I take on these theories as my truth? Or did I have to find my own truth from within – my journey to find it only just having begun?

Chapter Nineteen

I couldn't believe I was there doing this. I hated hippie, I yucked-out at smug-faced Yogi types, I couldn't stand motivational quotes and I made a point of never sharing anything remotely motivational or inspirational on my Facebook pages and blog – I don't pray for miracles I *bloody well* hunt them down.

Yet, there I was sitting in a circle – 'sharing' what had brought us here – my Reiki training course. Sharing!? In a circle of weirdos? This was not my kind of thing. At all. That was, until now.

Now I too was a metaphysical, spiritual weirdo, who also saw things, felt things … and said things like, 'Ooooh, the energy in here is really good.' And, 'Yes, that really *resonates* with me,' nodding in that way the spiritual do which looks smug, but really, it isn't. The rapidity and speed of my complete and total metamorphosis from hardcore, cynical atheist to a peaceful spiritual explorer being still shocked me sometimes. How quickly can someone change their *entire* belief systems? I reckoned I was on fast forward: I was doing a spiritual transformation on 'Ritalin'.

I held the sharing crystal in my hand as instructed by the Reiki Master and began my story. My throat instantly clogged up, tears spilling as I told the other participants of my story: Hana's tumour, the devastating fallout, my quest to heal her – finding little help here in Australia, the travelling – the feeling that I'd won only to be dashed by tumour regrowth and weight gain. Then my sudden and bizarre awakening … The other participants listened horrified as I relayed it all – the memories of pain and sorrow threading their way through the air to them.

'And now, here I am, with hands that are constantly radiating energy. I can't control it, it hurts me! I have to flap them about sometimes to cope with the intensity of it.'

'You have a gift,' the Reiki Master said quietly, before laughing a little. 'Although I'm not sure what it is yet.'

'I feel it too – a strong sense of purpose with all of this,' I agreed. Not a healer! I wanted to yell out – yet in spite of that, there I was doing my Reiki training, not really knowing why. I was also wondering how I would be able to start sharing this on Nurse Naomi – surely everyone would think I'd gone mad?

'You'll know what it is in time,' he said.

We began our class – our training to be Reiki practitioners, getting the background before our 'attunement'. With my Darth Vader-esque reading ability and normally insatiable curiosity to 'know' everything, I would have usually read up on Reiki training before attending the course. But perhaps, because I didn't really know why I was doing the course, aside from my supercharged hands indicating that I may be 'good' at giving Reiki, I hadn't actually read anything about the training before signing up and I wasn't expecting this 'attunement' business.

He took us apart, one by one and conducted this ceremonial aspect of being an 'attuned' Reiki practitioner. I sat on a chair and he hovered around me, holding his hands over me preparing to draw certain sacred symbols in my auric fields.

'Do you want this?' he asked quietly.

My eyes sprung open surprised at the interruption. 'Hmm,' I nodded.

'Is that a yes?'

Well, duh, I wouldn't be here if not! 'Yes.'

I closed my eyes and opened up my hands – he held his hands above different parts of my body, then over my shoulders – a gushing sensation rushed down like a waterfall, or golden rain, in waves over my body, swirling and entering into me then pouring limitlessly out of my hands and feet. When I opened my eyes I could no longer see his face but the face of an older gentlemen there – I had to blink repeatedly to come out of trance so that I could see *his* face again.

Then, later, during class practice, it was my turn to lay on the bed and receive Reiki. The sensations were the most amazing, intense sensations I'd ever had in my life. It was so much more incredible than any physical sensation I'd ever had because it encompassed both physical and non-physical aspects of myself – my physical body *and* my energetic form which I felt extending out like a cloud around me. Waves of energy rushed up and down my body, emanating from wherever participants where holding their hands – I could tell where someone's hands were being held over my body without looking as that was where the energy originated. The energy waves were pulsing and humming – it was truly a state of complete ecstasy; I could have just lain there forever in that state of pure bliss.

I used Reiki daily on Hana and Maryam. Hana absolutely loved it and would rapidly fall asleep during a session. Afterwards she'd wake up and lisp, 'Hmm that was reeeeeally nice!' It was such a beautiful experience to be able to simply place my hands over my child and let unconditional love pour out of them and for her to enjoy the experience so much! There was such naturalness to it, it felt like something that I should have always done and should be done by everyone, as if it was an inherent part of our nature.

Maryam was very sensitive to the Reiki energy and had to be in the right state to receive it. The first time I held my hands over her, around her heart chakra, she broke down in tears within about half a minute. 'That feels funny,' she sobbed. 'Stop it, Mummy.'

Within time, late evening, Nour would often walk in the door to find both girls lying on the floor, me sitting at their heads with a hand over each. And if ever Maryam saw me giving Reiki to Hana, she'd simply pull away the hand that was closer to her, away from Hana, onto herself so she could get her fair share of energy.

I gave Nour a session – he was, as usual, open minded about my latest endeavors. 'OK, I'm falling asleep now,' he mumbled after half an hour.

'Did you feel anything?' I asked him enthusiastically.

'No, sorry,' he yawned. 'Absolutely nothing. I tried, Nounou, I really *tried* to feel it.'

I laughed and got up ready for bed, too. It didn't matter – he trusted me enough to let me continue my journey even when it didn't make sense or seem real for him, that was enough for me.

The ease and naturalness of hands-on healing as a healing modality itself was revealed in how quickly the girls also began to channel this energy – like me, they found that simply talking about it made their own hands ache and then flow with energy. Hana would find that whenever she held her guinea pig, Chocolate, her hands would pour out loving energy to her little pet. We were discovering that channelling eternal and loving, healing energy was in our inherent natures as spiritual beings, and it was truly phenomenal and a privilege to be able to experience it with such intensity.

'I heard back from the journal! They liked the case report, but they want changes.'

I was chatting to a co-author about the Oxytocin Case Report. I had found a new co-author who was lovely and had helped me get the paper in tip-top shape, ready for submission. I scanned the suggested corrections.

'Hmm, they want us to cease her treatment, then do the whole thing over again with blood levels and psychometric tests before and after to "prove" what we observed?' I read astounded. 'This is crazy. A case report isn't a study! We were simply reporting our observations!'

After thinking over the comments for a day, I was ready to send a response – one last-ditch attempt to convince them to publish the report as it was, as opposed to recreating the experiment purely for the sake of another attempt to get published. I just hoped that the reviewers would see the sense in my comments:

Firstly, the patient in the report commenced this regular dose of oxytocin two years ago now and it is part of her ongoing hormone replacement therapy. We do not think it would be clinically viable or ethical to ask for oxytocin therapy to be ceased and recommenced at this late stage purely for experimental purposes. There are three reasons for this:

A. Oxytocin has been observed to impact positively on her quality of life. Asking her to cease therapy for this experiment we feel presents us with a moral conflict over acting her in best interests and our desire to share this paper with the scientific community.

B. Because the impact of oxytocin on the rest of her hormone replacement is still unstudied and unknown, we are opposed to altering a well-established part of her regime without knowing how it may impact the rest of her medications.

C. The patient has recently been diagnosed with a regrowth of craniopharyngioma and current priorities are on treatment to deal with this.

Secondly, this case report does not purport to be an objective trial – it is fully stated that the results are anecdotal in nature and that further research needs to be done. We believe that sharing these parental observations is in the interest of the medical in scientific community as they stand and we hope to conduct further objective structured studies ourselves in this area in the near future.

I stirred, luxuriating in that feeling you have as you emerge from deep restful sleep, knowing that something good is happening – the feeling you'd get as a child on Christmas morning, or waking up to a birthday. I'd been waking with this wonderful feeling for weeks now – peace flooding through me before I even had a chance to open my eyes. At this point I was sleeping on a king-size mattress on the floor in our spare room, both girls sprawled either side of me. Even since we'd returned from our trip to Egypt and the UK we'd found sleeping in our usual room too difficult – after I'd started my research on dirty electricity and the negative health effects of wi-fi exposure I'd deduced that we were most likely unable to sleep there due to an increasing sensitivity to the electromagnetics in the kitchen of the neighbouring apartment. Quite literally, the head of our bed was up against the microwave and dishwasher area of the kitchen next door. We didn't mind crashing on the floor like this – the girls slept better with me next to them and, besides, it was a countdown until we moved into our dream house. Although I must admit I had been fairly embarrassed when one film crew had popped over for an update and asked to film Hana in her room.

'Umm, well at the moment we're kind of squatting on the floor in the spare room,' I'd said. 'There are toys and clothes strewn all over the place!'

'Ah well, we'll just have a look,' they'd said, sure I'd been exaggerating. Their faces said it all when they flung open our bedroom door.

'Yes, literally squatting,' I confirmed, wondering if they thought we were total pigs. The thing is, the whole apartment was a mess, crammed with stuff that needed to be sorted out and given to charity – we didn't even have proper furniture, our dining-room chairs were second hand when we'd bought them 10 years earlier as impoverished students. Now the cushions on them were stained, ripped with stuffing pouring out. Although Nour was now earning more – when he'd started out with his clinic and limited referral base, money had been tight – our priorities for the past two years had been saving Hana. Before then we'd been too skint, forking out for a Bondi Junction rent with two young kids to provide for, to afford nice furniture. Besides, we were quite happy sitting on beanbags rather than a sofa any day.

I slowly got up out of bed to avoid too much rustling of the bedclothes so as not to stir the girls. I carefully avoided Nour's mattress, which was now squished at the end of our king-size mattress, as he had finally come to the conclusion that sleeping in the main bedroom was difficult. We were crammed like sardines in the little second guestroom! It was 4.30 am – if I was lucky, I would wake at this time to sneak in 30 minutes of meditation before Hana woke up. Sometimes she would wake up anyway and come out to the lounge and meditate with me in the darkness, but I relished the time alone before each day to connect with myself and the energy around me.

I sat up straight on the small uncomfortable red sofa that we had recently been given, clasped my crystals in my hands and drifted up and out of myself with my familiar pieces of music. Only months ago, a TV producer, in awe of how I had coped with the past two years, had asked me whether I meditated. I had snorted my response, 'No way! I'd die of boredom.'

Until my awakening, the idea of meditation had been deadly boring and something that new age hippies might do on Bondi Beach in their Indian-style clothing, brightly printed baggy trousers or loose flowing long skirts and headscarves. And if not them, then the 'active wearing' (usually Lululemon) Eastern suburbian 'yummy mummies' post yoga. Definitely not my style – I'd rather be doing sprints up and down the beach, mentally shouting 'Rahhhh!' at those icky spiritual weirdos. Yet now, meditation wasn't optional for me – it was something I *had* to do! And it came so naturally – there was no 'trying' to get a blank state of mind – within seconds of commencing meditation I'd slip into a delicious trance, tingly all over my body, feeling as if I was lifting out, or expanding perhaps into the room around myself. And I would quickly feel ecstatic – pure waves of bliss flowing through me almost instantly. I could allow some thoughts in and out – thoughts weren't an issue for me. Meditation allowed me to connect with bliss and helped me get through each day. Often my crown and brow chakra, or 'third eye' area, would rush with energy – such a strange buzzing sensation I once mistook for a fly. Coming round from meditation was more tricky however – as I frequently felt woozy and sometimes couldn't move my limbs for a few moments after deciding to end the session as I would try to reintegrate with my body. I'd open my eyes and simply stare down at my arms and legs as if they belonged to someone else – beginning to lift or move them was like shifting lead. I heard the bedroom door open but 'felt' the sound as an energetic shift in my auric fields – hearing energy as a shift in my energetic fields was a new development for me. There she was, up before the birds could start singing as always.

I reached out my arm to Hana and she climbed on to the couch next to me.

'Wanna meditate with me?' I asked. She nodded, still warm and sleepy as she clasped a couple of her own crystals, and closed her eyes. As she went into trance, I felt our energies mingle powerfully – together we drifted up and above Bondi, dancing in the orange sunrise on the horizon. Me and my angel baby.

Chapter Twenty

Hana was lying on the couch, her cheeks stained with dried salt from her tears.

'I can't bear it, Mum, my headache is so bad.'

I was holding my hands over her and they were pouring out Reiki like a river of love. I waited for the familiar soothing peace to descend over us then I silently told her soul: *Baby girl, when you are ready to go, you go ... I will love you forever, but I don't own you, baby girl. You aren't mine: I let you go.*

And at that precise moment I knew my love was the strongest it had ever been, deeper than the blue ocean and more eternal than the space with galaxies spinning away from us above. This was unconditional love. Peace settled like a thick cloak of warmth around us: nothing could penetrate it. The power of my love made me brave as, for the first time, I dared to stare the possibility of losing her in the face. For me, this meant accepting that, although I must always keep trying to save her, ultimately, I would accept that my daughter's longevity was beyond my control.

My readings on reincarnation enabled me to make this decision – to let go. The past life stories illustrated souls that came here to Earth to learn certain lessons – some people called these lessons 'karmic'. If this was the case, then I felt that allowing for an element of 'predestination' was applicable here – had Hana and I 'signed' Soul Contracts stating that this would all happen? I asked myself whether I had come here to learn that her life and her soul journey was not mine to control or save. I felt I needed to learn to be at peace in the midst of her pain and suffering, without making it my own or being broken by it. Then, when peace began to rain down, I knew I needed to let her go. I could clearly see Hana's spiritual journey as intrinsically linked to mine, but also separate, and so I began to accept that she had a right to chose when she wanted to go. My ferocious battle to keep her alive needed to end.

'I love you, Mummy. I love you, Mummy. I love you, Mummy,' she murmured as the rush of energy began to flow out of the palms of my hand, stinging the tips of my fingers. My heart swelled with love and gratitude and I let that feeling transfer into the energy flowing out of my hands.

Silently, I spoke to her higher self, her soul. *You are beautiful and I will love you for eternity. But I let you go! You are not mine. I love you, but you are not mine. I let you go, baby girl.*

She couldn't hear with her human ears, but her soul must have heard as she instantly looked up at me with her crystal blue-green eyes, shining that unearthly light she radiates, a light that old ladies and some sensitive individuals are so drawn to, like they can see an angel inside of her.

'Mummy,' she said knowingly – it was the following day and we were walking in to school, enjoying the fresh morning smell wafting off the Eucalyptus trees – 'We are going to be together for ever and ever.'

I sucked in a lungful of that wonderful air, but it was really the beauty of her words that I wanted to absorb into every single cell in my body. 'I know ...' I said, squeezing her hand. 'I can't wait.'

It was time for Hana's repeat MRI. Because of her ongoing headaches and my inability to figure out how the natural treatments were affecting her and my panic at not being able to try all those I wanted to do to reduce her tumour, I knew that the odds that her tumour being stable were low. As she lay on the MRI table, the machine whirring, humming and clunking around us – this time with a TV crew filming from the viewing room for an update – I smiled. I channelled Reiki to her feet as she lay there, quietly snoozing for the duration of her scan.

The tumour had grown a teeny bit, but it was bigger nevertheless – this time without hesitation and with a clear conscience we booked her in for surgery.

Within hours of posting on my Nurse Naomi blog that Hana would have surgery an amazing thing happened.

'My hands are literally POURING Reiki,' I gasped. This was uncontrollable and I had no explanation for this outpouring of energy from my hands except that it was the pure love and good intentions of my readers.

'They really do care ...' I mused. 'This is proof that the love of other humans really can impact upon others in a positive way.' I held up out my hands and marvelled at that power of people and the power of love.

The energy outpouring continued solidly for three days. I would dream of the energy pouring out of my hands because it didn't stop overnight. In fact, at night I was more aware of it pouring out of my feet too. Then in the day I'd be forced on occasion to place my hands over Hana just to channel the powerful energy to her – I didn't want to waste it!

'We are going to cruise through this as if it is easiest thing we have ever done.' I kept repeating this to Hana, and myself, as the days leading up to her surgery approached.

Stroke, haemorrhage, blindness, further brain damage, sudden death – yes, these were all possibilities but nevertheless I believed in my mantra, I truly believed this surgery would be a piece of cake – but I was prepared to face anything.

'How many days shall we say you will be in hospital for?' I asked Hana, refusing to dip back into the dark memories of the endless two weeks in ICU two years prior.

'Um, shall we say three days?' she said.

'Good one!' I agreed. 'Let's aim for three days. It'll be our little secret! Maybe because we want it, it will happen like that!'

I spent the days leading up to her second surgery meditating regularly. The moment I sensed any fear or nervousness, I would grab a couple of crystals, put on some relaxing music and go into trance. By doing this, I was able to stay in a very peaceful state – and this peaceful energy I felt radiated off me, affecting everyone else in the house too.

'You seem so peaceful about this!' my sister-in-law commented as she FaceTimed us in the car during the drive to hospital.

'Nounou is the most peaceful of all!' agreed my mother-in-law from the front seat – she had flown out the day before from Egypt to help out.

In the hospital, I settled Hana down with some activities after getting her into her gown. I put on a gown and hat, too – ready to accompany her to the anaesthetic bay. I did a crazy dance in my outfit and made her laugh.

Then it was time to go.

This was it.

Again.

'Mummy,' she began crying when she was cannulated – it hurt. Then the shot of midazolam simply made her confused and inconsolable – so much for my peaceful storytelling induction that I'd planned. Over her cries, I began stroking her face and told her a story while the noisy OT bustled around us, getting ready.

'Look at that blue bird,' I marvelled. 'It is dipping, swooping and diving over the waterfall, which is pink! And the rocks are bright blue. Now, if you fly a little higher, you'll be able to cruise above the mountain tops. And what can you see when you look down from there? Houses made of flowers!'

I looked up at the porter who was looking at me, confused, or bemused or simply intrigued by how calm I was, I couldn't tell. The surgeon's assistant walked in as we transferred Hana onto the operating table and her cries escalated.

'Now, now, listen to me,' I said in soothing tones, 'and let's take a deep breath and smell those flowers together! Hmm, there are daisies, roses, pansies – so many beautiful flowers in these houses!'

'OK, time for the induction,' the anaesthetist said. He was under strict instruction from me to give her an IV induction. I would never force the gas induction on her ever again.

'Now, my little blue bird.' I bent over to kiss her cheek and whisper in her ear, 'You are going to have a beautiful flight over these mountains!' I continued murmuring into her ear as she began to guzzle, the first signs she'd gone under.

'That's good. She's asleep now,' the anaesthetist said. I kissed her on her chubby smooth cheek once more. The question *'Is this for the last time?'* was hanging there, but I had no attachment to it. My bubble of peace was impenetrable.

I went back to the room, put on my meditation music and let myself slip into a light trance while my mother-in-law played with Maryam. The room felt full of energetic presences to me – support and love. Then, I could feel Hana with me – she was laughing 'silvery' laughter, tossing back long hair on a cloud. The sensation she gave me was pure joy – like her name in Arabic: 'Hana' – 'Joy'.

It wasn't long before I heard footsteps down the hallway as the surgeon's assistant and a couple of medical students headed our way. They came in the room and closed the door – closing the door was never usually a good sign …

'The surgery is done. It was very successful – he is a master of this technique, he got the tumour out in one piece, but here's the thing …'

I braced myself as Nour pulled himself up taller next to me.

'He wants her home today …'

I let my mouth drop open in shock and joy! Home today? Then I felt a jolt of triumph pour through me – this was it! This was the power of positive thinking! We had engineered this – I felt it in my entire being.

252

'... but we know we are going to get resistance to this from the ICU. They aren't going to want to let her go home.'

'Oh my God!' I gasped. 'That would be amazing. We had a terrible time in ICU last time, we couldn't get her out!'

'That's exactly what he's worried about – he's done an amazing job and worries about her safety in the ICU here. So you need to think about what you want to do.'

I looked at Nour. We weren't up for a battle against healthcare providers – as much as we never EVER wanted to step foot in a hospital ever again, we couldn't now guarantee it. We certainly did not want enemies here nor to taint our reputation further by discharging her against medical advice only hours after major brain surgery.

Hana was crying for me in ICU – a small bandage was sewn in with the stitches over her right eyebrow.

'You did it, baby! You did it!' I kissed her and she began to settle with my presence. 'Sleep off the anaesthesia,' I told her and held my hands over her to give her Reiki. I knew how weird I'd look to the ICU staff, but it did not bother me in the slightest. Two hours later she was still sleepy, so I got out my homeopathy and selected my trustworthy phosphorus.

'Um, what's that?' One of the registrars came to an abrupt halt at the foot of Hana's bed when he saw my impressive array of homeopathic remedies lying neatly in their small yellow case.

'This is a homeopathic remedy, phosphorus,' I explained laughing a little. 'It's excellent at reversing anaesthesia – but don't worry, mainstream medicine thinks this is all "woo-woo".'

'Ah, um OK,' he said, flushing a little in annoyance and a little in embarrassment at my audaciousness. Later, as the medical team did their rounds, I was still at Hana's head, stroking her, channelling Reiki without making too a big deal of it – perhaps most people just thought I wanted to keep my hands on her.

'There is absolutely no way she can go home hours after neurosurgery,' the head consultant told the team deliberately within our earshot. 'But we can look at discharging tomorrow to the private hospital or to home.'

Later that afternoon Hana was sat up in bed, colouring-in and munching on the salad that I'd made and packed early that morning.

'This is phenomenal,' I murmured to Nour. 'I wish we could take her home today.'

'There is no way we can do that,' he said.

'I know,' I sighed, 'but he has the same fear that we have – the longer she is in here, the longer it'll take to get her out! Just make sure that there are NO unnecessary interventions tonight when I'm gone, please, don't let them do anything. She's eating, she's drinking – if they start tinkering with her IV fluids …'

He nodded, the circus of two years ago still as fresh in his mind as it was mine.

I carried a sleeping Maryam up from the garage into the lift then slipped her into bed with me, but I found it hard to sleep. I wished I could be both here with her and also with Hana in ICU to make sure nothing silly was going on. I drifted off for an hour until a text message woke me up – I'd kept my sound on of course so that Nour could keep in touch.

It was a message from Nour:
they are just about to change the catheter because it's leaking

WHAT? STOP RIGHT NOW! I texted back and then rang immediately.

'What the hell are you saying?' I hissed in the darkness.

'The old catheter was leaking and so they have to put in a new one. They've just put on some anaesthetic cream on ...'

'Over my dead body!' I yelled at him. 'Nour! We said no unnecessary interventions! You know how much it hurts having a catheter put in. Don't you remember from two years ago after her first surgery, the animal howling?! Tell them right now, no catheter, she is well enough to use a bed pan or they can weigh nappies, *for Christ's sake*!'

'Hang on, the doctor is here,' Nour said and the phone went dead.

Livid, I began pacing the living room in the familiar half-lit glow from the street lamps eleven floors down. This was *exactly* what I had been talking about! Why put the girl through the excruciating pain of a new catheter when she would be discharged first thing in the morning?

He rang back a minute later. 'OK. He has agreed not to put in the catheter.'

I sighed. 'Nour, remember, this girl is going home tomorrow, her surgeon wanted her home today – no interventions that aren't lifesaving.'

Sleep was impossible after that and my stress levels had pinged from peace and tranquility to a feral desire to get her out of hospital immediately. I spoke to the surgeon again the next day who made his perspective clear.

'They will try to kill her if you don't get her out.'

Although others would think this melodramatic, I didn't – I totally agreed with him. After what we'd been through, I'd witnessed this myself. However, it was ultimately unedifying because he was unwilling to officially document that she was ready to be discharged. This put us in a position where, if we discharged her against medical advice and something happened, we could get into serious trouble.

'What are they running through this line?' the assistant surgeon had come to check on us. 'Don't tell me that's normal saline? If it is, you've just signed up for a week here …'

'What could I do?' I protested. 'If I overstep the mark and start dictating what to do and discharging her against medical advice, you KNOW that they could get DOCs onto us. Come on, you know the system.'

'I totally agree,' he said, 'but we've also seen them screw up too many times. You've got to think really carefully about what you want to do.'

The next day was unpleasant as I petitioned constantly for the removal of Hana's multiple lines which were causing her intense pain – she spent the whole day crying loudly as the 'team' tried to figure out where to send us. I knew I was getting on everyone's nerves, but sitting next to her while she was in constant discomfort and yelling with pain was intolerable to me – her advocate! Her voice!

We wanted her home but they didn't want to send her home without medical supervision. There was no room in the private hospital and the public wouldn't take her as she was a private patient. We couldn't get out of ICU! It was stressful, never-ending and frustrating – all made worse by Hana's constant howling due to the pain in her arms from her lines. There is nothing quite like the disempowerment of a parent who wants their child out of hospital, who is better able to care for them than the system but isn't allowed to do so – by the system!

But … the hell ended when the results of an electrolytes test came back normal and a few phone calls to Hana's very disgruntled endocrinologist. The ICU were attempting to pass over responsibility to him, but he didn't want to take it! I found this annoying – *I* was willing to take full responsibility. After two years of managing her, how could I still not be trusted to gauge her state of wellness?

Yet … we were home by dinner!

Hana was bathed, in a fresh set of pyjamas, eating a fresh meal then tucked up into her own bed by eight o'clock. I stepped into the shower, having the urge to wash my hair and get all of the day rinsed off me in the burning hot soapy water.

I could now breathe again. I felt a little ashamed that I'd let myself get stressed that day, particularly after the peaceful state I'd been in the day before, but the pressure of wanting her out of hospital away from intervention had been so intense, I'd cracked. But it was over now. Could I dare to hope that we'd *now* find the 'normal' we'd almost achieved six months before?

Chapter Twenty-one

The day Hana told me she wanted to die was quiet.

She was sitting at the table working on her mindfulness colouring book. I knew her headache was bad – that was why Maryam was playing in the fairy garden in the late afternoon sun, but she was stuck inside. Her eyes half closed, face slightly slack, the way she looks when the pain is really severe.

We had moved house a week after Hana's surgery, six weeks earlier. Her immediate recovery had been rapid and mind-blowing; day three post op she'd asked to go to Centennial Park to read her book. There had been minimal pain – she hadn't even needed paracetamol for pain relief, homeopathic arnica and hypericum were enough. She was back full-time at school, loved our new house surrounded by trees, a little creek, nature all round! It was truly idyllic.

But her eyebrow and head pain had suddenly began to increase – my instinct was this was part of the healing process, and the assistant surgeons had agreed, but it really affected her quality of life. I was pottering in the kitchen, about to join Maryam back in the fairy garden outside when she silently looked up at me, reading my every thought. Her crystal blue-green eyes watching me across the kitchen, quietly observing me, taking me in. She knew me as I knew her, at that moment I truly felt our bond, we had loved for thousands of years – *we had loved for eternity* – and we both knew it.

'I want to go back to where the angels are, Mummy.'

Her voice was soft, reflective. I instantly stopped what I was doing. I commanded the world to stop spinning: It stopped. Then I reacted, but on two completely different planes.

Oh, no, please no. Not those words! My conscious mind recoiled at hearing those words for the first time, a whirlpool spiralling downwards. My physical self flinched, my stomach and heart wounded like someone had stabbed with me a knife.

Please no: Human Me.

Simultaneously my soul reacted in complete opposition to my physical self.

Of course, my higher self or spiritual self whispered. She had known this was coming. My subconscious, superconscious self – whatever you want to call it – had been waiting for those words. I had been able to feel the fatigue in Hana's 'being' for a very long time. Two and a half years of intense suffering! Yes, I knew we'd had triumphs along the way, many many triumphs. We still had triumphs to come. But she was tired. She had been pushing for wellness for so long.

Denying her hunger. Pushing forwards with her weight. Working with chronic headaches, ankle pain, surgical pain. Pain, so much of it! And then the exhaustion – being tired, but going to school, staying up till bedtime, keeping busy to distract her*self* from her *self* – whatever it was currently 'doing' to her. Now her post-op surgical pain permeated everything she did. Her eyes met mine.

I know. I know, baby, my soul soothes hers, *I feel it too, and it's OK to feel it.*

'Really, darling?' physical, Human Me says, rushing over to her. I knelt down next to her and held her in my arms. 'How long have you been feeling this?'

Tears instantly spilled down my cheeks. I wished I could hold them back as I didn't want her to see me cry. I wanted her to feel free to tell me whatever she felt she must without worrying about making me sad: I could cope with anything! I WOULD cope with anything! But the tears didn't listen and poured like a waterfall.

And I wondered, for the umpteenth time how many times a human heart can shatter and still glue itself back together? I'd come here to find out.

'For a while.' She looked down. I wondered just where her mind had travelled secretly over the past few weeks when she hadn't shared her innermost thoughts.

'You *will* go back there one day, my love. We all will.' *Not now baby, please don't mean it* – this is Human Me, again.

'But I want to go *soon*,' she whispered forcefully then began to sob, desperate, tired sobs.

Yes, my dear twin flame and I release you, my soul sang silently, radiating joy and peace. *I will lead you there, your hand in mine.*

I sucked in a breath, it was hard to talk while I was fighting those tears, but now was not the time to disintegrate.

'Even …' I bite my lip, my voice shaky as I wasn't sure I want to hear the answer, '… even if it took you away from us?'

260

From me? Human Me.

We will never be apart. We are closer in death than we are embodied. Soul Me.

She turned to look at me, face on, eye to eye: This child was afraid of nothing.

'Yes.' Then sobs of despair because she didn't want to say it, she didn't *want* mean it.

The hurt was phenomenal – that my baby would prefer to walk away from her physical existence rather than staying in my arms! I don't think I've ever tasted a sadness so bittersweet that day. Because I was *proud* she wasn't afraid of dying, I was full of ecstasy that she would walk so bravely into the light when she was ready!

That's *my* brave girl, *my* soulmate.

But oh, the devastation that I hadn't 'made it OK', that my arms alone weren't enough to make her want to stay. How could I be a better mother? Silently I turned my face heavenward. My heart fluttered angrily in my chest.

How can this be? Why can't I make this go away? Haven't I learnt enough for one lifetime? I don't want to learn anymore!

How can you learn from this level of suffering? How can you be GLAD that you are being moulded by this? A cynic challenged my inner mind. I had no response at that moment – my physical self was angry with my soul self and whatever 'spirit guides' I may have with me. They could all piss off right now: I was angry that I chose this, angry that I must play this part and act out this role.

So I held her and didn't say anything for a long time.

The world started spinning again, but this time out of my control as I held her tightly, fighting the tears so that Maryam wouldn't see them when her little face popped up from amongst the pansies and fairy garden to check where I was.

Outside the kitchen door the wind rustled the leaves on the trees in the garden, they breathed and whispered around us. Clouds moved quickly through the deep blue sky overhead, the smell of damp earth rising off our lawn. An oblivious bird squawked too loudly as it landed on the ivy-clad fence. It was all so real, so *physical*. And my body hurt all over, pierced by the splinters of my shattered heart.

I felt the burden of my embodiment press down heavily on my head.

Later, the lentil soup was cooked, the salad vegetables chopped and I'd picked up the shattered pieces of my heart – again. The pieces were glued and I think my heart must look warped and ugly from the repeated shattering and endless remoulding. But it still beat and I was still there and my love was stronger than it ever was before – so there must be some beauty in its reformation.

I would not fight her pain, I will embrace it while working to end it. I would accept her pain, not diminish its impact nor be frustrated by it. I must try everything thing I can to reduce it. I breathed in the cooling green light, filtered by the trees outside, the cooling evening breeze as it fluttered through the window. A water dragon sat on the edge of the pool, savouring the last of the late afternoon sun.

'Dinner time!' I called out and I let myself inhale deeply and actively welcome the pain her words bring me: *I am still learning, she is still teaching me. She is still learning, I am still teaching her.* I focus on feeling grateful that I am here as Naomi, experiencing this. It hurt … *It hurt so much*! But it also transformed and it enabled me to fully express the depths of my love, which was infinite. I didn't know it was possible to love so completely, powerfully and infinitely. Love was the most powerful thing in the universe – although so many of us have forgotten. I was grateful that I had remembered.

'I'm published!' I yelled at Nour down the phone. 'It got published last month and I didn't notice!' There was my name, 'N. Cook *et al*' under the abstract for the case report on Google Scholar, published in one of the most prestigious paediatric Journals of Endocrinology. Next I emailed our German Guru to tell him the good news to which he replied, 'Wooohooo!' and promptly referenced our paper in his first-ever paper on oxytocin. Talk about 'moving science'! I was filled to the brim with gratitude – thinking back to how powerless and alone I had felt embarking on this journey to help Hana two years before and now here I was, building a network of experts I could communicate with and contributing to scientific fields myself: I couldn't ask for more.

Chapter Twenty-two

He led me up into a cave in a mountain, then told me to look out at the valley. 'Shout into the valley,' he told me. So I did. He was my teacher, my husband to be, although I didn't know it at the time, a soulmate – *he* knew that.

My young voice echoed out into the valley. I looked at him for what next – there was always a what next with him.

'The only real thing is your thoughts,' he said. 'Like your voice, only your thoughts are real. Life is an echo of what you are thinking.'

The world I was stepping back in time to was hazy, cloudy around the edges. I understood this to be an energy I associated with my 'Spirit Guide' who I called Sebastian. I was deep in meditation, a past life regression led by Brian Weiss from an online course I was completing. I was lying on the red couch which was now in my office, clasping two crystals, one in each hand. I had recognised the energy of this older native American man to be the guide I had most regularly communicated with over the last few months. Sebastian … I was viewing a past life memory with this enlightened man, a soulmate of mine.

The metaphor in his words knocked me flat: *What you are thinking of – becomes your reality.* With that was coming another change – I was beginning to shift again. I'd read and incorporated all that I could on spiritual theories regarding reincarnation and truths from the well-known past life regression therapists but, once again, my constantly inquisitive critical mind analysed and wanted more.

I struggled with static theories. It seemed to me a human trait that, once they thought they understood something, by believing they pretty much understood it, thus reduced that concept to something static – it became a boxed-in, non-adjustable concept. I couldn't see that spiritual truths could be reduced to something non-adjustable. I also couldn't see how one person could be right and another wrong – for example, Michael Newton would describe how evolved a soul was by his subject's perceived auric 'colour' under hypnosis and he would then be able to label an individual as novice soul or advanced soul – even when the subject may believe or see things differently. What also niggled me were the trends between the differing regression techniques in producing experiences and information that correlated with that practitioner's interests.

Similarly, I struggled with the heavy focus on 'Soul Contracts' and the element of pre-determinism that some people thought must therefore 'govern' their life's unfolding. Surely, *surely*, I felt that once you have had the ability to recognise yourself as a divine being, *awakened*, you had the ability to change and resolve these contracts rather than be, or feel, forever 'bound' by them?

I had already been through a religious upbringing and abandoned the rules and rigid theories of doing and being, I didn't want to encounter similar didactic theories in my own quest for spiritual truths. So where to next? What did I need to now know?

I had got the bestselling book *The Secret* years ago – after all, everyone was making such a fuss about it. I started reading it but, upon deducing within minutes that that was how I already lived my life (I called it 'Cook Luck'), I promptly closed it and went back to reading dystopian YA novels about aliens and the end of the world. *The Secret* lay at the bottom of my bedside table, in amongst dusty forgotten odd socks, for five years.

When were moving house, I emptied the bedside table and threw away the odd socks and picked up the book, hesitated and reluctantly packed it into a box. 'OK,' I thought, 'I won't chuck it now. I'll review it once we've moved in, but seriously, after five years, it really needs to go to charity.'

We moved in, I unpacked *The Secret* and hesitated before placing it on my new bedside table. 'Fine, you have one month of it being on your bedside table again. If you don't read it, ditch it,' I poignantly advised myself. One evening, short of books on reincarnation by Brian Weiss (I'd pretty much read all his works and still hadn't found my 'what next') I picked it up heavy-hearted, sure that it would be boring.

*Everything that's coming into your life you are attracting into your life. And it's attracted to you by virtue of the images you're holding in your mind. **It's what you are thinking**.*

I was grabbed by these first sentences. For some reason, the words I'd once disregarded as 'I already do that' jarred me so much I couldn't put it down. Because this time round, life hadn't been swimming along, happy-go-lucky as it had pre-brain tumour. This time I had an uncomfortable truth to face. If this was *true*, then according to the Law of Attraction, I had attracted my daughter's poor health into existence (unknowingly) through my own thought forms, belief systems and deep unspoken fears. Let's say this was just a *little bit* confronting!

Yet … in realising this, admitting and connecting once again with the dark, unspoken inner fears I'd harboured for my children's health and wellbeing ever since they'd been born, there was something liberating and fantastic about this revelation. My heart began racing and, in fascination, I began reading out parts aloud to a sleepy disgruntled Nour who was trying to plough through a Dan Brown. He was probably also thinking, *'Oh boy, what next?'*

'I have to see this movie,' I thought. 'This weekend I *will* see it.'

That weekend arrived and I'd been too lazy to order the DVD online, but I still felt a sense of certainty that I would see it that night. On the way to buy hay for the guinea pigs from our new local pet store, I happened to glance into one of the last (ever) remaining CD/DVD stores – amongst a sea of hundreds of DVDs and CDs my eyes only landed on one: *The Secret*.

The movie had me spellbound – there were literal chemical changes happening in my body as I watched it. My palms began sweating and I was filled with a sense of elation. The energy of those awesome presenters intermingled with my own – not only did I love the message, but I knew in every inch of my entire being that the Law of Attraction was *true*.

As usual, in my instant thirst and greed to know more, I rapidly progressed to reading and watching others who supported the same theories: Raymond Holliwell – *Working with the Law*; Bruce Lipton – *The Biology of Belief*; James Allen – *As a Man Thinketh*; Joe Dispenza – *You are the Placebo*; Lissa Rankin – *Mind Over Medicine*. I then completed an online weekend paradigm shifting course with Bob Proctor.

The whole thing was so completely relevant to my situation with Hana, I was glued to my computer screen. His words of empowering wisdom on how to change your reality by changing your thought patterns was phenomenal and inspiring: 'I've seen so many incredible things happen, I believe anything now. Paradigm is a mental program that has almost exclusive control over our habitual behaviour and almost all behaviour is habitual.'

Our instructions were to visualise the realities we wanted to manifest, become so emotionally involved with them that we could 'feel' as if we were already there. Then, by the Law of Attraction, we were told that those desired realities would begin to manifest.

My course of action had now become so clear it was transparent … to manifest Hana's complete healing I needed to not only believe that it could happen but to become emotionally involved with it. I needed to feel as it was happening *now*. He informed us that doubt would not stop the workings of the Law of Attraction, but that doubt held in the mind becomes the picture and therefore reality corresponds.

What I needed to do was literally increase or shift my vibration to a higher level – a reality where Hana was completely healed and cured of her brain injury. How would

I do that? When my daily existence was one where I could plainly see she needed her medications to stay alive? I started meditating on this, but in my stomach I knew that I wasn't there yet – I hadn't made that shift upwards. Bob assured us that this vibrational shift would take repetition and discipline so, with complete faith I would get there, I continued my daily practice and meditative routine.

And so my peaceful state of acceptance with regards to Hana's state of health shifted. If everything around us is willed into existence by our thoughts and unconscious belief systems or paradigms – be they formed here or in another place in space and time, even in spiritual dimensions – then this meant I had willed my current circumstances into existence. How amazing then that I had the power to will it out of existence.

Could I, by using the power of thought, will into my reality a completely, miraculously healed daughter?

If, due to our inherent and continuous connection to the Oneness, the ultimate source of everything, we cause the entire perceived universe around us to 'be', it must mean that we are not a victim to any aspects of our reality. I could no longer find any whiff of peace in simply believing Hana and I had been fulfilling a Soul Contract by our suffering, now there was a responsibility back on me to 'make things right again'.

It was late one afternoon and I was getting close to leaving for school pick-up, after abstractly practising my poor skills at telekinesis, on the spur of the moment I googled: *Learn*

Telekinesis Sydney. What came up was a webpage about a healing modality called 'Theta Healing' which combined psychic senses, healing skills and was based on the concept that beliefs form reality and also recognised the role of the Law of Attraction as central to healing. I saw there was a practitioner course coming up.

I can't believe I've found this course right at this point of my life! I wrote to Mark, the instructor. *Is there a space for me?*

'Of course there's a spot with your name already on it,' Mark replied.

Excited about this new development and change to my spiritual path, I began to read Vianna Stibal's work about the development of Theta Healing: she wrote of instantaneous miraculous healings!

But then came back the feeling of longing. If life-changing, crazy, magical miracles were possible for others, then why not for me? Why not for *Hana*? I'd already let go of her to a certain extent – in the context of spiritual growth and karmic cycles, the suffering had made sense! But now there was something else, creating miracles – but this meant taking back the reins! How could I accept Hana's health as it was when there was evidence it could be eradicated with intention, thought and powerful spiritual healings? The peace I'd felt over the last few months began to evaporate and the restless longing for change grew in intensity.

'I don't know what command I need,' I told my partner at the Theta healing course four weeks later. 'I do believe I can facilitate Hana's healing, but I suppose what I doubt is my ability or power to facilitate it, even though others are able to heal others this way! OK,' I chewed my pen, 'how about you ask for a download on "the Creator's perspective and definition of what it means to be an infinitely ... powerful being?"'

'Oh, that's a good one!' she agreed. We were working in pairs, practising the removal of blocks to healing via connecting to the Creator or Source Energy in meditative or Theta Brainwave state before commanding 'downloads' relevant to feelings and beliefs we wanted to change. This 'download' involved receiving energy from this eternal energy source that some call God, some call Source or The One. For simplicity I used the word 'Creator' in the classroom, although I preferred to think of it as 'Source' energy.

So, as per our instructions, and after the morning's training in attaining rapid-onset Theta Brainwave states, we entered into a Theta brain state within a few seconds and my partner silently made the command. I opened my eyes as I felt the download pour down over me. Thinking that was it, I was about to say, 'That was good,' but then it suddenly got powerful – wave upon wave of energy began to rush over me, cascading downwards. She opened her eyes, looking rather shocked. 'This is intense!' she gasped.

My face was slack and eyes glazing over – this was like being on drugs. We both closed our eyes again. I guessed that was about the time I should have the courage to make the 'healing command' for Hana – feeling drugged and blissed-out like that removed my fear of a failed healing attempt.

I commanded that a healing occur to Hana's best and highest good and finished with the usual Theta Healing ending, 'Show me. Thank you. It is done, it is done, it is done.'

In my mind's eye I watched Source or the Creator's energy pour over Hana while she sat at the dining-room table at home, colouring-in. The energy, blue/white/silver energy flooded around her pituitary area and hypothalamus. I couldn't see anything else, I didn't know if the healing would be accepted – I hadn't asked her permission … but, as her mum, I felt there must be some leeway there. Besides, if on some energetic level she didn't want or 'need' the healing, it wouldn't be received.

I slouched down in my seat, feeling drunk, or totally high, or both. The waves of energy were not decreasing but increasing in intensity. My partner and I sat staring at each other giggling like mad women for about half an hour. When everyone left for lunch, we lay down on the floor, completely off our faces for the whole hour. Just before we were to return to class, I made a brute effort to shake off my wooziness so I could focus on the afternoon.

'I commanded that her healing take place,' I told Nour that evening. 'Whether or not that healing carries through will depend on any blockages she has that I am not able to pick up because I'm not yet psychic enough. Or it will mean that I need to do further work on myself first – if we find no concrete evidence of it, when Mark gets back from his trip abroad, I'll go and see him and ask for advice.'

I proceeded to tell Nour of Mark's own miracle story and what brought him to Theta Healing. A builder by trade, he'd developed a terminal infection in his spine. Sent home to die, he tried Theta Healing, and was completely cured of infection and pain – his wrecked spine completely healed, within days.

'I do believe in miracles,' Nour said putting on his pyjamas. 'It was YOU who didn't believe these things were possible.'

'I was wrong,' I said. Thank goodness I had been wrong! 'But we need to focus on SEEING her well, and believing it has already happened! This is called "manifesting" – we need to live in a state of gratitude that it has happened.' I was recounting all I'd learnt from Bob Proctor and others who used the Law of Attraction. Nour frowned, as he put his clothes away inside our walk-in wardrobe. 'Living in a state of gratitude for her miracle healing' was an unrealistic task when Hana's morbidities were shoved in our faces everyday!

'I'm working on it,' I said getting in between the sheets, pulling my duvet right up to my neck before picking up Vianna's next book for the advanced practitioner class I was already booked in for.

'Look at my muscles, Mummy!' Maryam chortled as she sucked in her non-existent tummy in front of the bathroom mirror, her ribs protruding like sticks. 'I'm like Daddy!'

I laughed, reaching out to tickle her ribs. 'Daddy has a six pack, hun. These are your ribs!'

Hana climbed out of the bath and began looking at herself in the bathroom mirror – she'd often just stand there, looking at her reflection quietly, sometimes looking carefully at her lap-band scars, other times she'd whisper, 'I love myself, Mummy.' This time she looked down at the fold of flesh where her breast met her belly, then pointed to it. 'Is this *my* muscle?' she lisped innocently.

'Hmmm, I think it's a skin fold,' I said before grabbing her gorgeous, soft belly and blowing the most deliciously loud raspberry into it. Sometimes I'd chase her around the house, with her squealing, just so I could burrow my face into her belly and inundate it with love.

Maryam roared with laughter and insisted I do the same to hers, which was tough with so little flesh to plant my lips on.

'Come on, sisty,' Hana said, leading the way out of the bathroom, her towel trailing behind her. Excited that a game was on the cards, Maryam grabbed her towel and they disappeared into the bedroom. Seeing her joy at playing with Hana hit me in the heart each time. It felt like a balloon of love, I adored every inch of that girl – how well she had coped with all that had happened, her patience with Hana, every time she opened her mouth to speak it was if the air was literally filled with flowers, or butterflies. How *could* someone be so beautiful? She had been a little candle for me during the darkest nights of my life.

It struck me then … and I almost laughed at how my adult mind had elevated *me* to the status of protector. All those years ago when she had curled up next to me at night, the little magnetised worm that I thought I had been protecting – I hadn't seen it until that moment; she had been there for me, *my* comforter and my little guardian angel – and what a beautiful soul she must be to have chosen to do that for me in a body so small and mind so uncomprehending.

Chapter Twenty-three

If this was my reality, the reality *I* wanted to change, it made sense to change *me* first!

Over those few weeks after the first Theta Healings, Hana began to change rapidly – she developed a healthier look in her face and eyes, she was happier, more steady in mood and had high energy levels, plus her daily headaches had decreased dramatically. I knew that something was happening, there had been a shift – but it wasn't enough, I needed more! So I booked a session with Mark to start working more on myself.

'I can accept my role in the manifestation of my surrounding reality, that this circumstance was willed into existence by my subconscious thoughts, or, if you want to refer to spiritual planning and soul contracts, you can say that. I can accept that I had some secret belief that if she was "sick" then I could keep her safe, I could shield her from the dangerous world out there. Like in that past life memory of her and me living on the edge of the village, I feel like it was to keep her safe. Yet, because she was murdered, she wasn't safe,' I said.

'If she heals, what happens?' Mark asked.

A rush of love flooded through my heart. 'I let her go like a bird,' I exclaimed. I saw myself opening cupped hands and a delicate feathered little thing taking flight. I could see that I hadn't been ready to do that – I could control aspects of her health and safety if she was sick by keeping her close to me, never letting her go. But not anymore. Now I was ready to let her go to live her own life without me controlling her safety.

'What I want to do is release you from the feeling that you NEED to heal her,' said Mark.

I looked aghast. 'Why? But I want to want to heal her. If I let go of that, she may not heal! And I want her to be healed! I want to want her be healed!'

'Can I give you this pen?' he said. Oh boy, that example again. He'd used it at the Theta Healing course and I didn't really get it.

'Yes,' I said, reluctantly playing along.

'Can I give you this pen?' he asked again, then repeated the process. 'Do you see, I'm in the state of giving – so nothing else can happen when I'm in that state.'

'Hmmm,' I agreed, sighing as he went into Theta state and gave me the download.

Before ending, he asked if I could bring Hana in to see him the following weekend after I had completed the advanced course. I agreed, excited that maybe he would be able to psychically see how to facilitate her healing.

'You're pretty much all good right now,' he said.

'I feel good,' I agreed, 'but I wanted to find the blockages with me! It'd be easier to deal with them that way.'

'It'll be interesting to see what she's carrying and, whatever she is carrying, will be sure to trigger you. In the meantime, you'll probably shift from this later this week. You can thank me for that now.' We laughed and then hugged goodbye.

The weekend passed with no clear changes in Hana, even though Mark had helped to remove a couple of my own blocks. Then, Monday morning, as I gathered up my crystals, a new, amazing piece of clear quartz and a lovely rounded smooth piece of blue apatite literally vibrated in my hands. I quickly entered into a deep trance state, visualising all I wanted to manifest. Then it happened ...

I shifted.

In my heart chakra I felt it – a wire of energy pouring out, connecting me to my dreams. And I suddenly 'got it'. By letting go of the need to heal Hana, I was able to now SEE her healed. My heart racing, I saw Hana walking around the house NOW healed, thinning down rapidly. I saw her walk out of school, laughing. I saw us repeatedly throwing her medications away. The sense that she didn't need them was so overpowering, the vision kept repeating itself. Then I began to visualise how I would tell everyone, how I would tell my parents, Nour's parents, Hana's doctors – the followers on my Facebook page and Nurse Naomi blog. The radiating beam of energy shooting out of my heart chakra felt more intense by the moment.

Now I had not only an intellectual apprehension of how my future would manifest, but I also had an emotional attachment to it. Now I could live on this parallel vibration but at a higher level for as long as it took for my physical reality to shift itself and correspond, which it now had no choice but to do. According to the law, it HAD to shift to match the reality I was projecting and living in – in the realm of thought.

The possibilities in this new world were endless. My heart rate picked up a little. Was I brave enough for this? Could I keep doubt out of the picture to fully realise and manifest all that I was desperate to bring into existence?

Then it was the weekend. I completed my second course in Theta Healing and my excitement grew on Sunday afternoon for Hana's meeting with Mark. What would happen? Would he be able to witness her entire healing? What would he be able to see psychically that I yet couldn't due to my immature psychic abilities?

'Wow,' Mark breathed after coming out of Theta Brainwave state to do a psychic body scan on Hana. 'You know you're here for pretty important purpose, don't you?' he asked.

Hana looked at him blankly, but nodded as she felt she was supposed to.

'I can see a lot of trauma from the surgery there, and also some energies that are not hers, from medical professionals who have a mainstream view on healing and perspectives on her prognosis,' he explained. 'There is also some guilt there that she has picked up. Hana, sometimes when people have operations, although they are asleep, they still hear what is being said around them and take that on board, even though it may not be true.'

Hana nodded.

'I'd like to clear these things and I'd also like to clear you of some past life things. Do you know about past lives?'

She nodded again.

'I think they're a bit funny,' he chuckled, 'but I want to clear those and also clear you of any agreements or soul contracts you and your mum made before coming here.'

So he went into Theta again and cleared away these acquired energies and thoughts from this life and previous lives.

'I want you know that it is OK to communicate,' he told her. 'I can see that there have been issues with communicating in the past, but that's over now. You are safe to say how you feel about things.'

Communication ... interesting, I thought, when Hana's illness had propelled my desire to communicate our personal journey to thousands of people I didn't know. He made the commands and she sat there, a bit hot and sweaty, slightly bored and wondering when she would be allowed to go home to have her bath, take her meds and go to bed. I felt myself enter Theta state with Mark – having been working in Theta state all weekend, the energy was very easy to 'get into'. I let it wash over me.

'What did you see?' I asked Mark eagerly once she was outside with Nour and Maryam while I debriefed with him.

'I saw bucket loads of healing taking place,' he said with his eyes sparkling.

'And past life stuff?'

'Past lives ... don't buy into that,' he said. 'It's brain candy – we always see whatever we need to see in order to then clear it, don't get caught up in the storyline.'

I nodded. I agreed wholeheartedly – the more I thought about how we were One, the individuality of past lives was disintegrating into a grand universal, omniscient consciousness anyway. I could incorporate the concept of past lives into my spiritual understanding, but I didn't feel anchored there anymore, I was ready to move forwards.

'But yeah, since you ask, I did see past lives, four of them,' he chuckled again. 'Where you and Hana were constantly at odds with each other in the same way you had anorexia in this life and she gets the opposite problem.'

I took this on board. It didn't mean this was 'true' – what it meant was that *he* needed to see this in order to continue to facilitate Hana's healing. The experience of past lives was just as beneficial to the practitioner as it could be the client.

I hugged myself with joy in the car on the way home: this was a whole new world we were living in – one of empowerment and creatorship and one of responsibility. I was about to witness a miracle and, better than that, it would be a miracle that I would share with the world!

Chapter Twenty-four

'Once upon a time, there was a bunch of angels who were deciding where to go next. They were hard-working angels and liked to help many worlds and planets, all over the universe. "Where shall we go now?" one asked the rest.'

Hana and Maryam stopped their colouring-in at the kitchen table as I began one of their favourite stories, their faces lit up, hanging on to my every word.

'Earth!' shouted Maryam.

'But listen, it will be a tough one!' I warned. 'Because in this incarnation, one of us will have to get really sick … there's a lot of work we can do there if one of us gets sick and then we share the story with the world. And there's something else – at first we will have to *forget* that we are angels.'

'It'll be really hard,' Maryam nodded. 'I won't be the sick one. Uh uh, not me please!'

'No. Who will be the one that gets sick?' I asked. 'To be honest, I'd quite like to be the mother who has forgotten she is an angel, who helps the sick one and then shares what she learns with the other humans.'

Maryam laughed with glee and pointed at Hana.

'ME!' Hana beamed. 'I'll be the one that gets the brain tumour. I'm strong!'

'And then we get to tell the world all about energy and the angel world,' said Maryam. 'Because, Mummy, YOU didn't know about it until Hana got sick.'

'That is true and that will be part of the story,' I added. 'I'll be the mum who doesn't know about energy and the angel world until my daughters show me. But who will be the daddy?' I mused, before continuing in a narrative tone. 'And they looked all over the local cluster of galaxies for a soul residing there that might be tempted to come and join these souls in their next quest. But no one put up their hands, because this quest was going to be a challenging one. No one was brave enough. So they had to ask further afield, and over there, in an area of the universe these souls hadn't been to before was a brave spirit (who liked sport)' – the girls burst out laughing – 'who said, "OK, I'll come with you, and be the husband and father so long as I can still do lots of sport?"' More laughter from the girls. 'Now,' I said, 'are you sure you want this? Are you ready to jump into a wormhole and appear inside my tummy at the right time?'

'YES!' they both chorused.

'Good,' I said, 'off we go …' and, giggling at their expectant faces, I took a giant leap across the kitchen as my 'angel self' leapt through the higher dimensions down into the twisting, heavy energies of the third dimension.

'I'm living in two realities at the same time. In one my daughter is healed, in the other she still has health conditions and still needs medication to stay alive. Yes, I know there have been improvements, the fact her Minirin medication almost quartered over the course of a few weeks is amazing! Not to mention the change in pituitary function.' A recent blood test had shown an increase in Hana's thyroid stimulating hormone – was this a sign her 'non-functional' gland was waking up? 'But I want more … God! If I can't heal my stupid athlete's foot,' I'd exclaimed, 'how can I facilitate Hana's full healing?'

I was talking to a friend from Theta Healing. I'd asked her for a command on 'worthiness' or being worthy to facilitate Hana's healing. When she had gone into Theta Brainwave state and asked for a feelings download of 'being worthy of giving and receiving instantaneous healings' I'd had a flash – a scene I'd never seen before. Me, a bearded fisherman on a boat in a huge cold lake surrounded by mountains – my son, Hana, tumbling overboard and my useless attempts to save him. I only had one arm, the other severed in a boating accident years before. Grappling with air with my arm-stub, I'd roared as my other arm reached helplessly down to my son who was already sinking like a stone. White-faced, he'd stared up at my own mask of despair and the waters closed over him like clouds meeting to cover up the sun. Never, never again was I worthy of anything. I hated myself more than hate could hate. Nothing good must ever come to me again.

But even upon releasing that past life trauma and downloading 'I am worthy of giving and receiving healings', I could still feel a blockage somewhere, maybe somewhere in my solar plexus. I hadn't found my bottom line yet … I still had more work to do on myself in order to facilitate

283

Hana's miracle healing. I believed it would happen, therefore it would happen: it must happen!

'I don't know what I need to do,' I told her. 'I'm working on manifesting a reality where my daughter is healed, where she doesn't need medications to stay alive and her pain is gone. I'm seriously living in that reality, on that vibration when she's at school, but the two realities haven't merged together yet.'

'But is it up to us to choose the miracle?' she questioned. 'You can ask for one, but can you determine *how* it will occur?'

I pulled a face. Of course I could determine that I wanted my daughter's miracle brain healing. Who wouldn't want that miracle for their child!

'I'm going to spend the next week in meditation and in Theta state,' I told Nour. 'I have more work to do on myself – Hana hasn't healed the way I was anticipating through my manifestations and even with Mark's help. I know the problem must be with *me*, so I'm going to get to the bottom of it.'

For perhaps the first time ever – rather than seize the precious moments of time with the girls at school by filling it with writing work, I didn't even open my computer. I grabbed my two favourite crystals of the moment, my meditation music and a notepad. I slipped quickly and easily into a Theta state and began asking Source Energy what belief systems I needed to change. I felt issues surrounding 'time' were really important to resolve – the timing of things was something that preoccupied and stressed me. I lived in a state where I wished I had five simultaneous lives to help me carry out all I wanted to do in this one. I also tried further downloads of worthiness, but still felt a blockage there, a rock sitting in my chest or stomach.

'Please guide me on what I am supposed to do next to help facilitate Hana's healing.'

The answer was pushed loudly into my head immediately. 'Do? Nothing. Just BE.'

'Be?'

'Yes, BE – like a star is in a state of shining.'

Hmm, I pulled out of the trance. Nice wishy-washy spiritual image (even though I did particularly identify with stars), but how could that help me heal Hana? I wanted solid, concrete answers here.

What was blocking me from facilitating Hana's healing? It was more than worthiness – it was more than an issue of 'time'. I needed to test myself for some other beliefs.

I got off the couch and picked up my pendulum. In Theta Healing, muscle testing is used to reveal or confirm subconscious beliefs. However, I had difficulties with muscle testing and simply couldn't trust myself with it at all. Using the pendulum seemed to work better for me – I had consistent 'yes' and 'no' responses to questions that I tested it with, already knowing the answers. The pendulum in itself was more than likely a form of muscle testing anyway, responding to teeny, unnoticed neuro-energetic or muscle twitches consistent with unconscious movements to 'yes' or 'no' feelings or energies evoked in subconscious and energetic forms – so ultimately I felt it was all the same thing.

'I am capable of facilitating Hana's healing' – it swirled in an anti-clockwise circle, yes!

'Hana is ready to heal' – another anti-clockwise circle, yes!

I can facilitate Hana's instantaneous healing right now – the pendulum swished side to side, no!

What? Urgh! The blockage was still there!

I began writing this time, digging further to find the bottom line – for once and for all:

If I *don't* heal Hana, what's the worst thing that can happen?
- She will continue to suffer.
- If she suffers then I feel disappointed by my failure to help her.
- If I am disappointed in myself then I feel disempowered.
- If I am disempowered then I feel useless and a waste of an entity.
- If I am a waste of an entity then I do not know why I am here.
- If I do not know why I am here, then I do not know the Truth on What and Who I am.

I don't know What and Who I Am!

And there it was – my bottom line! Despair rose up within me and I began to cry silently in physical form, yet I felt it roar into the infinite spirit world, I know it was heard – the sound of a soul who is cut off from all it knows – a lost soul. Sobs shook my ribcage as I came face to face with the truth of my quest to heal my daughter: *I simply wanted to know What and Who I was.* I'd thought that by healing my daughter I would find myself and be connected with my true essence – finding Truth for once and all.

I fell to my knees on the floor – funny, it was instinctive, to kneel and bow my head down in the position of prayer.

It was as if this religious stance was never learnt or taught but something we each carry within ourselves, the way we all surrender to the Source Energy or the Creator. I went up into Theta Brainwave state:

'Thank you for helping me realise what I am looking for. To my best and highest good could you please give me the highest perspective and definition and the Truth of What and Who I Am.'

A little while later I felt this 'truth' as I myself, as Naomi, ebbed away and I became part of everything else:

I saw creation, on every level – the physical through to the supernatural realms as a sheet of fabric, not just connected but the *very same thing*. Everything and everyone was me – we were all one being. Then I saw Hana, separate to me, but very much still me. I saw her face as she came running out of school and felt puzzled amusement, which was now my amusement via my recognised connection as a Creating Source. I felt a tickle of laughter – why was I expending so much energy being *attached* to Hana's healing? It seemed funny to me from here, I mused at my quest as Creator and, as embodied Naomi, tasting this divine perspective. I could not only see but *feel* that this ultimately wasn't real but an illusion that we were using for a higher good – and that we were all One anyway. Why was I so focused on the physical state – why couldn't I see that ultimately, it was perfect and it didn't matter?

Don't try – BE, in a state of Love. Love like a star shines.

Then it clicked. Love – the highest and purest form of creation! Love – the highest vibration that energy can be … If we create from here, nothing can go wrong. Love is perfect – it doesn't look for results, it doesn't look for proof, love simply *IS*. I snapped out of meditation – I had to write this down before I forgot any of it, and as I wrote I felt the words were being dictated to and for me on the page:

It never was purely about healing Hana, Naomi. It was about healing YOU.

And to heal YOU – you needed to find and feel the Truth on What and Who You Are:

An aspect of the Creating Source, a Divine being who creates in love.

Your *ego* wanted to see Hana well, because you love her in the physical and seeing her suffering *hurts you* – your ego. This attachment is ultimately an attachment to yourself because as you now feel and know to be true, you and Hana, and everything else are One.

'But ...' I fretted out loud to the pen in my left hand, 'I had thought there would be some benefit beyond me and Hana if I could share her miracle healing with others! Then they too could see and have hope, remembering What and Who THEY are too! I thought this was why I was here ...'

Your ego wanted to share these messages with others to awaken the sense of divine within them, you were attached to this. But this is your message:

You don't need miracles to connect with the Truth of What and Who You Are as a human – you simply have to look within and you will find it.

And it is this: Love.

A new song began to play on my phone, a tune I loved, but what was it called again? I checked the screen: *Heaven on Earth.*

If I could integrate my true identity with this perception of an embodied human existence, I would find it: Heaven on Earth. This was Nirvana. I lay my head in my hands, an enormous burden lifted off my back. I felt as light as a feather and no longer imprisoned by what I *wanted* to do and what I thought I *needed* to do. It was gone. I was completely and utterly free!

Love …

The most unlikely message that I, as a smart, critically thinking, yes − egotistical, analytical, and yes − ever so slightly proud individual, would ever contemplate sharing with anyone else! Spiritual wishy-washy and naff! Dramatic miracles were surely more *my* thing!

Love?

But this was The Truth. This was why I was here to learn this for myself and share it with others. The river of quietness that flooded through me was pure and divine, I was ready to BE now.

I closed my eyes and I let this love, the highest vibrational energy that is, pour out of my entire being like fire. Visions took over. There was Hana in all her perfection, running towards me out of school. My love engulfed her in fierce golden flames. I looked to see the phoenix that may rise from the ashes, but then I realised that it was my ego looking for the phoenix and I stopped. Because right now there was no phoenix, just my golden love fire, burning up her entire being, reducing her to nothing − *nothing* − but hot flames. And that was all I had to do as a creator − co-creator and essential aspect off the Creating Source – simply explode with love.

If only my love was enough to make it go away ... a mother's love should be enough.

Of course it was all about love! I'd known it all along.

'It is safe to face it here, darling,' I murmured, cradling my sobbing daughter. Her cries echoed throughout the whole of the downstairs but they were nothing like the empty, lost, hollow cries of post-operative Hana. These cries were touching something, recognising something more painful than anything she'd chosen to face up to before. She had begun to shift, the emerging post-traumatic stress was being stirred up by our energy healings, daily rituals of meditations, expressions of gratitude, and yoga. This time a strong yoga move overcame and filled her with memories and an untapped sadness she'd walled off in her head. As she roared in my arms, tears streamed down my own face – but they weren't of despair and sadness, but relief, love, joy and gratitude. I could feel energy clearing in my own chest, the ebbing away of a heaviness that I hadn't even known was there.

'When we come face to face with the things we most want to forget, bad or scary things that have happened to us, it's as if a wall has been knocked down inside our heads. A wall we build to hide things from us, things we want to forget. And when that wall is down, and we can see all the bad things we wanted to hide from, it hurts all over again.'

'The pain ...' she whimpered. 'Mummy, *oh Mummy!*'

As she allowed herself to face and integrate the traumas her tiny body had gone through three years before, the guinea pigs shrieked and cried in their cage behind us, echoing the palpable despair Hana was finally releasing and expelling for good.

The late afternoon sun was streaming down outside from the bright blue sky. Sunlight bounced off the tall green-topped ferns lining the creek and shards of light flickered off the turquoise pool that Maryam was splashing in, her laughter deafening her to the sounds of Hana's cries a few metres away, inside. The kookaburras cackled overhead and cockatoos screeched loudly in the trees. A wind shifted the branches as leaves fluttered to the ground we'd raked clear only a few hours before. Creation in this third dimension truly was beautiful.

'Don't worry, baby girl.'

She looked up at me, tears still pouring down her cheeks, her eyes searching for something in mine — a reflection of herself? I smiled through my own mascara-streaked tears, she was my mirror and I was hers. My heart bloomed love in my chest like a song — Heaven on Earth.

'No matter what happens, it is all going to be OK. It really is all perfect because we come from love and love is perfect. This is What and Who We Are, *perfect as we are* — even though it doesn't feel this way when we're in these human bodies that sometimes hurt us and make us forget. But *we* remember don't we?'

She nodded.

'You're healing now, and it is brave of you to heal. However your healing shows itself to us — whether there is brain healing or not — it doesn't matter because all that matters is that you become a loving and peaceful being that feels and knows it is "whole" and perfect as it is.'

She is covered in the golden flames of my love and so nothing else matters because that's how it was done in the first place and that's how it happens every day: A continuous explosion of love that is us – all of us – both enacting, watching and being, creating as time and history unfold freely, no attachment, no conditions. Some of what happens *seems* good and some *seems* bad, but it all comes from the one Source, a Source of Love, so, in its essence, it was and always will be perfect.

What happens next will simply be a creation by the beings that are me, Hana and all those who choose to experience this journey with us. The future may be different for everyone, depending on how it is *thought* to be, how it is *perceived* and whether our creative thoughts are anchored in our true essence, remembering What and Who We Are and that is *love.*

I kissed her salty cheeks that are both hers and mine and I looked inside myself, deep in my belly – hunting for *my* wound, the wound that wanted to see Hana pain free and physically healed and all our suffering gone forever and ever! But I couldn't find it – intrigued, I searched some more, but the wound had gone. The spot this wound had once occupied gnawing away at me, every minute of every day was now smoothed over.

It had been a trip to something like hell, she'd dragged me there defiant, kicking and screaming, yearning for the suffering to end so much I'd waged war. But then, in that darkness, she'd taught me that love *was* the most powerful thing after all, and with *her* birthstone she had pressed the buttons in my hand – waking me up.

She had broken me, but then she'd put the pieces of me back together – this three-year-long journey that I had thought was all about healing her, only to discover, like a child opening a surprise gift, that person who truly had really needed healing, was me.

Acknowledgements

Thank you to my biggest supporter of this memoir: My mum, who said, with an intuitive glint in her eye, that it would be a bestseller when I was in a place too dark to comprehend anything so amazing.

Thank you to my husband for his endless generosity in supporting both my crazy schemes *and* my wildest dreams: I have never felt truly anchored to Planet Earth – luckily I don't have to try because you provide the anchor that so easily slips out of my hands.

I'm not sure if I ever want my sweet girls to read this, as I believe this aspect of our journey will seem like a fairytale belonging to people in a different dimension by the time they are 18. I hope that they are so busy and so enmeshed in actualising their own incredible lives that reading 'Mummy's old book' will be a bore! But I will thank them anyway for their rainbow-coloured light, simply: I adore both of you – from your eyelashes to your toes. And I still carelessly believe I could stop the world from spinning – if you wanted me to.

Thank you to the medical doctors, specialists, healers, and everyone else who played a role in progressing our journey helping Hana and healing me. Even if your name isn't here – you know the impact you've had in our lives.

Lastly, thank you to my beautiful readers – the new and those who have been with me, step by step on this journey for the past four years; I'm certain that many of you are part of my soul family. I truly love you all and I will never stop feeling honoured and humbled by your love, support and strength. It is incredible to be on this journey together, *me and you* – sharing and learning together.

Naomi now works as a Reiki Master, Theta and Intuitive Healer. She continues to write, blog and share her journey:

Check out www.howshehealedme.com for more information on the memoir.

Connect with Naomi on www.nursenaomi.com for more on her journey to health and wellness and to see her journey 'in action' over the years.

Sign up for her Soul Health Weekly Bites emails on www.yoursoulhealth.com if you are keen to elevate your own Soul Health Consciousness.

Details about Naomi's children's books, aimed at inspiring and empowering children to harness their own health and wellbeing can be found at www.thelittlebushnurse.com

For those with an interest in the Stars, Cosmic and Intergalactic Origins – please check out Project Starseed www.projectstarseed.com

Find her on Facebook here:

@Naomi Cook – Nurse Naomi
@YourSoulHealth
@projectstarseedgroup

27240581R00164

Printed in Great Britain
by Amazon